THE
DABBLER'S
GUIDE TO
WITCHCRAFT

TILLER PRESS

An Imprint of Simon & Schuster, Inc.
1230 Avenue of the Americas
New York, NY 10020

First Tiller Press trade paperback edition September 2021

TILLER PRESS and colophon are registered trademarks of Simon & Schuster, Inc.

For information about special discounts for bulk purchases, please contact
Simon & Schuster Special Sales at 1-866-506-1949 or business@simonandschuster.com.

The Simon & Schuster Speakers Bureau can bring authors to your live event.
For more information or to book an event, contact the Simon & Schuster Speakers Bureau
at 1-866-248-3049 or visit our website at www.simonspeakers.com.

Interior design by Jennifer Chung

Manufactured in the United States of America

1   3   5   7   9   10   8   6   4   2

Library of Congress Cataloging-in-Publication Data

Names: Lyte, Fire, author. Title: The dabbler's guide to witchcraft : seeking an
intentional magical path / by Fire Lyte. | Description: First Tiller Press trade paperback
edition. | New York : Tiller Press, [2021] | Includes bibliographical references. |
Identifiers: LCCN 2021023898 (print) | LCCN 2021023899 (ebook) | ISBN 9781982174347 |
ISBN 9781982174361 (ebook) Subjects: LCSH: Witchcraft. | Magic. Classification:
LCC BF1571 .L98 2021 (print) | LCC BF1571 (ebook) | DDC 133.4/3--dc23
LC record available at https://lccn.loc.gov/2021023898
LC ebook record available at https://lccn.loc.gov/2021023899

ISBN 978-1-9821-7434-7
ISBN 978-1-9821-7436-1 (ebook)

THE
DABBLER'S
GUIDE TO
WITCHCRAFT

SEEKING AN INTENTIONAL
MAGICAL PATH

FIRE LYTE

TILLER PRESS

NEW YORK LONDON TORONTO SYDNEY NEW DELHI

CONTENTS

PART 4
THE TOOLS OF MODERN WITCHCRAFT

PART 5
SPELL CANVASES

INTRODUCTION

LET'S GO ON A JOURNEY. . . .

Let's say you have a boyfriend. For the purposes of this exercise, we'll call him Todd. So, you meet Todd. You fall in love with Todd. The two of you move in together; you buy furniture and maybe even a ferret—whatever couples these days do to mark the fact that they're, you know, a couple. Then the inevitable happens: Some friend or social acquaintance or person auditioning to be the evil character on a reality show sends you The Text. It's filled with screenshots of Todd on dating apps, Todd offering up his nudes as though they were business cards, and worst of all, Todd saying that the birthday cake you made him—the one he said he loved more than any other cake despite the frosting being a bit off—was trash.

It's enough to make someone reenact a Kelly Clarkson music video and tear his apartment to pieces. But then you remember that you also live there and if you rip up the pillows you'll just have to buy new pillows. And, sure, pillows aren't expensive, but these particular pillows were (they're those really good latex pillows that stay cool) and purchasing pillows is not something you want to do during a breakup.

That's when a helpful friend brings over some wine, some chocolate, a deck of interesting-looking cards, and suggests burning Todd's things. It sounds like a good idea. You get a metal bucket, a lighter, that favorite T-shirt of his that you wear to bed, a few photographs from happier times, and a stack of sticky notes. You cry. You scream. You light things on fire. You write all the little ways he made you happy, one per sticky note, and burn those. You write all the little ways he hurt you, one per sticky note, and burn those, too. You drink wine. You dance. You realize that as the fires of Todd slowly burn themselves out, you feel better. You look around the apartment one last time, grab your ferret, and leave.

This is magic.

And this is how it starts. The intrigue, the curiosity, the interest in magic and spells and real-life witches. If you're reading this, there's a very solid chance that you've wandered into a bookstore after getting a taste of it. Perhaps his name wasn't Todd and maybe you weren't burning all of his stuff after a bad breakup, but it could have been a friend who gave you a shiny rock to keep at your desk to keep your busybody coworker away. It could be an aunt who gave you a tarot reading during a warm summer night before a new school year started. Magic finds us in all sorts of innocuous places and points in our lives and afterwards leaves us wanting to learn more. It can provide a sense of strength in a moment when you feel weak, sway justice in your favor, fiddle about with the weather, or simply give you the confidence to captivate an audience during an important speech.

I'm willing to bet that's how you came to hold this book: you caught a spark of magic and a little voice inside you is wondering what's next. There are a lot of books that can teach you the basics of magic or witchcraft, and even more that will educate you on spiritual traditions such as Wicca or Asatru or Hoodoo. The writers of those books by and large have spent many years studying their subject, honing their skills, and hope to share that knowledge with all who seek it. This book is not that.

This book is for people who, at this moment in their lives, might describe themselves as "spiritual but not religious." Seekers who do not identify with any particular religious tradition but are nevertheless looking for what magic awaits them out in the world. Dabblers who feel a pull towards crafting a personal spiritual path but aren't sure how to start, what the rules are, or whether any rules even apply. People who might be seeking community in addition to magic.

In thinking about what I wanted to say and how I wanted to say it, I thought a lot about the tarot. It's said that the Major Arcana—all the cards you probably think of when you think of the tarot—Death, the Tower, the Lovers, et cetera—is the story of the first card: the Fool. In most decks, the Fool is represented as a youth looking off into the sky in wonderment with a sack of goodies tied to a walking stick slung over their shoulder. They're bright-eyed, eager, and perhaps a bit naive. They've set off on a journey and are about to take their first step, except they don't realize they're stepping off a steep cliff. There's usually a dog barking a warning to the youth, who may or may not listen in time. The lesson of the Fool card is that life is a journey and you should look at it with a sense of wonder and excitement, but you should be mindful when taking those first steps. You should learn to look for warning signs, listen to those who came before you, perhaps do a bit more research, squeeze in time for self-reflection, and maybe take a quick break from looking at the majesty of your surroundings to check in as to whether you're about to walk off a cliff.

The complicated truth is that there's a lot of cool stuff to explore when it comes to magic, witchcraft, and learning about different spiritual practices and beliefs. However, every cool new thing you can learn comes with a long history of people misusing said cool thing in ways that might take advantage of a person who's in a vulnerable space of self-exploration and spiritual seeking. Especially in today's world, a spiritual journey should be deeply considered, and therefore this book is for those who are seeking a connection with magic and the wonder immanent in nature with respect for others, an appreciation of science, and without the urge to drop half your paycheck on supplies to get you started.

I mentioned that this book will deal with the fact that some people you may meet might seek to take advantage of you. No, I don't mean watching out for bad witches throwing potion bottles at you in a dark alley in some kind of witch war. I mean people like fraudulent psychics, predatory group leaders, authors and speakers who make tremendous claims of powers and abilities without evidence for the sole purpose of making money or increasing their own fame. Equally, I mean the generations of teachers, writers, speakers, and others who have quietly and unapologetically been taking from the practices and cultures of oppressed minorities, profiting off of them, and making them part of witchy canon so much that it becomes difficult to parse out when it happened or whether it's even possible to separate the appropriated from the not. I know, all of that probably sounds daunting. It's easy to become jaded or a bit cynical once you find it all out. I'm hoping that by providing you with this information up front you can save yourself money, time, and heartache down the road.

What's important to know first and foremost is that nobody else owns your spiritual exploration—you can absolutely find both magic and community in a way that will enrich your life.

In addition, this book is something of a cautionary tale of lived experience. I've been reading and studying witchcraft and the history of modern Paganism for over half of my life. Beyond that, I've hosted the Pagan-centric podcast *Inciting A Riot* since 2009. (Insert hipster *I was making podcasts before it was cool* joke here.) I've had a lot of missteps and gotten quite a lot wrong in my attempt to dive headfirst into the vast world of magical scholarship, but each misstep has been an opportunity to sit in discomfort, learn, grow, and do better next time. It's easy to fear being wrong. It's easy to be afraid to make a mistake, because all the bits afterwards don't feel good. I felt this book was important, however, because I have always found it necessary to have honest conversations about topics that might place us in an area of discomfort. Or, to put it another way, I value saying the quiet part out loud.

There are a lot of introductory books on witchcraft, magical study, and Pagan spirituality, but there are aspects about *being* part of this community that are by and large left off the page. Stuff you might not learn until years down the road and think, *If everyone knew this, why did no one tell me sooner?* The reasons vary from "nobody buys a book about witchcraft to hear about the dangers of unethically sourced crystals" to "some of this doesn't make us look very good," but I disagree with that premise. I think there is a way to say the quiet part out loud. I think embracing an honest, nuanced discussion of the realities of both magic and the community that practices it prepares you to dig deeper, learn better, and fill your life with magic in a lasting and powerful way. That's why this book isn't filled with answers. Rather, it seeks to teach you that the biggest lesson a dabbler must learn is that being a spiritual seeker is less about coming up with correct answers and far more about asking better questions.

So here we are, ready to go on a journey together into the vast world of magic. I can't promise that it'll always be easy, but it's my sincerest hope that it prepares you for what awaits you in your future. Along the way, I'll help guide you through some basics, reframe some expectations, and show you how to think critically while undertaking your spiritual journey. You'll learn to recognize warning signs, spot good and bad logic, what to do with all those crystals and herbs you see everywhere, what the movie *Legally Blonde* has to do with witchcraft, and, perhaps most important, how to craft a spiritual life that is meaningful, personal, and filled with magic.

PART

1

WAIT . . .
SO WITCHES
ARE REAL?

> *"Where magic is concerned, there is always an initial decision, an initial willingness to let it enter your life. If that is not there neither is magic."*
>
> —Neil Gaiman, *The Books of Magic: The Road to Nowhere*

Yes, yes they are. What, you thought I was going to say no and fill the rest of this book with coloring pages? Witches are real people who take their spiritual journey seriously. Contrary to the comments sections of many a social media post or YouTube video, they aren't role-playing, attention seeking, or losing touch with reality. While there aren't a lot of self-identified witches, Pagans, or otherwise magically labeled practitioners statistically, there is no less validity to their spiritual path. But I can understand some of the confusion surrounding the initial reaction when finding out someone identifies as a witch.

Pop culture has given us many captivating portrayals of witchcraft, ranging from Wanda Maximoff in the Marvel Cinematic Universe to the iconic green-faced Wicked Witch of the West in *The Wizard of Oz*. As a result, you may have come to this book with a lot of assumptions about magic and those who practice it, and it's important to first take a second to pause and examine those assumptions for what they are. Complicated assumptions lead to complicated questions that are sometimes difficult or uncomfortable to ask. Like, "How much of the stuff in movies is real?" "I did a spell and nothing happened . . . why?" "Is witchcraft evil?"

As we embark on this spiritual journey together, we will hold space to explore the witch as a fixture of story, film, and how that both aligns with and is differentiated from the witch as a real-world spiritual practitioner. It's also important to address some of the messier topics such as why your magic doesn't always work and the urge by some to prove or legitimize the practice of magic with science. The witch, as both figment and fact, has existed outside the realm of story as well, oftentimes in areas of politics and social justice. In fact, given the rise in protests and witchcraft's visibility in those spaces in recent years, politically minded witchcraft may very well have been your introduction to the world of real magical practice as separated from the wand waving you see on-screen. You will also hear me wax poetic about how my very favorite witch in television or film of all time is on the Hallmark Channel.

Before we get going, I want to quickly and briefly define a few terms, as they will pop up many times throughout the course of this book. It should be noted that both these terms and the definitions I'm providing are always evolving, and they represent my current understanding of how the community views these terms. Since our community is small, decentralized (meaning there is no governing body or book of rules somewhere), and less than one hundred years old, the terminology we use is also quite young and in a constant state of evolution. Which is to say, these are *my* definitions, and it's perfectly valid if you don't align with them. However, for the purposes of all of us being on the same page, here is what I mean when I say the following:

- **WITCH** — A person who practices witchcraft and self-identifies as a witch.
- **WITCHCRAFT** — The practice of magic, typically involving spells, rituals, or other rites.
- **MAGIC** — The act of manipulating the natural world, events, or the self through spiritual means such as witchcraft.
- **PAGAN** — Can be singular (a Pagan practitioner) or used as an umbrella term (the Pagan community) to refer to a decentralized group of people who adhere to spiritual traditions often inspired by or reconstructed from premodern beliefs and/or reverence for nature as sacred. Some view this group as a religion with many denominations while others view it as multiple distinct religious groups.
- **MAGICAL COMMUNITY** — This is used alongside of "Pagan community" to indicate the group of people who pursue an understanding of spiritual principles or magical practice and do not necessarily label themselves as Pagan.

One last thing: One can be Pagan without being a witch and vice versa. Indeed, one can practice magic without adhering to any belief in a higher power.

All that said, this first part of my book is my attempt to help you parse out what witchcraft is, what it isn't, and how to start discerning for yourself the fact and fiction of magical practice.

POP CULTURE
and WITCHCRAFT

Who was your first witch?

For me it was Eglantine Price, the apprentice witch in *Bedknobs and Broomsticks*, who could turn people into rabbits, ride her flying bed to watch cartoon animals play sports, and, lest we forget, fought the Nazis with magically animated suits of armor. Disney's spiritual successor to *Mary Poppins* was so popular in my house I very nearly wore out my VHS copy.

Maybe for you it was the Evil Queen in *Snow White*. Sure, she was technically evil, but her wardrobe was fabulous and her stony castle lair, with its cobwebbed bookshelves filled with titles like *Black Arts, Alchemy,* and my favorite, *Disguises,* is goals. Seriously, she called down lightning into a wine cup. That's a witch I would invite to my Friday-night circle gathering. Maybe you conjure up images of the cotton candy goodness of Glinda flying in her magic soap bubble in *The Wizard of Oz* or Mad Madam Mim in that epic showdown with Merlin from *The Sword in the Stone*. And, if you're reading this book, it's very likely that those early childhood memories sparked something in you. A curiosity. Permission to, even for a moment, believe in magic.

The thing about witches in media is that they don't have to be historically accurate, because the witch has always existed in a unique space in culture as a being of both fact and fiction.

The best witches are inspiring. Eglantine had a tiny book that she would leaf through furiously to look up her spells before chanting the arcane words of power. (Though, I have to say, I always wondered why. The spell to turn someone into a rabbit is three words, and it's one of the only spells she knew. How hard was it to remember three words?) Do you remember those tiny New Testament Bibles that the Gideons would hand out? Well, I had a whole lot of those, which is what happens when you grow up in a very small town in Texas with a surprising number of churches, and I noticed they were just about the size of the spell book carried by Miss Price. Every time my little brother annoyed me, I would flip open the book and chant the spell that would turn him into a rabbit.

It never worked but not for lack of trying.

It's OK if your witch is a being of pure fantasy with their sparkly spells or flying brooms or talking cats, because that witch led you here. The witches you know, however, didn't always look like they do now.

From Fairy Tale to Film

I love birds. I've loved and cared for multiple birds as pets in my life. If you're looking for a pet and you like the cuddliness of a puppy with the personality of a kitten, get a bird. Fun fact about birds is they're dinosaurs. There is no point in the fossil record where scientists can point and say, "Before this was dinosaurs and after this was birds." Witches are like the birds of the fairy-tale world, insofar as they've sort of always been there. There isn't really a moment in myth or legend where we can point and say, "After this is witches."

They've been used for centuries to frighten young children, such as the monstrous witch who lived in a house made of sweets and wanted to literally eat Hansel and Gretel. They've been seen as goddesses, like Hecate from ancient Greece or Cerridwen from Welsh myth. Medea, another witch from Greece, aided the hero Jason in his search for the Golden Fleece, later marrying him, only to be left by him for another woman, which sent her—according to different accounts—into a revenge tour that included murdering a king, his daughter, and her own children. Russia has a trove of witch stories about Baba Yaga (who is sometimes one witch, sometimes multiple sisters), with her iconic hut that sits upon two large chicken legs. Depending on the story, she could be found eating a child or helping out a lost traveler.

As we moved from oral tradition to the written word, the witches of old started finding important roles in novels and plays. Shakespeare loved a witch, and so many of his best plays included them. There was Sycorax in *The Tempest*, who was banished to an island for practicing sorcery said to be so strong she could control the moon. The Weird Sisters of *Macbeth* foretell the events of the play and show up to help out every now and then but are neither a malevolent nor particularly beneficial presence. While Disney has ensured most people forgot this, the sea witch in the original tale of "The Little Mermaid" isn't the villain. She's simply a witch living in a dangerous part of the ocean trying to make a living selling witchy services in exchange for whatever an underwater princess is willing to barter.

Of course, there have been plenty of good witches, too. From Russia to various parts of Europe to right here in the United States, right alongside the nefarious witches out for children eating and revenge, there have appeared kindhearted characters who provide aid when it's needed most. They are sometimes conflated with fairies, such as various versions of the "Cinderella" or "Sleeping Beauty" stories, but often this has looked like a mother or grandmother figure who provides the main character with magical objects or helpful incantations that become useful when facing evil later in the story.

For a while, the earliest witches in film and on television reminded us of those iconic legends and characters, often maintaining an appearance that suggested they were something other than human. Like their more ancient counterparts, they could be fearsome or helpful. *The Wizard of Oz* from 1939 gave us two examples of witches, one with a monstrous green face, the other gliding through the air handing out shoes. Familiar names have popped up, giving new faces and story lines for history's most adaptable fairy-tale figure. Endora on *Bewitched* harkened back to the biblical woman who conjured spirits for Saul. Roald Dahl's book *The Witches*, as well as its subsequent film adaptations, continued a long tradition of witches being portrayed as otherworldly, monstrous creatures tempting children to their doom while wearing human skin suits. Hayao Miyazaki's *Spirited Away* gave us the sisters Yubaba and Zeniba, who are thought to be updated iterations of the Baba Yaga figure in both her malevolent and benevolent forms, respectively.

Over time, the appearance of the witch did start to become more mundane while retaining their supernatural gifts. Television saw Samantha on *Bewitched* wiggling her nose to solve all sorts of midcentury maladies. In 1986 *The Worst Witch* centered the young Mildred Hubble as the magical protagonist in a school for witches. One thing about the witch in media remained steadfast: their spells could do pretty much anything the caster desired, and they came with wicked special effects.

The nineties brought a wealth of witches and put them in more realistic settings that to this day have influenced an entire generation of practitioners. The heavily Wiccan-influenced, Goth-flavored Catholic school girls of *The Craft* told people that magic might look less like sparkling effects and more like a picnic in the woods with your friends and chanting over a cup of wine. (Though, sure, Nancy walks on water and Sarah changes her hair with a wave of her hands, but at least there were no sparkles.) Two years later the film *Practical Magic*, based on the book of the same name by Alice Hoffman, told people that witchcraft might look more like dancing in the kitchen with your family or blending a lotion infused with herbs and intentions. And while there are certainly special effects used when Jimmy's ghost refuses to leave Gillian alone, they were far more tame than previous installments in the Witchy Cinematic Universe. To this day many practitioners point to this film as one of their favorite depictions of witchcraft in cinema.

Sabrina. Willow. Prudence. Bonnie. Ingrid. Queenie. Hermione. From *American Horror Story: Coven* to Amazon Prime's *Juju*, witches have evolved from mythical creatures blessed (or, in some cases, cursed) with magic and touched by chaos to nuanced, human characters of all gender identities, skin colors, and socioeconomic backgrounds using magic in ways spectacular and ordinary. Their stories are less about their magic and more about their humanity. One needn't look further than reinterpretations of characters like Circe or Morgan le Fay to see that we are still a bit obsessed with these classic witches but want their stories told with a fairness or equity not enjoyed by women in literature previously. Though, we still have our child killers in the midst like the one in *The Witch* from 2015 who stole a baby and used it as a beauty treatment.

Whether you grew up wandering the literary halls of Brakebills or your soul calls Halloweentown home, those first images of witchcraft and magic are the ones that take hold in our hearts and minds. Something about that fictional witch feels true to you.

Because of this, it's easy to get a bit let down when you find your first book on "real witchcraft" and wonder why it's more "light this candle and think this intention" and less "witness objects flying about the room as you wave your wand and speak these ancient words of power."

I'll be honest, I still get a bit let down by that last one. And, yes, to this day if I'm cleaning the house and nobody's looking, I absolutely sit astride my broom hoping that today is the day it will carry me into the sky. So far it hasn't worked, but I live in hope.

The witches you grew up reading about in stories or seeing on your television have given you a set of assumptions about all sorts of things. Big things. Small things. Things you don't even know you have opinions about yet because you haven't needed to think about them much. This is called implicit bias, which is the academic term for all the stereotypes you unconsciously apply to people and subjects, affecting your understanding, actions, or decisions regarding those people and subjects. We're going to explore this a bit more in depth later, but right now I want to help you understand how these assumptions have seeped into your subconscious and how the often fast and loose portrayals of witches, magical practice, and certain belief systems can have far-reaching consequences.

The Case of Papa Legba

There's a push by screenwriters and studios to ground their stories in relatable settings and populate them with much more human witches that has begun to blur the lines between what is true and what makes a great plot point. Sometimes this is fairly harmless, such as watching Sally Owens blowing on a wick to light a candle in *Practical Magic*. The worst that happens here is your husband walks in on you trying to light a candle with your breath and then you have to smile and pretend you were blowing out a wax pillar whose wick is still white. However, other depictions can be quite harmful in ways both obvious and difficult to put into words (that implicit bias I mentioned earlier). Let's go back to the example of *American Horror Story: Coven*.

In January 2014, the figure of Papa Legba was introduced to the show. He was depicted as a black man with red eyes wearing a top hat adorned with skulls while snorting cocaine and stealing babies. The character was so instantly iconic that (as of this writing) a quick internet image search for the term "Papa Legba" fills your screen with variations of that depiction and that depiction only.

Except this isn't who Papa Legba is in the religion of Voodoo at all.

Anthropologist and Voodoo priestess Lilith Dorsey wrote extensively on the depiction and the overall treatment of Voodoo in the series. (Quick clarification on the following quote: Dorsey uses the term "Lwa." I reached out to Dorsey for clarification on the term, and she stated that a "lwa" or "loa" doesn't have a neat and tidy cognate outside the religion of Voodoo, but that one could consider them deities.) In one article she wrote:

> The show, in addition to falsely equating Legba with the Devil, seems to have collapsed his character with that of the Voodoo Lwa Baron Samedi, traditionally depicted with a Top Hat and images of the dead, as he is the ruler of the cemetery. The reality is that Legba is the wise teacher, the communicator between the worlds. I like to call him the gentle guiding paternal influence we all wish we had.[1]

I suppose a wise teacher and interplanar communicator didn't fit with the screenwriters' story. At the time I'll admit I didn't understand the problem with the depiction. (I told you that this book would contain many cautionary tales and mistakes from my own lived experiences, didn't I?) I decided that since the story being told was a work of fiction, anything factually or historically inaccurate in the portrayal of Voodoo or the deities of that faith were merely part and parcel of said work of fiction. I reasoned that if we can enjoy shows like *Xena* or *Supernatural* with their very loose relationship to myth, what's the harm in a show putting a new spin on Voodoo?

The problem, of course, that one learns with time and distance is that this singular portrayal has consumed the current conversation and understanding of this loa. The popularity of that one depiction has made it incredibly difficult for seekers wishing to learn more about Papa Legba or, indeed, the rest of the religion of Voodoo to do so without receiving mixed messages.

It's this muddying of the waters of history and culture that can become extremely problematic to the point that it's often difficult to parse out what is celebrating the beliefs of a certain culture and what is fan fiction. Furthermore, when it comes to the magical traditions of BIPOC (black, indigenous, people of color), their portrayals in media skew to the negative, leading to the belief among the general public that their respective spiritual traditions are somehow inherently evil.

Children's movies, horror films, and plenty of television shows offer up Voodoo as the magical practice of choice for the wicked and depraved. It is used as the strange and terrible magic in the film *Child's Play* wielded by the serial killer Charles Ray, allowing him to transfer his consciousness into a doll that then goes on a murderous rampage. *The Serpent and the Rainbow* sold audiences on the horrifying idea that zombies are the product of vengeful practitioners seeking to raise the dead and steal their souls. On the other side of the entertainment spectrum, Disney's *The Princess and the Frog* has seen its fair share of criticism from scholars and practitioners alike. Voodoo is even used by the villain in the live-action *Scooby-Doo* movie with the intent to murder Scooby and release demons to rule over the earth for the next ten thousand years. And, of course, the list goes on.

Voodoo in film and on television is often portrayed as a violent tradition practiced by people that studios seem to go out of their way to depict as savages. The media strips topics such as animal sacrifice, voodoo dolls, and zombies of their historical and spiritual contexts, twisting them to fit a plot that is often written to scare white people.

Let me digress for a moment. I am not in any way a scholar on Voodoo. There are far better voices and speakers from inside that community who could do a much better job teaching you than I ever could. (And I recommend you take a peek at the "Resources" section for some great books by those people.) But you do not need to be a scholar to see that the portrayal of Voodoo has an effect on the way the average person views Voodoo, if they regard it as a serious living religion at all. However innocent the intention of storytellers may be, there's a real and harmful impact on the way people associated with the tradition are discussed.

When Haiti had an earthquake in 2010 that killed in excess of one hundred thousand people and devastated the nation, evangelical pastor

Pat Robertson said that the catastrophe was due to a pact with the devil. He said the following on his TV program, *The 700 Club*:

> [Something] happened a long time ago in Haiti, and people might not want to talk about it. They were under the heel of the French. You know, Napoleon III and whatever. And they got together and swore a pact to the devil. They said, "We will serve you if you will get us free from the French." True story. And so, the devil said, "OK, it's a deal."
>
> And they kicked the French out. You know, the Haitians revolted and got themselves free. But ever since, they have been cursed by one thing after the other. Desperately poor. That island of Hispaniola is one island. It's cut down the middle. On the one side is Haiti; on the other side is the Dominican Republic. Dominican Republic is prosperous, healthy, full of resorts, et cetera. Haiti is in desperate poverty. Same island. They need to have and we need to pray for them a great turning to God. And out of this tragedy, I'm optimistic something good may come. But right now, we're helping the suffering people, and the suffering is unimaginable.[2]

Somehow the pastor recharacterized the Haitian Revolution as a wicked deal with the devil to run the white people off their island. This is incredibly reductionist. It asserts that all the people of color involved were Voodoo practitioners and slaves when neither was necessarily true. There were plenty of people of color in Haiti who were wealthy and free for a number of reasons; not everyone who was a person of color necessarily practiced Voodoo.

Just as important, Robertson's comments evidence a pervasive misunderstanding that if one is not a practicing Christian of some type, they are "lost" or possibly actively serving the Devil—capitalized here to indicate this is the Christian Devil, their Big Bad. This thinking is exacerbated if the non-Christian in question belongs to a polytheistic belief system, as this violates one of Christendom's Ten Commandments: "You shall have no other god before me." Of the current major world religions, those that include worship of more than one deity are mostly made up of people of color, Voodoo being one of them. It's impossible to hear the sort of comments Pat Robertson makes and not harken back to a time when it was seen that the civilized practiced Christianity and that any other type of belief system was for uneducated savages.

Equating Voodoo with evil, with Devil worship, and generally treating it as a dark and malevolent religion ties together these threads of bias that are bound up in racism and xenophobia and the misguided notion that colonization and forced conversion were good things that white Europeans did for the world. This type of thinking is harmful, reinforces stereotypes that are sometimes obvious and sometimes difficult to put into words, and comes from the ether of consumed media.

OK. This is heavy. Let's take a step back for a bit, because there will be plenty of time to parse out history later. For now, I'm hoping you'll take away the understanding that depictions of spiritual practitioners in media do more than simply tell fun stories. They influence how we see one another in deep and profound ways. They create hierarchies of importance, of goodness, and of virtue where none should exist.

The Realest Witchcraft on Television

Witches on television and in movies do more than influence our views on certain cultures; they also influence our understanding of the practice itself. I started this chapter with the idea that there are witches from fairy tales and fiction, noting that the figure of the witch is a unique creature that is both fact and fiction. The factual witch, the one you'll bump into in a bookstore (or the guy who wrote this book), doesn't share a lot of similarities with the witch in fiction. Except, perhaps, when it comes to taste in fashion, but I digress. My friends and I joke that if someone were to ever make a movie about "real witches" it would be the dullest movie ever made.

Watch as the witch drives to the bank to make a deposit. Notice that when he puts the money in the tube, the tube flies through the air and into the bank. Later he will do some grocery shopping, but no cash will be exchanged. He will simply wave his phone across a screen and magically the groceries will be paid for. At night, his dog will vomit on the carpet. Watch as he uses a mystical device to clean the carpet as though it never happened. Magic!

The reality of daily life for those of a witchy persuasion is neither as exciting as macro culture would have us believe nor as eventful as the media would portray. We aren't spending our weeknights stopping crime with incantations or potions. I know. I know. Mourn the disappointment. It's fine; we all had to.

Magic in the everyday lives of those who practice it, however, is no less potent and no less effective than the stuff you see on television. From the lawyer who pockets a stone before she goes into court because she needs a little extra boost of confidence, to the guy who ensures his résumé is anointed with a bit of oil before he hands it in to sway the odds in his favor, magic can be as intrinsically part of one's daily life and routine as brushing your teeth or walking your dog.

Now, don't laugh, but nowhere have I seen a more realistic portrayal of magic on television than in the Good Witch franchise on the Hallmark channel. *The Good Witch* was a made-for-TV movie that aired on the Hallmark Channel in January 2008, and it has since spawned six sequels and a TV show. The TV show is in its sixth season as of this writing. It's certainly possible that the magic on the show feels realistic because it's a Hallmark show and their special effects budget is on par with that of a high school production of *The Wizard of Oz*, but whatever the reason, it works.

Cassie Nightingale, the central character in the show, is most certainly a witch, but she's a witch who practices the kind of magic you'd actually be able to perform. Better still, she practices the kind of magic that gets results. There might be a dish baked and given to someone to open up much-needed lines of communication, or her intuition helps her be in the right place at the right time. She and the rest of her family use their magic to foretell the future, summon a lost item, break curses, improve their businesses, send an unwanted person away, and overall live a magical life.

This portrayal doesn't feel sexy, and I don't ever see Cassie Nightingale making Top 10 Witches in Media lists, but the funny thing is that when I talk to other witchy-minded writers, podcasters, bloggers, et al., *they* always list her as one of their favorites. She's the witches' witch. And, yes, there are plenty of ways to break down the wealthy, cisgender, heterosexual, white characters and jejune story lines that are the hallmark of ... well ... Hallmark, but the point about the magic stands.

I think it's important to recognize and celebrate these humbler portrayals of magic in media because it normalizes the idea that the witch you might meet at a coffee shop is as real and valid as some fictionalized Chosen One on-screen. It can be quite difficult to parse out the difference between the witch in media, the witch in fairy tale, and the witch in real life. That brings me to one final point before we move forward.

What Makes a Witch?

An interesting thing happens when you try to research witches. If you go to Google or Wikipedia—the place where most casual research begins—and you search for the word "witch," you're going to need to clarify some things. If you're on Wikipedia, you're going to be asked whether you meant "witchcraft" (meaning the use of supernatural abilities in myth and practice the world over since time immemorial) or possibly you mean "witchhunt" (meaning the search for practitioners of witchcraft, a search that still occurs in parts of world today, though there's more about that in the political witch chapter), or perhaps you're asking about one of the modern pantheons of witches as depicted in Terry Pratchett's Discworld novels or the *Witches of East End* TV series. See, the internet knows something that many witchy books and blogs seem staunchly opposed to accepting: the word "witch" doesn't always mean the same thing.

Sometimes the word refers to pointy-hatted women who ride brooms into the night sky and sing hypnotic songs to children in order to lure them to their deaths. Other times it is a scapegoat for adults in the developing world that kills men, women, and children who are perceived as some kind of threat. In some parts of the world witches are protectors, guarding their community against evil spirits, or healers who stave off all sorts of maladies through traditional methods. Still other times the word means the hopeful singer-songwriter next door who makes her own herbal tea and carries a piece of carnelian with her when stepping up to the microphone.

It's important to note this need for disambiguation because we should be cautious with language. Words morph depending on context, and it is important that we allow them to wear different clothes sometimes, to go off into the world and be their own entity. Otherwise, our language stays stagnant, and we don't get to invent new ways of conversing. It's also important to recognize that sometimes when television or movies or Pat Robertson tells you that someone is a witch, they could mean anything from an oppressed minority group to a superhero.

It should also be pointed out that, once you're behind the velvet ropes of Paganism or witchcraft, you realize that there are lots of ways to be a witch and nobody owns the term. You might also find that the practice of magic isn't for you, but you still appreciate the spiritual or religious traditions of some particular Pagan path. That's fine. You can be Pagan and not be a witch. Plenty of Pagan religions, like Wicca for example, don't necessarily overlap with the identity of being a witch or practicing witchcraft. You can be one or the other, both, or neither. The important thing is that you make this choice for yourself after consideration and study. Let me say that again for the people in the back: labels like "witch" or "Pagan" or "occultist" or whatever are self-applied. You get the honor of deciding what fits you and your spiritual practice best. Media doesn't normally make this distinction, and therefore it can take years to unlearn that predilection to conflate all of these terms.

Are You a Good Witch or a Bad Witch?

I realize that I'm giving myself away as an elder millennial when I bring up this reference, but I'm still not over the fact that after the writers made the character Willow (from *Buffy the Vampire Slayer*) a powerful witch capable of taking on Big Bad villains alongside Buffy in the fifth season, they immediately turned that newfound strength into an addiction that led to the character becoming the main antagonist of the following season. Why? Because according to the world of fiction, too much of the wrong kind of magic is dangerous, and if you perform it terrrrrible things will happen. (Insert thunder clap and rolling storm sounds here.)

However you got here, the one thing you've probably brought to this path from the media you've consumed is the understanding that there is good magic and bad magic. Left-handed magic. Dark magic. Black magic. There are all sorts of names for it, but by whatever you call it the assumption you're carrying about it is that it's a distinct and unique form of magic specifically wielded to harm others and possibly, by extension, yourself.

The natural inclination when it appears that there is some type of binary choice or spectrum between good and evil is to choose good. (I . . . assume . . . I mean, like, I understand if you want to live out your evil Disney witch villain fantasy, because I, too, am enamored with Ursula and the Evil Queen and Maleficent. So, if evil is your thing, go for it. Though I hear it doesn't come with a good dental plan, but they have a fabulous cape stipend, so in my opinion it evens out.) Social psychologists might say this is because we wish to adhere to social norms—such as generally being thought of as "good" and doing "good" things—not necessarily out of any personal desire to be a good person, but rather to be *thought of* as a good person. We are far more consumed with how we are perceived by others than unpacking what choices fit our personal understanding of morality.

The felicific calculus you're mentally performing when you hear that something is labeled "black magic" isn't usually whether you should learn more about a given spiritual practice before making a rational decision regarding its inherent virtue. It's usually "OMG what if Brenda finds out I dabbled in the Dark Arts?! She'll tell everyone I'm a devil worshipper and then I'll never be allowed back to brunch!"

The truth about "black magic" as a term and an idea has a long and fraught history. It's bound up in a murky mixture that is part early Christian demonology, part classism, and, especially in recent centuries, part racism. I am not a professional historian, so I'll leave the parsing out of the details to those best suited to the task (hint: check the further reading guide in the back of this book for the fascinating and problematic history of this term). What I do want to answer up front for you is a question that you might be wrestling with in the back of your mind if you're new to this topic:

Is there such a thing as "black magic"?

When people ask this, they typically mean a kind of magic that is inherently malevolent, harmful, and possibly dangerous. As I said earlier, there are a lot of implicit biases and straight-up outright misinformation that have likely led you to believe that at least some types of magic are to be avoided. While there might be a bit of truth to the idea that, since magic is a tool and witchcraft is a skill, there are certain techniques that could be a bit advanced for a beginning dabbler, I want to reassure you that we are still only talking about tools and skills.

A salad fork can be used to pierce a crisp bed of romaine lettuce just as easily as it could be used to stab someone's eye. There is no bad magic or good magic; there is just magic. It is a natural part of our world and a natural part of each of us. You shouldn't approach any part of it with fear, but, rather, with respect and appreciation for its origin and evolution.

Forget what you've been told by *Charmed*. Working a little magic to improve your life, as well as the lives of your family and loved ones, isn't against some cosmic rulebook. You are not going to get spanked by the Witch Daddy. (Unless you ask nicely and set ground rules first.)

What Can You Take from Television?

It might say a lot about me to tell you that when I was a kid one of my favorite TV shows was *Judging Amy*. It aired from 1999 until 2005 and starred Amy Brenneman with Tyne Daly playing her mother as a juvenile court judge and social worker, respectively, living in Hartford, Connecticut. The series was loosely based on the life of Brenneman's mother, herself a judge on the Connecticut State Superior Court. (Sidenote: This was also the first time I saw Tom Welling on television. He played her child's karate teacher and eventual love interest, and, coincidentally, played a key role in me figuring out I was—and still am—very, very gay.) Unlike the various *Law & Order*s and *CSI*s and other sundry crime dramas of the day, this show was the first I'd seen that centered family law and seemed to make the case for justice and fairness and that sometimes those things didn't equate to years and years of punishment. It inspired me.

I ended up going to college for a degree in criminal justice with an emphasis in juvenile studies. Then I worked for a few years in the juvenile court system, during which time I came to the harsh understanding that the real world wasn't like *Judging Amy*. There aren't quite as many happy endings or neatly wrapped-up cases as on television. However, it doesn't mean that there isn't some basis for what I saw on-screen, and it doesn't mean that the early love that TV show inspired in me didn't eventually become a deep and abiding passion for ideas like justice and fairness.

There are plenty of archaeologists who will tell you that they pursued the career after watching *The Mummy*. Plenty of folks in the medical field will cite *Grey's Anatomy* or *Scrubs* as the spark of inspiration behind their choice to go to medical school. Since the early 2000s crime labs have reported an uptick in applicants who became interested in forensics after watching the TV franchise *CSI*.[3] At the same time, not a single one of those people will tell you that their daily reality matches up with the media portrayals that inspired them.

Witches on-screen, in books, in plays, in myth and folktale, have their place as part of a good story. They're a fixture of literature and tales told around campfires, in film and on television, and it would be quite dull if they suddenly conformed to real-world limitations. One should be cautious when taking in media to remember that what you see on-screen is fiction and especially cautious when that fiction is borrowing from an oppressed culture, examining not just the stories we consume but also the ways in which the stories are told as well as the ones who are telling the story. Always do more research before believing that the Voodoo in the horror movie is factual. But don't be afraid to let the witches of the screen beckon you into believing, if even for a moment, that magic is real.

The truth in the case of real-life witchcraft is often just as strange and interesting and engaging as fiction, though, perhaps, without all the sparkly bits. It is important that your expectations are tempered, because chasing after the magic you see on the screen or in your favorite fantasy series will either lead you to several dead ends or empty your wallet from buying into false promises. The witch from fantasy might have brought you here, but it's the rich tapestry of the mystical mundane that will keep you endlessly fascinated as you continue on your magical journey.

CHAPTER 2

WHAT CAN MAGIC DO?

W hen you were a kid, did you ever play that game "light as a feather, stiff as a board" at sleepovers? You sit around in a circle and say some words and then place your fingertips under someone who is lying down or sitting in the middle and attempt to lift them. If you do it wrong—say one person doesn't actually lift but pretends to—then it fails. If you don't have enough people, it will likely fail. If you are not acting in perfect concert, it will fail. But with enough people, a little prep work, and some luck you can actually lift someone off the floor with little more effort than carrying a few heavy shopping bags.

In the movie version of "light as a feather, stiff as a board," all sorts of mystical things can occur when you do the chant in a circle of friends, as long as it's late at night and there are candles lit and at least one of you is secretly a witch. (I don't make the rules of cinema.) In *The Craft* Rachel True's character is left floating in midair, suspended by magic until someone's mother walks in, breaking their concentration and the enchantment.

But is any of this "real magic"?

Well, that depends. The word conjures up all sorts of images from the fantasy genre, most of which defy physics or look really painful. (Seriously, Hermione's transformation into that half-cat thing doesn't remotely look fun.) With all those images floating around the ether, it can be difficult to ascertain two things:

1. Are people serious when they say they believe in, and actually perform, magic?

2. If so, exactly how crazy are they, and how fast should you be running in the opposite direction?

The answers to these questions, in my case, are "yes" and "quite" and "hopefully faster than me unless it's dinnertime; then you're fine because I'm hungry and this burrito won't eat itself." (Unless, of course, it's magic, too.)

All joking aside, I understand that the notion that magic is real and can affect you and the world around you elicits a range of reactions, which is perfectly valid. If you've told your family and friends about your beliefs, you are also likely no stranger to raised eyebrows and questions about your grip on reality. However, as a thought experiment, I want you to temporarily remove the idea of magic from shooting fireballs out of your hands or raising the dead. Instead, I want you to think smaller. Much, much smaller.

Mundane and Minor Magics

Every now and then a sort of story gets passed around online asking you to believe that humans might possess supernatural abilities. Sometimes the label is superpowers, other times it's magic, and depending on what is currently playing in a movie theater near you, it could be called something else. The gist, however, is always the same. Maybe people are magical, but magic doesn't look like what we think it does. Different versions of this hypothetical exist, but they almost always include a list of examples. They include things like:

- Nobody knows why, but James always makes the best coffee in the office. He uses the same coffee, filters, water, and machine in the break room that everyone else does, but his always tastes better.
- Susan has never broken a bone. She's been in a couple of car accidents and took a bad tumble where she landed on her ankle, but she's always walked away fine.
- If you give Malcolm a plant, any plant, he can make it thrive. One time he dug out a couple of crispy,

brown ferns from my trash that I was planning to
throw away, and a few weeks later they were green
and thriving on his windowsill.

The argument being made is that perhaps magic is less the flashy stuff that makes for a good TV show and more of an undefined set of quiet, subtle, inexplicable ways in which our lives are improved.

It is easy to get bogged down trying to explain the mechanics of magic, mostly because you can't. (Sorry . . . don't know if I was supposed to say "spoiler alert" there.) Some people liken it to prayer, where you ask a deity to make something go the way you want it to and hope that deity is feeling generous. Others try to use the trappings of science to explain it, complete with different types of measurements and instruments and studies and documentaries that all claim to prove how magic works. Further still you'll have a new trend in self-help come out every few years, such as the Law of Attraction, and people will point and nod in agreement. When these are reviewed with a more critical lens, they are often found wanting.

The Law of Attraction, as an example, which is often restated as "thoughts are things" or what you think (positive or negative) becomes what you bring into your life, is deeply flawed. The principle only works for those privileged enough to be financially secure, physically healthy, and supported by societal infrastructures. Marginalized groups and those without financial security, whom society is not built to support, did not become stigmatized, oppressed, or underserved because they weren't thinking positively enough. Likewise, the same is true for those with chronic or terminal illnesses and those with disabilities. Turning magic or spiritual seekership into pithy bumper sticker quotes is inherently problematic, as it ends up being reductive and incomplete.

While I hold out hope that one day I'll pick up a broom and it'll carry me off into the sky, I feel the most important thing we can do when introducing someone to the concept of magic is discuss its limitations honestly and openly. At its core, magic, as I have come to understand it through study and experience, assists with weighting the scales of possibility in your favor. This is why witches aren't, for example, making a profession out of winning the lottery. Millions of people play the lottery, and for very high jackpots—you may be one of them—but you have a better chance of being bitten by a shark while being struck by lightning in the middle of accepting your Academy Award than you would actually winning outright. Magic works best when you are attempting to achieve a realistic goal, utilizing both magical and mundane efforts.

If you want a job, all the spells in the world likely will not make your phone ring with job offers if you are not putting out résumés, turning in applications, and doing the legwork associated with obtaining a job. Magic might help get your application noticed or give the interviewer a more favorable view of your responses. Perhaps magic might make you more confident in your interview and less likely to trip over words or sit in awkward silence while trying to find an original way to answer the question "What is your greatest weakness?"

There are all sorts of spells in best-selling books on witchcraft detailing how to change the way you look or meet a lover or find a lost pet. Unless you're equally changing your lifestyle, putting yourself out there, or hanging flyers and organizing search parties, all you're really doing is lighting a candle and talking to yourself. Like a birthday wish without the cake. Intention without action does not typically lead to a positive outcome.

ALL JOKING ASIDE, CALL A DOCTOR

Plenty of situations call for magic to be secondary to mundane action. Medical issues are perhaps at the top of that list. If you're told you have a malignant tumor, for example, casting spells, lighting candles, and making lovely smelling oil blends can certainly be something you do . . . after you have taken appropriate medical actions as prescribed by your health professional.

Proving Magic with Science

There's an uncomfortable overlap between those who believe in the practice of magic and those who have a distrust of medicine and science. It is not uncommon to find practitioners using the language and tools of science to bolster their claims while ignoring or even denigrating the scientific method, which seeks to test, in a replicable way, the veracity of their hypothesis. Another way of stating this that my friends in the scientific community use is that researchers attempt to "break" or disprove the hypothesis. A hypothesis is an educated guess about the way something works, but in order for it to be scientific and testable there must be a way to disprove it. Basically, the researcher must be able to conceive of an observation that would disprove—or falsify—the hypothesis. We move forward in scientific thought when we conduct experiments that could potentially disprove our hypothesis.

There's a trend of people who support their arguments with science but are only using the trappings of science—the language or tools of scientific research—without ever creating a testable, falsifiable hypothesis.

This is most often seen in paranormal entertainment programs. I'm using the term "paranormal entertainer" to delineate between those who perform good faith paranormal investigation and those who seek to create an entertaining media product oftentimes through bad faith methods. These programs rarely depict an accurate portrayal of real-world paranormal investigation. A favorite tool of the paranormal entertainer is the EMF (electromagnetic field) meter. These meters are designed to warn users of potentially dangerous radiation levels, but when the meters are repackaged and marketed to paranormal entertainers, it is alleged that they can detect the presence of ghosts and other supernatural presences. The issue is that the specific EMF meters typically used can be set off by most types of electronic devices, old wiring, and a host of electromagnetic waves. (And when you're surrounded by cell phones, camera equipment, voice recorders, et cetera, it's not hard to start finding alternative reasons why a low-grade electromagnetic field detector could go off.) Because it's scientific equipment with a legitimate use, entertainers can occlude exactly what it is that the meter is detecting. In these programs entertainers always tell the audience they found at least some type of paranormal phenomenon, and they misuse quite a bit of equipment in their attempts to prove their findings.

The issue is not relegated to paranormal entertainment. Sometimes you will hear about studies that allegedly prove the existence of magic. At the very least, some claim that these studies prove our intention, or our will, has real-world effects beyond our internal thought processes. While this has certainly softened in recent years, a cursory search through witchy blogs, vlogs, and other media finds that the idea is still very much alive.

A name that comes up regularly is Masaru Emoto. If you're a millennial or younger, you might not know his name, but you have almost certainly heard of two of his more infamous experiments.

Emoto is the pseudoscientist who claimed our emotions could affect the molecular structure of water. He even wrote a *New York Times* best-selling book about it. He would expose water to different images, terms, and even music. He then froze that water and took pictures of the ice crystal structure. Allegedly, negative emotions and images created ugly or violent crystal structures while positive and beautiful images resulted in equally pleasing crystal structures. OK, so far so good—it makes a certain amount of intrinsic sense. What quickly became clear, however, as others attempted to replicate this experiment was that Emoto had employed the same strategy that anyone who has ever taken a group photo with a bunch of drunk friends has used: he took lots and lots of photos and then settled on the one that worked for his purpose.

He also claimed that this experiment worked on rice. He put cooked rice into different containers and spent a period of time saying specific phrases such as "Thank you!" and "You're an idiot!" to the containers while leaving one alone as a control. According to Emoto, the rice receiving the negative comments rotted while the rice receiving gratitude eventually fermented and created a nice smell. While many have also attempted to replicate his results, the scientific community has been unable to do so. In fact, many state that Emoto's experiments seem almost purposefully irreplicable. Nevertheless, their popularity lives on in the pseudoscience and magical communities among the ephemera of supposed proof that "thoughts are things."

Remember, for the claim to be supported by the scientific method, there must be some observation that could disprove the hypothesis. Yet so many practitioners, paranormal entertainers, and others in and around the magical community who skew science to support their claims ignore the observation that might disprove them. Or, like with Emoto, findings could be taken out of context, painting a picture of evidentiary support that isn't supported. There is a fine line that the modern, informed magical practitioner must walk between what is provable and observable and what must be taken on faith. The learning of magic itself is a bit like the scientific method, in that it is based on observations, results, and replication. The important idea for experienced practitioners and dabblers alike to keep in mind is where the goalposts should be placed when it comes to matters of spirit. Do you always need proof? If so, what kind of proof do you need?

Magical practitioners operate a bit like scientists in that we make observations about the world around us and the ways in which magic seems to affect it or come from it. This could be taking certain actions during a particular moon phase or painting your door a striking color. We don't make it a habit of injecting truly falsifiable parameters into our spiritual beliefs that often, and I'm not saying we always need to. There is plenty of space for a spiritual journey to coexist peacefully alongside an appreciation for science while acknowledging that parts of the journey will go outside what is able to be proven. We'll get into this a bit later, but for now a good rule of thumb is that if it isn't hurting anyone—including yourself—and it isn't causing you undue fear or paranoia, then there's room for faith.

OK, So Magic Is . . . Fake?

The problem with this attempt to cloak the effectiveness of magic inside debunked studies and pseudoscience is that it obfuscates whether we need the proof at all. I would posit that the need for legitimacy on paper is wrapped up in the economy of magical practice. There are a lot of people trying to sell you books and herb blends and soaps and oils and candles blessed under a full moon while the practitioner chanted and spun in circles counterclockwise.

Because the magical community is decentralized—meaning there's no leader or book from which knowledge and rules originate—it's difficult to determine who's being genuine and who's attempting to make a quick buck from a gullible seeker. In all this uncertainty, one question remains: Is magic real?

Ostensibly, this question is why so many people cling to studies and gadgets and YouTube documentaries. I think the answer to the question is as easy as asking, Did magic work for you? Did you obtain employment if you performed a job spell while doing the mundane work required in conjunction with the spell? If you were seeking a lost object, was it found? If you were attempting to open communication after a fight with a lover, did you?

Sometimes the end results of the spell aren't necessarily positive. You might get a job, but your boss is terrible. You might find the missing object, but it could be broken. You could open communication with your lover only to realize the relationship isn't worth pursuing. Magic is real, but it's the expectations put upon magic by Hollywood, by those trying to sell you something, and by people hoping to get famous that set seekers up for failure.

For magic to be successful, it must be possible. You're not going to summon up a blizzard in the middle of summer, nor are you going to attract a movie star you've never met to your front door. You will not jump off the roof and fly, nor will you reanimate a corpse. But if the clouds are full and there's the possibility of rain, you might tip the possibility of it raining in your favor. If you're having trouble making friends, a charmed stone carried in your pocket might help make that next attempt at an introduction feel less awkward or help you feel bolder.

Take the slumber party game I talked about at the beginning of this chapter. "Light as a feather, stiff as a board" actually works. For real. I'm not kidding. We understand the science behind it. Try it with a group of friends. Everyone gives it a go of trying to lift the person in the middle, failing, and then coming together, chanting, and making a concerted effort to lift the person. It's possible for it to succeed, because of the even distribution of weight among multiple people who are working in concert. Is that magic?

I wholeheartedly believe in magic, and if I can leave you with one last thing in this chapter, it's that magic is a natural part of our world. Therefore, it is perfectly acceptable for an act of magic to have a scientific foundation, for the result to be measured and understood. There are acts of nature, ways to manipulate the elements and ourselves, that lead to real, lasting transformation that toes the line between what is science and what is magic.

The lifelong smoker who's able to cope with their addiction after hypnosis. The calm a person with anxiety can feel after writing what troubles them down onto a piece of paper and burning it or sticking it in a jar in the freezer. There are known reasons why these things work on our psyche, but that does not make them any less an act of magic.

Or, as one of my favorite authors of fiction, Terry Pratchett, once wrote, "It doesn't stop being magic just because you know how it works."

CHAPTER 3

WHEN MAGIC FAILS

I have hosted a podcast exploring topics of magic and spiritual seeking for over a decade, and the one question that pops up in my inbox more than almost any other is "I did a spell and it didn't work. What did I do wrong?" What's even more curious is that when I talk to other magical content creators, they say the same thing. Whether you're dipping your toe into the cauldron for the first time or you've been dancing under full moons for decades, there have been times when your magic simply didn't work.

"But Fire Lyte," you ask, having just read chapter 2, "you just made this big case that magic is real and works! Doesn't it seem counterproductive to write a whole chapter immediately afterwards about how . . . it doesn't?"

Well, dear reader, that's exactly why this chapter needs to be written. You see, despite being one of the leading questions many dabblers ask, it's not a topic that's approached often. At least not publicly. Mostly because, in my experience, authors and content creators want to focus on what magic can do and all the ways they've successfully implemented it in their lives. Some attribute this mentality to social media, wherein we show a version of ourselves that's perfectly angled, digitally edited, and possibly sponsored by a questionable tea company. However, the urge to tell others how successful we are at doing a thing—in this case spell craft—rather than showing the daily struggle to become and remain successful isn't solely a product of social media, nor is it remotely novel.

When you're trying something new, especially something in the realm of woo-woo, it is very easy to toss your cauldron into the trash when you did all the "double double" by the book, but the "toil and trouble" didn't manifest. Go get your cauldron out of the trash, because that's good cast iron and we can just scrub it off and try again.

So, for Real This Time . . . What Is Magic?

There is a lot of debate about what magic is and isn't even among experienced practitioners. A lot of the reason for that is that defining magic is wrapped up in spiritual commerce. In other words, magic is often defined by those in the public sphere seeking to decide who *owns* magic. These folks will create a convenient meaning that skirts falsifiability and in some form or fashion intimates magic is not something you either possess or can master without their assistance.

The two most common ideas surround heredity and lineage.

People who claim to be hereditary witches tend to espouse the notion that some people are born with magic and others aren't. Sometimes it includes a claim of a blessed family line, sometimes not. No real rhyme or reason. This is a fun theory because it does all the things humans like best. It tells us we're special. It tells us we're different and better than other people. It gives us an explanation for why we might feel like we don't fit in with families or certain groups. The threshold for being a hereditary witch seems to be fairly straightforward. You ask yourself, *Do I feel like I was born a special, magical being capable of performing great feats of the supernatural?* Then you say, *Yes,* and someone sends you a welcome package of quartz crystals, a wand, and a sack of glitter to throw upon entering or leaving a room. (Note to self: great business idea . . .)

The lineage folks have a few more rules. While they don't necessarily state that people are or aren't born with magic, they are more than happy to tell you how they come from multiple generations of practitioners. They also typically stretch an unbroken line between them and someone involved in the Salem Witch Trials, or perhaps further back to an accused witch in Europe or another historical figure who was featured in a History Channel documentary about people who were involved in the paranormal.

Some will tell you they're magical because of who they were in a past life or because they visited a holy site or were blessed by a shaman or are channeling this or that deity. The list of reasons people will give about why they're more magical, or at least better at magic, than you is endless.

Now, since I do not know each of these hypothetical people personally, I couldn't attest to their level of good faith, genuine belief, or motivation for what they're saying. What I can tell you unequivocally is that there's no locked door you have to go through, literally or figuratively, to practice magic. Let me say that again: you are free to practice magic no matter who you are. There might be initiations you must go through in order to join a specific spiritual group, but that is a wholly different thing.

Magic doesn't depend on who you were in a past life, who started your coven, or whether you can trace your ancestry back to Lila, the Great Druidess of the Sea (not a real person, but that gives me an idea for a novel). When you venture out into the world, if someone starts telling you one of these stories, just nod along. Let them get it all out. They've been holding it in a long time hoping someone would ask them. Or you could do what I do and act like you just got a very important text message that requires you to move twenty feet in the opposite direction in order to respond.

It is a part of the natural world, and accessing, manipulating it, and improving your use of it is a skill. In that way, magic is simply a tool, a birthright that belongs to everyone, and witchcraft is a set of skills employed to engage with that magic. Yes, it takes practice, study, and dedication, but so do a lot of things. Like singing.

When You Miss the Note

Let me digress for a moment. I'm a gay man, and while I like to pretend—as most people do—that I'm not a stereotype, stereotypes exist for a reason. In this case, I am that reason. I love me some pop divas. (Apologies to my editor and all lovers of grammar for that sentence structure.) I love a breakup song with a big, range-y (not a word) chorus and lots of belted high notes. The problem with almost all of those songs is having to sing them live, night after night, to a crowd of thousands of people who all have smartphones, social media accounts, and secret hopes of attaining viral fame.

We've all seen it happen. Or heard it, as the case may be. The singer who reaches for that high note when singing "The Star-Spangled Banner," whose voice sounds as though it is this side of recovering from a cold. So when the lyrics "o'er the land of the" ramp up, you're white-knuckling your $7 hot dog and $12 beer wondering if their fatigued vocal cords are going to hold up through that last high note. Then it happens. The singer's voice seems to shred to bits at the start of the word "free," but she still continues, seeming to hope that this is all a bad dream and if she keeps trudging through all those shreds they will coalesce into a single, beautiful note and this will all be over. It doesn't happen, of course, and then the entire news cycle for the following days is about how this legendary singer botched the United States' national anthem.

Suddenly everyone online whose social media profile photo consists of a white person in the driver's seat of a car wearing wraparound Oakley knockoff sunglasses they bought at the Dollar Tree is laughing about what a terrible singer she is. Compilation videos are made. Certain parts of the internet decide she's "canceled." She "ruined" the national anthem.

The problem is that while, sure, the singer failed to hit that one note in that one performance of the song, we've all seen and heard that singer give dozens, if not hundreds of pitch-perfect performances over the course of her career. We've heard her perform crisp melismas with ease and stood in awe watching her belt a note so high few other singers on earth could hope to attempt it.

Failure is the most temporary thing in the world. Failure feels bad, yes, and if you happen to fail on live television in front of millions of people it probably feels worse, but few people really care about your failures for very long. You gave a bad performance? Shake it off and wow them next time. Your terrible dancing was witnessed by your crush? Laugh it off and realize it's part of your charm. You tried to make an award-winning macaroni and cheese recipe you saw on television featuring a dozen different, very expensive, types of cheese and ended up sort of burning it and also not buying nearly enough yellow cheddar and it's Thanksgiving and your grandmother is having to be nice about it? OK ... well ... that last one was me, and I moved to a different state shortly afterwards, which is really the only thing you can do in that specific scenario.

The point is that, as cliché as it sounds, failure is simply part of growth and improvement. Failure also means that you tried, which is a lot more than many can say.

This is more than a motivational speech. This is a friendly but essential reminder that, since magic is a skill, it requires practice, study, and effort. When you're doing all those things in your course of learning, you'll figure out how to make magic work best for you. As with other skills—running, painting, baking—there are basics everyone learns, and then there are the things each person does to make that skill work for them.

Runners will figure out how to hold their hands, open or closed, while running, on which part of the foot to land in their stride, and how to breathe. Two painters can choose the same medium and the same subject, but they will likely choose different brushes, create gradients using wholly different techniques, and add in touches that make a piece theirs. And, of course, while baking is certainly a science, if *The Great British Bake Off* has taught us anything, it's that innovation and imagination is the soul of greatness. (And also that no matter how good you are or how much you practice, sometimes the tent is too hot and your ice-cream cake melts.)

So sometimes a spell fails because it does. Because that's what happens during the course of learning and trying something new—or something old. However, that last point about baking reminds me of something.

Circumstances with a Capital C

A few weeks ago I made a loaf of wheat bread. Now, this book is being written during the 2020 coronavirus pandemic, so it should be noted that absolutely everyone is baking bread. All the time. Because of that, a lot more people have begun to realize that baking bread can be difficult to get right. This particular wheat loaf recipe is one I have taken to making at least once or twice a week for the last several months. I thought I'd perfected the process.

Except, for some reason, on this particular day, the ball of dough that normally forms during the kneading process had turned out lumpy and misshapen. I thought I did everything the same way that I do every other time I make the loaf. I added the ingredients in the same way, kneaded it the same way, let it rise the same. But, on this day, the bread was less the lovely brown loaf with a slightly asymmetrical domed top that I normally make and more something that my five-year-old niece might make out of

Play-Doh. (However, reader, I ate it anyway because it is still bread and I was very hungry. Tasted fine. After butter. And strawberry preserves. Did I mention I was very hungry?)

The reason my bread didn't turn out was because of the circumstances under which it was baked. Sometimes the air is too humid, or it's not humid enough, or the kitchen is too cold. Besides the ingredients themselves, like the fact that your heaping teaspoon of salt might've been a bit over-heaped, the circumstances under which you make bread can make all the difference between the loaf turning out and becoming a freshman year art project.

One of my favorite depictions of magic in media is from the work of the author Lev Grossman. He wrote a series of books called The Magicians Trilogy. You might have seen the TV adaptation, also called *The Magicians*. Now, you might be confused if you're familiar with the material as to why it's one of my favorite depictions of magic in media, as I devoted an entire chapter of this book to, in part, celebrate the types of magical depictions in film and on television that do so without special effects. And, well, *The Magicians* is chock-full of them. The thing that the TV show, and especially the book trilogy, gets right is that once you've learned the "right way" to do something from a book, the efficacy of magic can boil down to the Circumstances. (Yes, capital *C* Circumstances.)

In the novels you not only have to consider things like the tides and the moon phase, the temperature, where certain stars are in the sky, but also where you are in relation to those things and even what you had for lunch. You can perform the same spell multiple times and get a different result, or none at all, if the Circumstances are not right. In the real world, you'll often find people telling you something similar. For example:

- Don't perform spells to improve your business while Mercury is in retrograde.
- Perform banishing magic while the moon is waning.
- Sweeping your floor at night will sweep away your wealth.

These are not the Circumstances I'm talking about. To be frank, if you're in need of something, waiting for weeks or even months for the stars to be arranged in the correct alignment in the heavens while the moon is in the correct phase means that the moment will pass you by. If you need to perform magic, then do so. All that other stuff, astrology, moon phases, et cetera, is more like a weather forecast. If your goal is to exercise and there's rain in the forecast, you might not choose an outdoor hike but opt for some time on a treadmill at the gym or a workout in your living room, but rain in the forecast doesn't mean that you can't exercise at all. You could even decide to exercise outside, though you might make some adjustments to your wardrobe for health and safety. Same for magic: you can achieve your end result despite where Saturn happens to be hanging out at any given time.

What I mean by Circumstances is far more personal. Effective spiritual work is far more dependent on your internal weather, as it were, than the cosmos. In my experience your emotional state, focus, and intent have far more to do with achieving your desired result. That shouldn't be received as some type of revolutionary concept, either. It's applicable to a lot of different types of skills.

Have you ever gone for a run outside simply out of habit? In the winter? In Chicago? (Sorry . . . perhaps this is just me.) It's cold. It's dark. You would much rather be in bed, and it's not like you plan on getting out of your sweatshirt and leggings for another five months anyway. So, perhaps you run slower than you normally would or for a shorter distance, or you might just skip the run completely and get an extra thirty minutes of sleep. You can go through the motions of running, but you won't quite get as much out of it had you put on your kick-ass workout music, gotten focused, and put an intentional effort into it.

This type of failure can be attributed to multiple root causes. There could be lots of reasons in your internal forecast that contribute to spell failure. Let's examine a few of the most common.

INTENTION FOG

Sure, a "Make It Rain Tomorrow" spell sounds fairly straightforward. You want to make it rain. Tomorrow. But so many different kinds of magical workings require a bit more internal searching before you can home in on your desired end result. The ubiquitous love spell comes to mind. Are you lonely and looking to fill the void with any human-shaped person?

Or is the kind of relationship that you're seeking more of a friendship or indicative of work you should be doing on yourself with a therapist? Not having a clear understanding of what you need quite often leads to an undesirable result or no result at all. Defining one's goals isn't solely part of a solid spiritual practice, but it's part of good life advice. When you're starting a business, it's a pretty accepted idea that you should know not only what you plan on offering the public but also what success looks like in a year, in five years, and so on.

Clearly defined intentions help you not only work for what you want but also understand what "success" looks like for you. Is success in that love spell getting married? Finding someone to go on adventures with or sit quietly beside you as you both spend your evenings reading? What do you need out of that relationship now, next year, in five years? Knowing what you truly want is key to understanding whether you've been successful.

EMOTIONAL LIGHTNING

You know that feeling you get when it's been a busy week and you flop on the couch thinking you're about to settle in to stream *The Office* while eating a whole gallon of ice cream with a spoon, but then your mom calls and tells you she's on her way to your house in thirty minutes? Your ability to clean your house is suddenly fueled by a mixture of panic, desperation, need, and knowing. You want to get the house clean. You need to get the house clean. You also know that if you put in this effort right now your mom will walk into a fairly clean home and you can relax and enjoy her visit. (And you know the look she'll give you if the house is a mess.) Those are, in my experience, the right conditions for successful magic. It's a special combination of knowing what needs to happen, clearly envisioning your intention and the path forward, perhaps a hint of desire, and then actively putting effort into ensuring it comes to fruition.

The thing about lightning is that it doesn't strike the way you think it does. When lightning strikes the ground from a cloud after all the right conditions are met, the bright flash that you see actually comes from the ground, not the cloud. Clouds send out all these little negatively charged spurts, and when it latches on to the right positive area on the ground, flash. The same is true for magic. You're never going to get that flash, that intended result, if you're simply going through the motions. The most effective spells I've ever worked have been ones where I not only knew my intention but also needed it, felt it deep in my spirit.

SCATTERED SHOWERS

So you know what you intend; you've got all the right emotions and inner work ready. You've lit your candle and cast a circle and said all your fanciest words. You're done ... right? That might work on television, but that's not how it works in the real world. (I know, I know, I was disappointed, too.) It's a bit of a cliché to say, but it's called witch*craft* for a reason. It's a craft. A spiritual practice. It's work.

A spell to get a new job doesn't work if it's just a green candle and a lot of wishing really hard. I've known a lot of spiritual practitioners with all sorts of deep knowledge and years of expertise and not a one of them has ever said that their job spell resulted in a recruiter calling them up out of the blue to offer them a job to which they hadn't applied. It's the same with rain. If you get a deluge immediately after planting your seeds, followed by no more rain or watering on your part, your garden won't grow. If you sow a field of corn and the rain only comes every now and then, some days a downpour, others a drizzle, you likely won't get much corn. But if you work with the weather, supplementing a lack of rain with diligent watering and monitoring of the crops, pruning when and where needed, and overall being an active participant, you are far more likely to grow a healthy, vibrant crop come harvest season. Here, the rain is like magic. It can certainly help, and in some cases it might even do most of the work, but it still requires active, mundane participation on your part.

While you can certainly consult the stars, the tides, the moon phase, soil acidity, an almanac (yes, those are still a thing), they can only tell you the circumstances outside. Effective magic requires that you align your combined magical and mundane efforts with your internal Circumstances to bring an intention to fruition.

Sometimes People Lie

I cannot have an honest discussion about the failure of magic and spell work without talking about the very real fact that people lie about their own success. All the time. Online. In person. In books. In interviews on podcasts and television. People lie. What I've always found so odd about lying in a spiritual context is it's never necessary. The truth of magic is, to me at least, marvelous. Plenty of people, myself included, attest that magic has transformed their lives for the better without pretending it is more than it is. So, why do they do it?

When the topic is magic, it can be difficult to parse out what is and isn't true. Knowledge of the practice and various traditions of magic is wrapped up in folklore and fairy tales and Hollywood spectacle. Unfortunately, the truth is also muddled by those attempting to capitalize off of others, preying on fear and ignorance while bolstering claims of their immense magical gifts and experiences.

The reasons are varied, and sometimes they don't exactly make our community look great (which . . . again . . . is why most folks avoid having these conversations directly or at least in black and white). Whether it's a professional, or would-be professional, witch or spiritual teacher, or curio crafter or paranormal entertainer, the reasons for falsehoods in the witchy community are the same as in any other community: money and/or influence. In either case, these folks have a vested interest in you believing that they are powerful witches or warlocks or psychic mediums or whatever other title they assign themselves. They claim to perform great feats of magic, possess secret knowledge, or, in some cases, set themselves up as the only person capable of saving you from some dark force. But . . . why lie at all? Surely, if magic is real and there are millions of practitioners out there who will tell you it is, then why do some people take it too far?

The psychologist David J. Ley, PhD, wrote an article for *Psychology Today* in 2017 titled "6 Reasons People Lie When They Don't Need To"[1] where he talked about . . . well . . . the title pretty much says it all. He discussed the typical reasons why people lie, and they are exceptionally applicable to our spiritual community—after all, people are always people, witch or not. Three of the most common motivating factors are as follows:

1. **This version of the story is important to them.**
   This could be based on undue pressure the person is putting on themselves despite the fact that the issue

at hand might not be that important to the person they're lying to. Did you really visually see a fully embodied spirit, or was it perhaps a feeling you got or an image in your mind's eye? These differences likely wouldn't matter to the person hearing the story, but the person telling it feels a pressure to entertain, to impress.

2. **The truth gets in the way of their narrative.** Were you ever a teenager who got a ticket or wrecked your parents' car? If so, you know you couldn't completely lie to your parents. The truth was evident. But there was a way you told the story that made you look far better than it could. You weren't looking at your phone; you didn't see the speed limit sign. (But, really, no speed limit sign in the United States reads 85 mph down a backcountry road.) There's a narrative you're clinging to that's better than reality, and the truth would be an inconvenience (and possibly lead you to more trouble).

3. **They don't want to let you down.** This is very often found in those who have hung their shingle out in the world and are making a go of being a professional metaphysical purveyor in some capacity. To gain traction, customers can't just believe in the truth of the claims; people have to be impressed by them. Think back to my earlier discussion of paranormal entertainers. You can never leave an investigation without finding some kind of proof, right? Thus the urge for these entertainers to try to convince you that a sound is really a spirit, or that a blinking light on a misused piece of equipment is evidence of a manifested otherworldly entity. The same is true for those selling divination and spell work. They will ask probing questions and use your answers to rearrange the narrative in a way that conveniently proves their mystical prowess.

The failure of magic can be attributed to a lot of things. Sometimes it's because it's a new skill you haven't mastered, but that's why we call it practice, right? Maybe the magic failed because it wasn't the right tool to begin with or you failed to take appropriate and proportional mundane action to achieve your means. Perhaps your expectations went far beyond what magic is capable of achieving. Remember that magic is most effective when it is reasonable, clearly defined, and possible. No matter what, though, you should always feel empowered to ask questions but, moreover, to seek answers to those questions. Simply asking questions without seeking answers will not serve your spiritual growth. While those answers might feel uncomfortable, they're necessary because standing in truth is a far more powerful position than standing in uncertainty.

The RISE *of the* POLITICAL WITCH

itches are an indelible part of stories and children's movies and Halloween and, apparently, TikTok. When we think of their portrayals, we tend to focus on all the magic that they do that requires a special-effects budget. How they changed their eye color or turned the head cheerleader into a pineapple. What gets missed in our recollection is how closely aligned witches have always been with politics. Body politics. Governmental politics. Social politics. Gender politics. In ways big and small, from King Arthur's court to a protest in your neighborhood, witches have been right there influencing events, protecting themselves or others, and using their gifts to balance out the scales of injustice. Much of that forgotten or unspoken discourse is coming back to the forefront in recent years as our ever more interconnected world is experiencing massive, rapid social awakening and transformation. Old stories are being revisited and traditional tales mined for feminist undertones, queer identity, and racial justice.

One of the reasons people come to magical practice is to give power to the powerless, to those who are not represented or accepted or protected by society at large. If recent events have sent you reaching for your wand and cauldron when voting doesn't seem to be enough, you might be interested to know that you are joining a long and powerful tradition of witches actively (to borrow a phrase) crafting the change they wish to see in the world.

★

There is a legend that some in the magical community mention anytime a discussion includes the following ideas: the effectiveness of magic, politics, or the early days of witchcraft in the modern era. The legend originates from a man named Gerald Gardner, known as the father of Wicca. As the story goes, in the summer of 1940, when the British were bracing for a possible invasion from the Germans, a group of witches met at night in a town called Highcliffe-on-Sea.

They went into the woods, as all the best witches from stories do, and created a circle, placing a light (accounts differ whether it was a lantern or perhaps a flashlight, as they couldn't risk a bonfire) in the direction of Berlin. They stripped off their clothes and danced naked under the stars, chanting and combining their intentions into a collective of energy known as a "cone of power." The story goes that their chants were the same chants previous groups of witches used in a similar ritual in the 1800s to turn back Napoleon. And, once this cone of power was raised, Gardner says they directed the energy into the mind of Adolf Hitler himself. This tale is recounted in Gardner's 1954 book, *Witchcraft Today*. Here's what he says happened:

> They met, raised the great cone of power and directed the thought at Hitler's brain: "You cannot cross the sea...." ... I'm not saying they stopped Hitler. All I say is that I saw a very interesting ceremony performed with the intention of putting a certain idea into his mind... and though all the invasion barges were ready, the fact was that Hitler never even tried to come.

Other than the account by Gardner, there's no historical evidence that this ritual, known as Operation Cone of Power (which is an admittedly great name), ever happened. To be fair, however, if you and some friends went out into the woods to strip naked and chant, how much evidence would you have that you did?

Whether this event happened exactly how it is described in the multiple retellings by Gardner, or whether it sort of happened how it is described by Gardner, or whether it's all completely made up doesn't matter at this point. The tale has served to help create a center point upon which many modern witches construct a timeline of magic being used for purposes greater than themselves. It's quite common in literature and film and on television to see spells be crafted for the purposes of winning love or banishing a meddling neighbor. It isn't often that you see witches depicted on the front lines of war (well, with the exception of our gal Eglantine Price) or influencing elections or attempting to magically ensure the outcome of a Supreme Court ruling.

And yet, in recent years, that is exactly what witches are doing, and they're doing it loudly. From the Women's March in 2017 to the Black Lives Matter protests in 2020, you cannot miss the signs held or costumes worn by people reviving the symbol of the witch as a warning to those in power. The witch of fiction and folktale is a person who is sometimes seen as weak, powerless in the face of oppression, but gains revenge and rights wrongs using magic. It's easy to understand why you see signs like "Hex White Supremacy" or "Witches Against Walls" being held by black-clad, pointy hat–wearing protesters. This isn't a new phenomenon, though.

Reexamining Salem

On the topic of witches and political oppression, no college lecture, podcast episode, coffee shop meetup, or stitch and witch knitting circle would be complete without mentioning Salem, Massachusetts, and the witch trials of the 1690s.

When we talk about this period in our history, it's jarring to many to find out that the entire arc of the Salem witch trials started, ran its course, and ended in the span of fifteen months. I realize I didn't live through the witch trials, but this fact always feels so odd to me. It feels wrong somehow, doesn't it? That such a short time could have this type of lasting impact on us that we still use the term "witch hunt" frequently in political and social discourse?

From February 1692 to May 1693, 172 people were charged with the crime of witchcraft, with 14 women, 5 men, and 2 dogs executed.

Stories about this period so often focus on the trials themselves. The executions are often the first thing you learn about, specifically because there is always one guy in the crowd who wants to be the one to tell you that nobody was burned at the stake in Salem. (It's true, but the expression on that guy's face is so smug you kind of wish it weren't.) Beyond that, the other piece of the trials you hear about is the idea of "spectral evidence." This is a form of evidence allowed in actual courts of law that was comprised completely of visions, dreams, pricks along the skin, and other supposed occurrences that accusers claimed they experienced and attributed to the "witch" in question.

So, you could say something like, "Goody Jenkins came to me in a dream and slapped my face and tried to choke me because I said her butter wasn't churned properly," and the court would enter into evidence that Goody Jenkins absolutely attempted to cause you physical harm via witchery. It would be accepted as fact, the veracity never questioned, and the only way to keep your neck from the hangman's noose was typically to admit to the nefarious deed and then point the finger at someone else.

You might have noticed the disparity between the number of people accused in Salem (over 200) as opposed to the number of people executed in Salem (19). That's because with the exception of one person, Samuel Wardwell, all those who confessed were granted reprieve. What's interesting is that Samuel, along with his wife, Sarah, and their daughter, Mercy, all confessed the day they were accused, but Samuel recanted the testimony, as it was coerced. "Honesty gets you hanged at Proctor's Ledge," my mother always says. (My mother never said that.)

OK, so you're asking yourself why I'm giving you a history lesson in the Salem witch trials when you could have googled this information for yourself. It's because we only ever talk about the trials themselves. The middle bit. The hangings and the dunking people in water and the weird little bird who was also the Devil. We talk about Giles Corey, who was executed for witchcraft by being pressed under rocks and when asked whether he would confess he simply said, "More weight." (What a badass.) The point is we talk a lot about the "what" of the trials and rarely about the "why," which I find far more interesting.

Folklorists, historians, sociologists, and strange little nerds like me find this period of time fascinating because it is an incredibly harrowing example of a social epidemic. Much like a virus can cleave through a population, so, too, can virulent ideas and beliefs. When you look at what was happening in and around Salem right before people started leveling accusations of witchcraft, you might see societal conditions that feel like they could be the story of your own town right now.

A number of theories about how and why surges of witchcraft accusations and subsequent executions exist. Some say that the almost exclusively male medical profession sought to eradicate midwives and other traditional healers. Others say that the act of accusation was a convenient way to separate a wealthy widow or single woman from her property or inheritance, especially if you wanted to own her land yourself. Some blame syphilis. In the case of Salem, some blame fungus.

Paul S. Boyer and Stephen Nissenbaum's book *Salem Possessed: The Social Origins of Witchcraft* laid out that the people of Salem were divided by things like class and geography long before anyone thought to blame witches for their problems. That is not to say that there were not people practicing folk magic in Salem before, during, and even after the trial period. What makes Salem unique is the skewing of those folk practices as Satanic—when viewed with a Puritanical lens—as well as the introduction of spectral evidence. One interesting take that offers a level of nuance completely void of the spiritual involves economics and climate change.

In 2004 Dr. Emily Oster, professor of economics at Brown University, argued in a paper published by the *Journal of Economic Perspectives* that the root cause of the trials in Salem wasn't pacts with Satan in forest clearings or witches trying to astrally drown their enemies. Instead, she argues that economic deterioration and food shortages are the reasons why the town was suddenly rife with witches. Her paper takes a look at the centuries-long period known as the Little Ice Age, which was a period of cooling typically referred to as happening between the sixteenth and nineteenth centuries, which also happens to line up with the dates for the majority of the witchcraft trials in Western Europe and the Americas.

Her paper goes on to look at how periods of economic downturn and food scarcity combine to aid in the type of pernicious paranoia that extends one's hand to point a finger in accusation of another. Her conclusions cite a number of other researchers who suggest that economic downturns don't just lead to an increase in accusations of witchcraft but violence of all types. She cites research that suggests lynchings rose in the American South as economic well-being deteriorated. Further research is cited to suggest poor economic conditions are associated with an increased chance of civil conflict, or in her words, "citizens blame other ethnic groups for deterioration in economic conditions."[1]

Basically, when things go wrong and it appears we have no other evidence or reason, we start looking for witches. Sometimes, though, we don't go looking for witches. Sometimes, when things go wrong, we become the witches.

The Reclaimed Mantle of the Witch

Divorced from fiction, the word "witch" has, for some groups, become a reclaimed term in a sociopolitical context. They are not necessarily practicing magic or divining the future, but rather crafting a vision of the witch as a figure from history that the patriarchy overlooked or put down. No longer a victim of circumstance or the boogeyman of the uninformed, she is here to level the playing field and, yes, perhaps cause a little chaos along the way.

If you have existed on the internet in any capacity in the last decade, you've no doubt come across the story of the Night Witches. They were an all-women regiment of bomber pilots who flew for the Soviet Union in World War II from 1942 until the end of the war. Posts on social media have renewed interest in the regiment because of how fearless they were. Their signature tactic was to turn their plane engine off as they neared their target, gliding until they were within striking distance. The sound of the night air rushing over the plane allegedly sounded like the sweeping of a broomstick, and thus they were named Night Witches.

These women did not carry parachutes for the first two years of their operation because the bombs aboard the planes were already too heavy, and they couldn't risk the extra weight. Men did not accept them as equals. They were given obsolete aircraft and ill-fitting uniforms previously worn by the men. Yet, by the end of the war, the Night Witches were the most highly decorated female unit in the Soviet Air Force.

Jump forward a couple of decades, and you'll find the formation of the group known as W.I.T.C.H.—Women's International Terrorist Conspiracy from Hell. Though the acronym has taken on other meanings since the group's formation in 1968, one thing has remained the same. The intention of the group was to aggressively combat the patriarchy, and they kicked off their string of protest actions during October 1968 when they glued the door latches of the New York Stock Exchange shut. When the (male) bankers couldn't get in, chaos ensued. One of the organizers claims credit for a sharp decline in the Dow but also stated that they didn't think of themselves as "real" witches but used the imagery of the witch as a powerful woman.

The group would go on to stage protest demonstrations against the Bell Telephone Company (now part of AT&T), the Chicago Board of Trade, President Richard Nixon's inauguration, and at least one restaurant where they asked women why they were willing to let men buy them dinner. W.I.T.C.H. was revived in 2015 in Chicago in order to protest housing rights in the city. They then organized and joined other protests against the forty-fifth president of the United States, Donald Trump.

In fact, a lot of people joined in witchy protests against Donald Trump. And, as in decades past, the people who were taking up the moniker of the witch interpreted the word differently. For some, they literally mean they are witches, casting spells and influencing the world with their intentions. For others, though, they see the witch as a figure of righteous anger, a figure who can topple patriarchal institutions that protect the wealthy and powerful. Even, possibly, a presidential administration.

#HexThePresident

There is perhaps no more visible example of political witchcraft in recent years than the viral hex targeting Donald Trump. While there were certainly many magically minded people who were taking action against the divisive former president leading up to, during, and after the election of 2016, this organized event is credited to a witch named Michael Hughes who created a Facebook event titled "A Spell to Bind Donald Trump and All Those Who Abet Him" that originally took place at the stroke of midnight the evening of February 24, 2017.

A binding spell is used to prevent a person from acting in a certain manner. It is not designed to harm or somehow cause a specific, direct negative effect. You might remember a binding spell being used by the character Sarah in the movie *The Craft* in which she wrapped a photograph in ribbon while chanting in an attempt to prevent Nancy from doing harm against others and harm against herself.

Despite not being acts that are intended to cause direct harm, binding spells are nevertheless a controversial action. Many believe they affect the target's free will. And, sure, people who practice magic will attempt to twist air currents for hundreds of miles to alter the weather or charm a lottery ticket to eke out a win of hundreds of millions of dollars over millions of other players, but stopping someone from doing a bad thing? Apparently, that's controversial. So, late February 2017 was an interesting time to be part of the magical social media world, as everyone had a hot take.

Hot takes or not, this spell went viral. Celebrities and social media influencers participated alongside regular folks who were tired, scared, and otherwise felt as though their voices were going unheard. Just as in days gone by when marginalized people turned to the witch as a source of inspiration and empowerment, people donned their black hats or their hoodies or fuzzy slippers, gathering with friends or strangers or alone, and lit candles and chanted and hexed the (now former) president of the United States.

Donald Trump was not magically expelled from office. Looking back over his term as president, one cannot find any measurable tapering off of his influence after February 2017. And with so many people doing so many spells aimed at him at once, it can cause you to wonder—possibly assume—that magic isn't real and doesn't work, and if I believed that this would be a very short book. But this act has inspired dozens, if not hundreds, more group actions aimed at not only the United States' politicians but other political figures around the world. Further, the internet has helped witches and magical practitioners and curious dabblers alike connect to cast spells to aid the environment, protect protesters, and sway Supreme Court appointments and decisions as well as a host of other matters across political ideologies and with varying degrees of reach.

I also participated in the hex on Donald Trump in February 2017, mostly because of how I felt in November 2016 and every hour of every day since then. I felt powerless. Hopeless. I worried for friends and loved ones and people I'd never met who were feeling targeted and scared, worried that their civil liberties could be taken away with a tweet. My husband and friends gathered and performed our version of the hex and drank wine and spent time in community with one another. If there's one thing I'm sure of from that night, it's that the spell had a profound effect on my mental health.

It felt good. It felt like release. It felt like protest. If I've learned anything from studying political witchcraft, it's that it is as much an act of protest as it is an act of magic. It is people finding power when they are told they have none, and if the magic itself does no more than inspire people to have hope where they had none before, to be prepared to take to the streets when necessary, to be kinder to one another, then it's a worthy and worthwhile act to continue.

There are a lot of reasons why people call themselves witches. Whether the word means something spiritual or political or social to you, the end result is the same in a sense. By the time my spell was completed and all the candles had burned down and my friends and I were drinking wine and looking up at the stars, I felt like a weight had lifted from my shoulders and something that had been knotted up in my stomach had untangled itself. I felt lighter than I had in months, and I was able to use that renewed energy to much more clearly focus on making necessary change in my life and my community.

The magic had been worked and something in the world had changed: me.

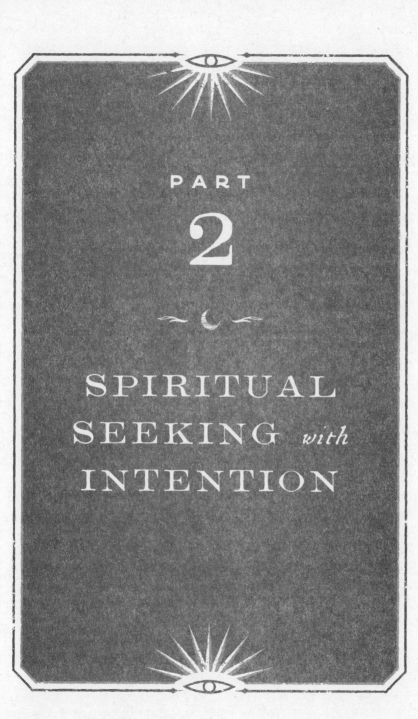

PART

2

SPIRITUAL
SEEKING *with*
INTENTION

I just want a version of the occult that isn't built on plunder, but I suspect that if we could excise the stolen pieces, there would be nothing left.

—Elissa Washuta

The last several chapters looked at some of the ideas you might have held before you ever picked up a book on magic, where those ideas came from, and started peeling back the layers of expectation versus reality. As we move forward in our journey together, I want you to start asking some deeper questions about the nature of spiritual exploration itself. Not only why people go on spiritual journeys in the first place, but why are you—*you*, specifically, right here reading this book from an angle on your couch that would make your chiropractor scream—going on *this* spiritual journey.

Building out a new spiritual life is no easy task. You're learning new things and exploring new concepts, and as you do, you're peeking in windows to other cultures and adapting an amalgam of these practices to your daily life. Remember that the point of this book isn't to tell you what to do to build your practice but to teach you how to ask better questions so that you can make your own informed decisions. That's what this part of the book is about: asking deeper questions of yourself, of the information you're learning, and whether we're all just making it up.

CHAPTER 5

WHY ARE YOU HERE?

So far we've covered a lot of ground. I've talked about reasons why you might have gained an interest in witchcraft, the history behind how witches are perceived, the finer points of how Hallmark nails their portrayal of magic, and . . . somehow . . . World War II. I know. I was shocked by that last one, too. In short, I've done what in corporate speak is known as talking about "the why behind the what." Now, though, it's time to pull the focus back to you, your journey, and where you go from here.

People come to magic and witchcraft for different reasons, and they want different things out of it. As you start to build your own practice, it's a good idea to continually ask yourself why witchcraft and Pagan spirituality interest you. Perhaps think deeply about the media or literature or past experience that sparked your interest and why. You don't need to have answers right away, and those answers may change with time, but coming up with a list now will help you with some of the topics later. (Didn't know there'd be homework, did you?) If nothing else, having a foundation of poems, books, media, et cetera, that sparked that pursuit of magic can be incredibly helpful during times when it's hard to believe in anything. I know it helped me.

I was that kid who would spend his weekends out in the woods making witch's cottages out of trees and logs and whatever else I could find. I would pick berries and leaves and weeds and carry them back to my cottage to be used in magical remedies that weary travelers would seek me out to procure. I dug little pits where I pretended to build fires and hang a cauldron and speak magical words over the imaginary simmering liquid held within. I did all this simply because I had fallen deeply, irrevocably in love with magic in first grade when a stage magician came to our school and performed a routine that absolutely transformed my worldview. He made one of our teachers disappear from the audience and reappear in a glass box onstage. He created fire with his hands. He could pull flowers out of his sleeve.

I can trace my love of Greek gods and superheroes and ghost stories and all things spooky back to that one single, fateful day. That spark of inspiration became a lifelong love of seeking magic wherever I could find it. It wasn't until high school band, when I was sitting next to our first chair French horn player (I was second chair), that I found out magic was something real that you could really practice. She had a book by an author named Scott Cunningham called *Earth, Air, Fire & Water* that introduced me to a world of legitimate magical beliefs.

I wish I could say that the trajectory between each of those moments of small magic until now was a single, exponential, upward swing, but it wasn't. I've gone through periods of doubt, periods where big, existential questions like "What happens after we die?" made me spin off into an anxious mess for months at a time. It's important to note that it's completely normal to go through this, and it's completely valid if you don't exactly come out the other end of it with satisfying answers to Big Questions. That's the thing that I think I've come to appreciate about this spiritual path. We don't have answers. We have interesting ways of exploring questions and are open to possibilities.

But it's important to know why you're exploring in the first place. If you're hoping for a neat and tidy understanding of the universe, I have some good and bad news about that. The bad news—I always do bad news first—is that there are no neat and tidy answers about the universe. Ever. Those who try to tell you they have it figured out are probably hoping to sell you something. The good news is since there aren't really any right ways to believe, it's pretty safe to say that you can't do it wrong.

I've talked before about how magical practice and Pagan spirituality in a broader sense are decentralized systems of belief. This means that there is no single governing body determining what we believe. There is no book whose words we are forced to interpret or bend or attempt to contextualize in the modern day. There are many good things about that, but the one thing it means that can throw people off is that we lack surety about the Big Questions. There is no chapter and verse to look up, to put your faith into, when an uncomfortable question arises. It's work. It's a breaking down of how you used to see the world and building up a new worldview. It's hard for many, because there are no direct cognates to plug and play your newfound spirituality. (Though many have tried.)

What you get instead is like an open world RPG without an owner's manual where you're the protagonist and the goal is to discover how magical the world really is. Sitting on this side of the journey thus far, I can tell you that I have far more appreciation for simply gazing at the way sunlight filters through leaves or the feeling of a billowing wind curling around your body. The natural world is a place filled with wonder and magic, even if the answers to the Big Questions aren't answers as much as they are invitations to ask more questions.

Spiritual Nones

Stop me if you've heard this one before: "I'm spiritual but not religious." Once upon a time, this phrase had the connotation of being uttered by someone who was being obstinate about committing to a given religion. I can almost see the kind of person my parents think of when they hear this phrase. I feel like they think that person wears a lot of vests and necklaces. I don't know why. I don't make the rules.

Chances are good that if you picked this book up as part of your spiritual exploration, you might identify with that phrase. The Pew Research Center has been diligently keeping track of the various spiritual affiliation trends in the United States, specifically as they relate to "religious 'nones'"—or those adults who self-identify as either atheist, agnostic, or "nothing in particular." In 2007, this group accounted for just under 16 percent of adults, and by 2012 that group accounted for one-fifth of US adults (and one-third of adults under the age of thirty).[1] In 2017, that number had increased again to 27 percent of all adults in the United States.[2] Pew was also quick to point out that this growth is happening across political affiliation, age range, gender identity, race, and socioeconomic background. More people, generally, are moving away from religious affiliation but still think of themselves as "spiritual." And, if past is prologue, that number will simply continue to rise.

What does this tell us? Growing up in the kind of environment I did, religion wasn't a choice, nor was I ever led to believe it could become one. I was raised a Southern Baptist, because that's what my parents were. That's what "we" were. Your family's religious identity was something conferred upon you at birth and seen by them—and the world around you for the most part—as an immutable part of who you are and who you're going to be when you grow up.

However, what the data tells us is that in recent decades a growing number of people looked around, looked at themselves, and realized that their spiritual path doesn't have to be predetermined by birth. The numbers are even greater in younger generations. Thirty-five percent of millennials, those born between 1981 and 1996, categorize themselves as "nones" compared to 17 percent of baby boomers. And it's not because 35 percent of millennials were raised without religion. Pew tells us that only 9 percent of adults state that they were raised without a family religious affiliation.

In 2018, Pew polled self-identified religious nones and found out something interesting. Only 37 percent of that group stated that they did not believe in God (I'm using the capital *G* because that's how they phrased their question and reported their data). In fact, a minority of religious nones (31 percent) are atheist or agnostic. Far more respondents stated that they categorized themselves with the "nones" because they disagree with certain religious teachings (60 percent) or do not like the positions churches take on social or political issues (49 percent).[3] This data seems to suggest that plenty of people are open to belief, open to spirituality in a general sense, but not at the expense of their broadening social and political consciousness.

I've been in your shoes, and I know it can be scary. It's OK to sit with that uncertainty and fear for a moment. It's OK if that moment takes weeks, months, or if you never quite shake that feeling of being unmoored in society. It takes a lot of courage to defy a label, to transform a part of one's identity, and I don't think that's talked about or appreciated enough. Whether you found this path when you were a teenager or you've come later in life, or whether you're still trying it on for size, simply acknowledging to yourself that you might not wish to identify with the religion of your upbringing is a big step.

I also want you to know that it's perfectly valid to dabble without fully committing to a new spiritual home, and it's also completely valid if you never really feel like you have found a spiritual home. I bring up these demographics because I want you to know that you're not alone. Sure, the nones aren't likely to be as easily found in groups, and that can be difficult because humans are social creatures by our very nature. We want to seek out a group, even if only to know that one exists if we need support or community.

Labels are complicated and comfortable, and the urge to immediately replace an old one with a new one is strong. Take your time, though, and hold space for your right to experiment, to choose, to cobble together a new spiritual path.

However . . .

Get Ready to Work

I've done a good deal of talking thus far about why magic does or doesn't work, about why people come to this form of spirituality. While I certainly don't want to make it seem as though you're about to be Cinderella before she meets the fairy godmother, working day and night at thankless tasks with only local vermin for friends, I do want to set the expectation that you do have work ahead of you.

We all come to this path with a set of preconceived notions about spirituality, other cultures, and about our rights to the teachings from those other cultures. Asking people to wipe their proverbial slate clean is an exercise in the ridiculous, as it's impossible to do. Instead, I will caution that your task is to welcome discomfort when it arises. (Notice I didn't say "if," because discomfort is absolutely ahead of you.)

Have you ever changed jobs? You got used to where the break room was and which manager didn't care if you went five minutes longer on your lunch. You were accustomed to who was in charge and what the rules were and the breadth of room you had inside those rules to find your own way of doing things. Then you applied for a job making a little bit more money at a new company, and suddenly you don't know where to put your sandwich. You're cutting your own lunch by two minutes because you want the people in charge to think you're someone who . . . I dunno . . . eats fast. You get it.

Suddenly your world is smaller. You don't know how much space there is to make your new day-to-day life your own. Now take that idea of discomfort, a discomfort signed up for and welcomed, and expand it to encompass bigger ideas like the definitions of "good" and "evil." The concepts of life, death, afterlife, rebirth. How you define what is and isn't moral if you're no longer bound by what a book written thousands of years ago says. You now have permission to believe, permission to explore and rewrite your understanding of the universe, but with that comes an obligation to think critically about what you select to be part of your new paradigm and why.

Up until now there are likely parts of your spiritual beliefs or traditions that are there because they were the way your parents did them, whether they resonate with you or not. It can be jarring to suddenly realize you get to choose these for yourself, and the temptation is to start inserting new terms and ideas into comfortable slots in your mind. That's a bit easier and less problematic with new and exciting concepts like holidays. Suddenly Halloween gets so much more interesting and magical when you learn about Samhain, and you'll feel like you get two Christmases once you discover Yule.

Belief, as I've come to understand it, is far more vast than the transactional "I believe in You, so please give me This" relationship many end up having with some deity or other. It is a way of understanding the big and little lies we tell ourselves about the way the world works. Breaking down what you believe isn't simply no longer believing that Sky Daddy will smite you for wearing mixed fabric. It's about deciding *why* you believe. In anything. At all.

See, when you talk about belief with most people, they end up thinking you're talking about a deity. In the witchy community, or around Halloween, discussions of belief can involve ghostly encounters or warnings of dealing with faeries. But these are still far easier to believe in than the big beliefs.

Terry Pratchett, renowned author of the Discworld series, gave me one of my most profound moments of understanding on the subject of belief in his book *Hogfather*. If you've never read it, it's a story about how Death stands in for the Discworld's version of Santa Claus after said Santa figure (the eponymous Hogfather) is temporarily indisposed due to a conspiracy to assassinate him. It's my favorite Yuletide/Christmas story. Pratchett has this way of writing delicious fantasy satire that wraps up great truths about the world in palatable, pleasurable packaging. The great truth of *Hogfather* is summed up best by this bit of dialogue between Death and his granddaughter Susan:

> "All right," said Susan. "I'm not stupid. You're saying humans need . . . *fantasies* to make life bearable."
> REALLY? AS IF IT WAS SOME KIND OF PINK PILL? NO. HUMANS NEED FANTASY TO BE HUMAN. TO BE THE PLACE WHERE THE FALLING ANGEL MEETS THE RISING APE.
> "Tooth fairies? Hogfathers? Little—"
> YES. AS PRACTICE. YOU HAVE TO START OUT LEARNING TO BELIEVE THE *LITTLE* LIES.
> "So, we can believe the big ones?"
> YES. JUSTICE. MERCY. DUTY. THAT SORT OF THING.

Death explains that the universe doesn't inherently possess Justice or Mercy, but that we impart those ephemeral qualities upon reality as though there is a cosmic scale somewhere in a far-off galaxy ensuring things generally remain fair and even for everyone. The message here is that even this act of belief in the general goodness of the universe, and by extension our fellow man, is indeed a leap of faith that we have to work up to believing. They're big, messy concepts, so we start with small things and work our way up.

Choosing your spiritual path, especially a magical spiritual path, isn't simply falling in love with folklore and myth and the magic immanent in nature. It's not about the fun spells and shiny rocks and rituals you can perform under the full moon. It is a purposeful choosing to reorient your perception of the universe in such a way that you can believe in the big things—the inherent goodness of humanity, that the arc of morality bends towards justice—by being open and intentional in your search for spiritual growth and understanding. That is not to say that one *must* believe in ghosts and fairies and divine beings in order to believe in mercy, truth, and justice. Agnostics and atheists and "spiritual nones" have just as much claim to believing in those things as anyone else, and that is equally valid.

What I'm acknowledging here is that you have a choice, not only about what you believe but also about why you believe it. Don't rush into anything too quickly. Dabble. Explore. Learn. It's fine. If you've been waiting for permission, then here. I'm giving you permission.

Being "spiritual but not religious" can mean practically anything you want it to mean. Adding magical beliefs, witchy practices, and exploring minority religions can, again, look like almost anything. (Even if you don't like vests and necklaces.) The point here is to open your eyes to the idea that exploration doesn't simply mean finding new names for your established worldview. It means completely unlearning the notion that you have to have a set system of beliefs. Humans change as we grow and interact with the world. So, demolish your old vocabulary and do some inner work unpacking why you are on this journey. Be willing to feel uncomfortable, to be wrong, and to use that discomfort to broaden your "why."

CHAPTER 6

SETTING YOUR INTENTION

So, reader, what *is* your end goal? What do you hope to get out of your personal magical journey? Do you seek the structure of a new religion like Wicca, or perhaps you're more interested in exploring mystical practices with or without a belief in a divine being (or . . . beings), or maybe you simply like thinking deeply and critically about interesting things? In any of those cases, having at least a vague idea of where you want your journey to take you will help you to develop a plan of getting there successfully. Why? Because of *Legally Blonde*.

I Have a Point, I Promise

Remember when Elle Woods (the film's protagonist) thought her entire life was going to be finishing a degree in fashion and then becoming Mrs. Warner Huntington III for . . . ever? Her intention was based on a set of expectations handed down by both her family and society. Being a supporting character in someone else's very charmed life was about all she wanted. After Warner dumped Elle, we are shown her immense academic potential when she becomes singularly focused on getting a high score on the LSATs, but her intention was still relegated to getting back together with Warner and reestablishing her status as his adoring wife. It wasn't until she realized that was never going to happen that she really came into her own and altered the way she approached her education. No longer was it a means to win back a man, but Harvard became a means of finding herself and charting a path to a future that centered her needs.

I know ∴. . . you didn't ever think you'd read a book about witchcraft that based a chapter on *Legally Blonde*, did you?

I think it should be established early that neither of Elle's potential pathways is inherently bad. If she were to become Mrs. Warner Huntington III, it's possible that she could have gone on to live a perfectly fulfilling life. Plenty of people are quite happy and content to throw themselves into the role of supportive spouse. Nothing wrong with that. Perfectly valid. Eventually, though, Elle realized that it wasn't a possibility for her. (And, let's be real, she dodged a bullet. Warner was a tool.)

Remember how in the last chapter I talked about breaking down your concept of why one pursues a spiritual life? Many people are tempted to try to fit new information into their established understanding of how to be a spiritual person. (Yule = Christmas. Spells = Prayers. Et cetera.) Figuring out your "why" requires opening yourself up to new ideas, to being wrong and often uncomfortable. Elle realized this, too. She thought she would be able to plug her new life and teachings at Harvard into her established understanding of how the world works. Insert a law degree in the place of fashion merchandising. Put Warner back in the boyfriend slot. Pinkify absolutely everything. Her worldview doesn't have to change.

It wasn't until Warner made it very clear that he was never going to take her back that she realized her new journey wouldn't be as simple as plugging and playing new into old. She had to set a new intention. She had to be willing to be wrong. To be uncomfortable. To realize that not all of her established ideas were going to suit her new journey. And, because of that, eventually she found a new kind of success.

What? Like It's Hard?

Unlike getting a law degree, taking on a new spiritual journey doesn't come with a syllabus. You are to be forgiven, however, if you went to a bookstore and came away thinking it does. There are plenty of books in the "Witchcraft for Dummies" or "Paganism 101" genre. These books are the bread and butter of multiple publishing houses for a reason. (Heck, this book technically falls into that category.) So, it's easy to think you could pick up one of those books, read it cover to cover, do the stuff inside it, and be done learning the basics. Right?

Well, there's a problem with that logic. While we like to call introductory witchy books 101-style books, there is not a direct correlation with actual 101-style textbooks. If I were to take a World History 101 or Chemistry 101 class, the book I would likely be assigned would not have a single author. Oftentimes textbooks are written by several people in coordination with fact-checkers and consultants, each with advanced degrees and years of experience in both higher education and research, who help determine what needs to be included in order to ensure the topic is sufficiently and exhaustively covered. It's done this way so that you get a more robust understanding of the subject matter and so that the information you learn is (at least in theory) representative of an objective understanding of the facts rather than a subjective one.

For example: in a science textbook it's far more important to know *why* the sky is blue rather than the emotional impact the blue sky had on the author.

In the realm of spirituality, however, these 101 books are typically an introduction to that author's subjective point of view, personal experience, and ways of understanding certain information. There is little fact-checking (if there were, we wouldn't have spent several decades with witchy books touting a long-debunked theory that 9 million women died during a period called the Burning Times); instead, the onus is on the reader to perform their own analysis of the veracity and effectiveness of the material.

Again, full disclosure: this book does the same thing. I've selected topics, injected my perspective, and presented the information that I believe is important for you to learn. By necessity, I've also had to leave plenty out. If I'd included an exhaustive examination of all of Pagandom, its history, and every type of metaphysical practice under the witchy umbrella, this book would be thousands of pages long and . . . well . . . I probably shouldn't be the person writing that book. I am lacking in PhDs, and I don't have that kind of attention span.

Curation isn't inherently a bad thing. Many literary genres don't need to present their information in a textbook format to be successful. If I'm reading about travel, for example, I expect that an author might include their favorite restaurants or a unique recommendation for an all-night dance hall. It's interesting, but not necessary, to include topics such as the historical development of the local school system or the political structure chosen for local governance. Spirituality is one such topic where it is important to seek out facts and the history behind our perception of those facts, but it is also important to understand the experiences of others.

Which is why so many witchy books read less like textbooks and more like travelogues of the divine. Because of that, and because there is no one right road to travel, it is important to understand that crafting your spiritual education will be more difficult. There is the urge to create a bit of a cult of personality around the first author you read or the first one you like. Don't beat yourself up. We all did it.

I remember after reading my first Scott Cunningham book, suddenly my entire witchy worldview was Cunningham. Luckily, for everything I wanted to learn, there was a Cunningham book for that. His encyclopedias of herbs and stones were basically sacrosanct in my mind. When I got my first apartment, I tore into his book on creating a magical household. I saw little need to go outside his writing for my education, because it all seemed to provide a practical, inexpensive, meaningful guide towards enhancing my spiritual path and improving my witchcraft. I read other books, but I always compared them to Cunningham's accessible writing style.

Of course, I was learning all of this in the early 2000s. Before YouTube had taken off. Before podcasts were a thing. Back when you had to sort of hope you bumped into a fellow witchy person at a coffee shop somewhere who would be nice enough to talk to you and recommend a book. (Sidenote: I did end up bumping into a witchy person at a coffee shop, and she's still a dear friend to this day. In fact, had I not met her, I doubt I'd be married to my husband. Never underestimate the importance of random witches in coffee shops.) To find others of like mind, we trolled online message boards for who might have converted their garage into a crystal shop or which tea shop was also a place where magically minded people met up regularly. It all felt very underground and secretive, which was certainly fun but made learning difficult.

I've Come to Join Your Study Group. And, Look, I Brought Sustenance!

These days information is far more accessible, but, more important, other witches are more accessible. There are thousands of people who've made YouTube channels and podcasts and Facebook groups and blogs and Instagram accounts and . . . I assume . . . several other types of social media that I am now too old to learn or care about. You get the idea.

The advent of social media combined with the fact that we are all walking around with a recording studio in our pockets means that learning from others is easier than ever. That also creates a really helpful path for self-learning. Here are some tips I've picked up that helped me create my path.

LIKE THE BOOK?
LISTEN TO THE AUTHOR

Go to your favorite podcast streaming service and type in the name of the author of your favorite witchy book. In many cases, they've been interviewed at least once. Go listen to that interview. You can do the same thing on YouTube. It's a great opportunity to understand how the author came to their conclusions, how they learned their craft, who influences them, and what didn't make it into the book. (That's usually the stuff I love the most.)

LISTEN TO THAT PODCAST/
YOUTUBE CHANNEL/WHATEVER

If you liked the interview with that author, subscribe to that podcast. Go listen to their other episodes. Chances are, they have other authors you've never heard about and other perspectives you hadn't yet come across. What's great about many of these shows is the variety in their topics. I know with my own show, just in the last year, I talked to an art historian about ghosts, an author of queer YA fiction, a homeschooling mom about the facts and myths of that style of education, and an expert on Slavic folklore. While books are forever fixed points in time, representing information the author believed was true and important at the time of their writing, media such as podcasts or vlogs evolve with time and act as a good challenge and balance to what you're reading.

LISTEN TO OTHER SHOWS

Not all podcasts or other internet media are interview-style shows, so searching for particular authors or creators might not lead to finding them. However, once you've found voices you like, listen to what *they* listen to. There are so many incredibly interesting niche podcasts to be found going deep into very specific topics. For example, if you're interested in crystals, *Borealis Meditation* is a podcast specifically about the intersection of science and magic as it relates to crystals, gems, and minerals. The hostess, Kathleen Borealis, is an actual geologist and geophysicist who breaks down complex geological topics and marries them with magical knowledge and folklore. What you'll quickly find by listening to a variety of voices is that no two witchy people have the same set of beliefs or practices.

READ NONWITCHY BOOKS

I realize it can seem counterintuitive to tell you that your magical education will require reading books outside the witchy section of the bookstore, but I truly believe they might be even more important towards your spiritual development than the witchy books themselves. Art history will help you understand symbolism and visual metaphor. Chemistry and biology will help balance out the information provided about the natural world. Invariably when people come to this spiritual path, they look for reading lists. When I'm asked for such a list, I tell people that I believe you need a well-rounded mundane education as a basis for spiritual exploration. In my opinion it will help you when you're unpacking your experiences or assessing what you read, and critical thinking skills like these are essential. This advice isn't relegated to just books, either. It goes for documentaries, lectures, public events, et cetera.

AUDIT FREE CLASSES

Did you know that a number of colleges and universities allow you to audit some or all of a class for free? Oftentimes you can do it from the comfort of your home. There are a number of classes you can take in comparative religious studies, world history, art, and more. If you're interested in it, you can likely take a class—or ten—on the subject. I got a lot out of auditing different comparative religion and sociology courses from Harvard in my early days via iTunes U. Want to learn the history of witchcraft? Want to explore the science behind working with plants? Want to learn a language so you can read and understand ancient texts? These classes are often free or far more accessible financially than taking the class for a grade, and they can even come in the form of handy prerecorded lectures that you can download and watch on your own time. As we explored in earlier chapters, there's plenty to learn about the cultures from which modern Pagan practices originate as well as the philosophy and theology through which they are viewed. It is important to have this education in order to put what you read in the witchy section of the bookstore into its proper context.

DO THE STUFF AND
WRITE DOWN THE RESULTS

This is the fun part. (OK . . . I think all of this is fun, but most people prefer wand waving over studying the development of in-group dynamics.) We call witchcraft a practice for a reason. Try out the stuff in the books you're reading. Light those candles. Meditate with those crystals. Dance under that moon. Take notes along the way. This can be done in a journal, an app in your phone, or a series of sticky notes. Be honest with yourself. If the book tells you that a certain stone improves communication, but you don't find that to be the case for you, make that note. Over weeks, years, decades of doing this you'll eventually figure out what works for you, what makes sense for you, and what doesn't align with what the books tell you to do.

I'm Not Scared of a Challenge

Being in charge of your own magical education can seem daunting, but figuring out your intention, making a plan, seeking out sources, and then keeping track of your progress along the way will set you up for success. My simple advice for you in this regard is to keep your education balanced. This is why part of my suggestions for creating your personal syllabus involves auditing classes and taking in nonwitchy information. If something feels off or weird or wrong or not fully genuine, that mundane education will help you figure out why you're feeling that way and help you seek out better resources.

So, you've figured out why you're on a spiritual journey, and you've started chasing those impulses down many wonderful paths to help you learn more. Now it's time to figure out what you're going to do with that knowledge and where you want to go from here. It's work, challenging work, but incredibly rewarding. Oh, and if you want to wear pink while you do it, that's totally fine. And encouraged.

CHAPTER 7

The ETHICS of DABBLING

As a dear friend of mine begins stories, way back in the long, long ago, when I was a spunky college student taking my first Comparative Religious Philosophy course, we had this guy in class. We've all had this particular guy in class. (In retrospect, I'm increasingly concerned that I've been this guy in at least one class.) For the purposes of this story, and the fact that I am now an elder millennial and do not remember his name, I'm going to call him Dave.

Comparative Religious Philosophy was an eye-opening course for me, having been raised in a staunchly conservative Southern Baptist Christian household. It compared and contrasted the major tenets and philosophies of most of the world's major living religions. If you take some of the advice from the last chapter and choose to audit any course, I highly recommend making one of them comparative religion, as it will ideally demystify and humanize beliefs with which you aren't currently familiar. Or it should. Unless you're like Dave.

For most of us, the weekly three-hour class flew by in a riot of discussion and engagement. For Dave, however, these three hours were a battlefield. (Sidenote: Please never take a class in school with your purpose being to somehow convert all the students and professor to your Thing. Even if your Thing is Tupperware, that's . . . not how classes work.) Dave showed up every week more and more consumed with the notion that the fact that this class was being taught at all was heresy of the highest order. He argued with the professor, himself a Zen Buddhist, begging him to call out these other religions as false, their gods as imposters or devils attempting to lead people away from the one true god. The professor would kindly remind Dave that this or that religion was several thousand years older than Christianity and therefore it would be difficult to state that the gods of that religion were demons in disguise when the disguise itself wouldn't be conceived of for thousands of years.

It didn't work. Instead of understanding that this was a class and that the course material was filled with the legitimately held beliefs of billions of people around the world, Dave only thought about how the material affected him and he took it all quite personally.

I would like to think that I haven't been Dave at some point, but that would be a convenient editing of my history that isn't supported by facts. The truth is that we all have a bit of Dave in us, especially those of us possessing more societal privileges. The trouble so many of us run into as dabblers starting out on our respective spiritual paths is that we immediately center ourselves, our needs, and our comfort levels. We codify every new bit of information within our existing frame of reference. I wish I could tell you that this never goes away, but you will always have to check in with your respective privileges, audit your language and actions, and make adjustments. Doing otherwise can lead to hurting people and communities around us.

So far in this book I've talked about how so much of modern discourse and thought surrounding witchcraft, magic, and the broader umbrella of Pagan spiritual beliefs is wrapped up in layers of politics, inequity, racism, and innumerable other forms of implicit bias. This chapter is going to explore the ways in which our automatic impulses keep us from learning and growing, especially when presented with new information that contradicts or challenges our current way of thinking, as well as the ethics surrounding engagement with new ideas and cultures.

Yes. This entire chapter could be summed up with a "Don't be like Dave" meme, but I have a word count to hit, so leave me alone.

Grounded and Decentered

Living through 2020 means having lived through a number of Very Big Conversations around social issues such as racism, xenophobia, transphobia, and more. Whether you've engaged with those conversations directly, watched silently on social media, or simply picked up the gist in the ephemera of being a human being in the world, you've likely heard the term "centering." The wellness and New Age spirituality worlds talk about it in terms of meditation, and in that context it means something like "letting go of your stresses in order to come back to yourself."

However, in conversations regarding privilege and social learning, centering oneself is kind of the exact opposite. "Centering oneself," in this context, is a reactionary term meaning that you have allowed the stress of a certain topic or situation to cause you to ask the same question that every protagonist in a romantic comedy has asked when confronted with the idea that the lovable best friend character might have a life of their own: "How can I make this about me?"

The mistake that Dave made during our semester in Comparative Religious Philosophy was in thinking that the existence of and learning about other beliefs and practices affects him personally in some way, that the class was a challenge of his beliefs. In short, he made each item on the syllabus about him instead of taking it as an opportunity to understand others and find commonalities among our fellow man. See, some folks have this idea of zero-sum bias, thinking that life is a competition with winners and losers. You might think of this in terms of politics, where one side's gains are seen as losses for the other side when the reality is that any advancement should center the betterment of all citizens. Socially we've seen this in areas like marriage equality, where the right for LGBTQ+ individuals to marry is seen as some kind of threat to the marriages of heterosexual couples as though marriage is a finite resource and only some should have it. Dave was exhibiting spiritual zero-sum bias, thinking that other people holding beliefs unlike his own—even, perish the thought, in opposition to his own (gasp)—somehow threatened or invalidated his beliefs.

We're all guilty of this at some time in our lives. Centering oneself is a reactionary response we have to a number of different situations. This isn't always about major societal ideas, either. Often this behavior shows up in well-intentioned, innocent ways. Take grief for example. People have been dying as long as there have been people, and yet for some reason we've never gotten a handle on how to react to another person's grief. My husband, on the one hand, experienced a lot of loss as he was growing up, and it's made him view death with a bit of pragmatic distance. He's also a veterinarian and has seen death on a daily basis for decades. I, on the other hand, haven't experienced as much loss in my life, nor have I been around people who have lost beloved pets every day of my life for multiple decades. Whereas my husband's impetus when seeing someone else grieve a loss is to acknowledge that it is a sad thing while not involving himself unless specifically asked, I . . . tend to want to jump in and figure out how I can help make this time in someone else's life easier.

Do you need food cooked? Your house cleaned? Can I tell you a joke to lighten your mood? Would you like to see pictures of my dog? Do you need any errands run? Would you like to talk about the deceased?

Some of those are fine. It's good to show up for people when they need and want it. Caring for the people who matter to us is a way we show them that we love them. Other reactions, however, are not fine, especially when they are unsolicited. Something as simple as *I know you're sad and I don't know the proper way to react, so here's a photo of my cute dog* could be well-meaning, but it immediately centers you, your dog, and your expectation of warm fuzzies and compliments on your cute dog. The glaring and most problematic version of grief centering, however, is the classic: *Have I told you about a time I have also lost a person I loved?*

When someone else is processing a loss, many of us often try to find a way to relate to the uncomfortable feeling of being in the proximity of another person's strong emotions by summoning up a memory of a time we went through something similar and sharing it. For example, say you have a standing coffee date with your friend Emma. When you arrive, she's visibly upset, and she tells you that her favorite aunt passed away yesterday, and the funeral is in a couple of days. You ask if there's anything she needs and she says no, but that simply coming here and being with you was what she needed so that she could get out of the house. You tell her that you lost your grandfather a few years ago, so you know what she's going through.

Emma might be fine with this comment. You two could have the kind of relationship where this is not seen as an intrusion on her grief process. Or she could suddenly be burdened with having to say all the obligatory things we're supposed to say when someone tells us they've lost someone. Suddenly there's a moment in the conversation about Emma's grief when it isn't about Emma's grief anymore. It's about you and your loss.

Centering oneself is typically a response to a time of personal discomfort. As we've seen in recent years, with the advent of social media bringing to light many of the quiet things we all had previously decided not to say out loud, those of us with different types of intersecting privilege are having to confront ideas that make us uncomfortable. As with the preceding interpersonal examples, the initial response for many is to ask, "But what about me?"

Rachel Elizabeth Cargle wrote a brilliant piece on problematic centering in an article for *Harper's Bazaar* August 2018 titled "When Feminism Is White Supremacy in Heels."[1] Her piece is a deep dive into the ways white feminists tend to wield calls for unity or positivity as weapons against BIPOC. Specifically, she touches on different ways in which those with privilege either erase marginalized people from conversations about themselves or redirect the entire conversation towards the privileged. I've already talked about the concept of centering, but I wanted to spend a bit of time on a few other topics Cargle discussed: tone policing and spiritual bypassing.

Oftentimes we assert our needs and comfort level in a manner called tone policing, which is when you tell a marginalized person who is expressing grief, pain, or anger that they'd be better served by saying things "nicely." From the privileged person's perspective, this draws on their experience of believing that if you're nice enough and patient enough eventually you'll get your way. From the marginalized person's perspective, this is often received as trivializing or delegitimizing their very real feelings or earned outrage. Alongside tone policing is the white savior complex, which is when a person with privilege (such as white privilege) is confronted with the ways in which they have directly contributed to white supremacy, xenophobia, et cetera, and instead of listening and learning they trot out the long list of ways in which they have helped that marginalized group in the past. Sometimes these are big things ("I was at X protest!") or medium things that further exhibit their privilege ("I donated X money!") or even really small things that they think are big indicators of allyship ("I shared a heartwarming video on Facebook!"). (I'm not kidding about that last one.) It's also a problematic trope that comes up in movies—looking at you, *Green Book* and *The Help*!

One of the topics that Cargle discusses is also one of the biggest issues we see in our community. It's called spiritual bypassing. As she says, when confronted with the realities of complex social issues such as racism or homophobia many people try to "love and light it away." They call for unity and kindness and peace, asking people to light candles and send good vibes. This term was originally coined in 1984 by the psychologist John Welwood, and it refers to the prioritizing of spiritual beliefs or experiences over psychological needs.[2] In this way it is used as a defense to either sidestep or ignore difficult, uncomfortable, or wholly problematic issues. These issues don't stop being issues for the person or group in question after you lit your candle and sent good vibes, and pretending that this spiritual action is sufficient minimizes real suffering. These ideas closely align themselves with toxic positivity, or focusing on maintaining a positive mindset no matter how dire the actual circumstance might be. The downside is that those who are directly affected by the racism or transphobia or xenophobia are then painted as aggressive, angry, mean, et cetera, because they simply aren't being positive enough. They're not being victims in a way that is seen as respectable to those with privilege.

What does any of this have to do with learning about witchcraft? you might find yourself asking. A lot. Why? Because so many different cultures and social groups intersect to make our modern witchy, magical, Pagan community. I want you to understand early and have it reinforced often that not every conversation, book, or piece of information you come across is for you or about you.

I know. I know. We don't like being told we aren't allowed in the clubhouse. And it's uncomfortable to hear that not every space is specifically for you, but that doesn't mean you cannot learn more about it, celebrate it, or even, sometimes, participate in it.

Is It a Gate or a Window?

As plugged into social media and the internet in general as our society at large has become, it's mind-boggling to think that when I was starting out on my own witchy journey the only way I had of meeting other like-minded people was to hope I randomly bumped into them at a coffee shop or CD store. And that they were nice. And that I wasn't awkward.

And that they had any interest at all in pursuing a friendship. Seriously, I can probably trace most of the choices I've made and people I've known back to a single patio table at one particular Starbucks. (Give me a break; I'm from a small town, and this was our only coffee shop for at least thirty miles.) I did get pretty lucky in the beginning. I made a wonderful core group of like-minded friends who welcomed me without question and didn't try to poke holes in the labels I applied to myself, which was a big deal for a young gay guy in East Texas in the early '00s.

It wasn't until several years later, once I'd gotten a little experience and knowledge and a better internet connection, that I began engaging with the online Pagan community.

Oh my, was it different.

Just like the real world, the online world is filled with labels and assumptions. Unlike the real world, it's a bit more difficult to overcome one's immediate assumptions about you. The labels and identifiers you use imply your intentions, your prior knowledge, and your experience, whether or not any of it is accurate. For example: if you say you're a Gardnerian Wiccan (a Wiccan tradition whose members can trace their initiatory lineage directly back to Gerald Gardner), people immediately assign a set of personality traits and beliefs to you. The online world is filled with character limitations and short attention spans. It contains all the world's knowledge and invites you to connect with it . . . if you can find it among all the other arrangements of words and images floating about masquerading as good information. It can be difficult to find an inroad into learning more about subjects about which you are passionate.

No matter what your thing is—rock collecting, Star Wars, the economic policies of ancient Chinese empires—there's a network of enthusiasts, scholars, and content creators out there for you. If they let you in.

When I joined the online Pagan community all those years ago, I got a swift education in a pretty obvious idea: words mean things. At the time I recall that the online world was mired in determining what the words "Wicca," "witch," "eclectic," and "Pagan" meant. (I'm sure there were plenty of others, but it's not like I took comprehensive notes on the contents of early '00s Pagan message boards.) People argued over whether being a Wiccan meant you were also a witch, whether you could be an "eclectic" Wiccan, and whether any of it was technically under the label of "Pagan." Had this conversation happened on that coffee shop patio, I would be fairly confident that it would have been a bit more civil, and people would have walked away with at least a modicum of goodwill towards others. Instead, this happened largely online and thus it was a digital war zone. (People would even call it a "witch war" online.)

Why am I bringing up the petty squabbles of internet discussions from almost fifteen years ago? Because our society has only gotten more online and when you join that online discussion as a "witch" or "Pagan" or "spiritual seeker" or "mystic" or whatever other label you ascribe to, it causes other people to react, to decide whether they want to let you play in their sandbox. This type of decision—determining whether or not someone can join your proverbial club—is called gatekeeping, and it's a part of almost every subculture you can name.

Do you think of yourself as a "gamer"? Prove it. Name the ten most popular Xbox games from 2017.

Do you call yourself an athlete? Prove it. How much do you bench?

Do you call yourself an occultist? Prove it. What did Aleister Crowley have for breakfast the morning he began writing *The Book of the Law*?

Gatekeeping isn't a wholly terrible thing. In certain circumstances it can be a part of a check-and-balance system that ensures resources are being provided to those who need them. While we don't typically think about it, there are plenty of types of positive gatekeeping we practice in our daily lives. We say who can and can't go behind certain doors in a hospital or access sensitive information in protected servers. There are more neutral versions of gatekeeping, such as the assistant who determines whether your request for a meeting with an executive gets approved. If gatekeeping were relegated to appointment books and data entry that might be fine. Annoying, but fine. However, what I'm talking about is something else.

Gatekeeping in the context of this chapter is in regards to two things: 1) who has the right to claim certain labels or titles and 2) who is allowed to learn about, practice, and/or profit from various spiritual practices.

Something I noticed back in the early days of writing my blog was that quite a lot of time was spent by folks online telling people they shouldn't call themselves Pagan. They did it with other words, too—like "witch"— but "Pagan" really stuck in people's craws. Reasons varied, but it almost always came down to *your spiritual path doesn't look like my spiritual path and therefore it's wrong and you shouldn't get to use the same label as me*. (I swear you could almost hear them chanting "nanny nanny boo boo.") I took issue with that. Sure, words should mean things—if you call yourself a plumber I expect you to have a working knowledge of pipes—but the problem at hand was that we were telling people they couldn't call themselves a word we had yet to properly define. The word did not equate to an agreed-upon objective reality.

That's the difference between calling someone a plumber and calling someone a Pagan or witch or occultist. The dictionary definition hasn't quite caught up to the intent of those living practitioners who apply the label to themselves, mostly because the modern interpretations of these words are fairly young in the grand scheme of things. Some Pagan religions like Wicca weren't founded until the mid-1900s. (More information about the evolution of modern Pagan terminology, beliefs, religions, and practices can be found in *Drawing Down the Moon* by Margot Adler. It's a phenomenal, if dated, resource.) Suffice to say we're still figuring out what these terms mean, who gets to claim them, and why, which means telling people who feel the label fits their personal understanding of spirituality that they cannot use it or have no rights to it is ... well ... wrong.

Except when it's not.

See, there's another level to gatekeeping—that second point about who is allowed to learn about, practice, and/or profit from various spiritual practices—which we really need to dig into as it pertains to the realm of witchcraft and Pagan spiritual learning. I talked previously about how many different types of spiritualities seem to be placed under the Pagan umbrella. There's Wicca, sure, as well as Asatru (a Norse-based religion), nonreligious witches, Thelemites, Druids, and a whole host of groups with varying degrees of organization. What do those have in common? They originate from mostly white, European sources. Other practices—such as African Traditional Religions (ATR) or *brujería*—originate from the BIPOC community, often from conquered or oppressed racial minorities.

These traditions either survived colonization or were revived by their respective communities as a way of reconnecting with their ancestral heritage. The gatekeepers of these traditions are the respective BIPOC communities themselves, which is apparently a controversial idea. White people mistakenly, though unsurprisingly given the legacy of colonialism, cultural suppression, exploitation, and appropriation, feel that they can invite themselves into these spaces and then take what they like back out. (I mentioned before that we *really* don't like being told we can't do something, right?) But the fact of the matter is that if you are an outsider it is not and should not be your choice to participate in those closed communities. That's not to say that you cannot learn more about these traditions or that you won't be able to find someone to initiate you into the tradition no matter your ethnic background; it's that the invitation to participate should lie within that community and not with you. When I try to explain this, I usually ask someone to think about a Pride parade.

Pride parades are part of LGBTQ+ celebrations and are one of the most public types of ways in which our queer subculture engages in person with the rest of the populace. If you can physically show up, you can engage with the Pride parade. You can see drag queens in their natural habitat. You can get free rainbow sunglasses and rainbow pens and rainbow necklaces. You can even get rainbow food, though I will say I had a rainbow grilled cheese one time and that was not remotely how the gods intended cheese to be consumed. Basically, you can experience the full spectrum of queer identity and expression in one place. Many people, however, confuse access with permission to center themselves.

I wrote about this originally in 2016, just after a reporter had used gay social media apps at the Olympic Games in Brazil to entrap and out as many athletes as he could. Outing is an act of violence done to queer people, especially those from countries in which being outed as LGBTQ+ can come with a literal death sentence. I tried to explain that there are many spaces built by queer people for queer people where nonqueer people can participate, like bars and clubs and, yes, parades. Except these same cisgender, heterosexual (cishet) people need to remember that their needs aren't the ones that are important in those spaces. From bachelorette parties in gay bars demanding the DJ play their music to comments from the cishet community about how Pride parades shouldn't include certain content because it's not "family-friendly," nonqueer people seem to think queer-specific spaces are some type of gay petting zoo that should conform to their needs and preexisting stereotypes.

When I said this originally, I was overwhelmed by responses, mostly from white women, who said they should get to occupy these spaces because straight spaces aren't typically safe for women. Commenters told me they preferred going to gay bars so they wouldn't be preyed upon by men and they were glad to be in a space where they didn't have to worry as much about someone drugging their drink. Many women went on to tell me that since they paid their entry fee, they should get to treat it like their space, too, further threatening that if gay bars didn't like it they'd take their money elsewhere.

All of these things are valid in the sense that everyone deserves a space that is theirs, built for them and their respective community, with internal rules and common language and shared lived experiences that unite them. A safe space for their community without fear that they will be persecuted or further marginalized simply for existing openly and proudly as themselves. Everyone deserves this. White women deserve this. Disabled people deserve this. Furries deserve this. People who really, really love the anime *Sword Art Online* deserve this. No matter what piece of your identity you want to protect, whether it is an immutable part of who you are or something as simple as a beloved interest you don't want the world at large to ridicule you for, you deserve a space. However, you are not entitled to another community's space no matter how difficult you've found it to find a space for yourself.

Why? Well, as an outsider of a given community, you bring with you a set of biases, assumptions, and beliefs about how things *should* be done. You bring your privilege and your judgment, neither of which is typically very welcome in marginalized spaces. You bring loyalties that primarily lie with your in-group, meaning that you'll choose your own people if things get tough. Because of all of these and more there are things you will likely see that will make you uncomfortable and your discomfort might lead you to saying or doing something harmful to the community whose space you're occupying. In my example earlier of cishet people coming into queer spaces (such as queer-centric bars and Pride events) we see this in multiple ways:

- Centering and prioritizing the safety and security of nonqueer people in queer spaces inherently creates an unsafe environment for queer people. One example of this can take the form of cishet people having a problem with whom they share a bathroom, causing trauma to the queer person at best and possible physical endangerment at worst.

- Centering a celebration of your heteronormative marriage can be harmful and triggering to queer people. While we were awarded the right to marry in 2015 by the Supreme Court of the United States, recent SCOTUS appointments have many in the LGBTQ+ community concerned that those rights could be limited or taken away in the near future. Those fears aren't unfounded. Not only is our right to marry in danger, but states around the country are actively passing legislation meant to limit the rights of queer citizens. Access to healthcare, job security, and more are all targets of legislators who do not seem to see queer citizens as worthy of the same safety and security enjoyed by our cisgender, heterosexual counterparts. Mainly, if you've never had your right to marry litigated by a court you probably shouldn't decide to center such a celebration in front of those who have.

- Centering your requirements for when and how you should be entertained and then threatening to take away funds from minority-owned businesses if you are asked not to center yourself isn't doing anything except reminding that minority group that you were never someone they could trust. You're not with them for the long haul but rather to be temporarily entertained in a way that fits your needs and expectations.

What being a queer person in a queer space and being, for example, a black Hoodooist among a sea of white authors and teachers have in common is that neither individual can shrug off their intrinsic identity once they leave that space. Even in their own spaces or speaking from their own experience and culture they have to fight for legitimacy, safety, and equity.

One study titled "The White Space" by Elijah Anderson, a professor of sociology at Yale University, looked in depth at the power dynamics specifically of white people who by and large avoid "black spaces" while "black people are required to navigate the white space as a condition of their existence." In Anderson's paper he showcased how white people tend to view traditionally black spaces "with disgust, pity, judgment, and fear." The paper documents the fact that black people, specifically, start with a trust deficit that is almost impossible to overcome. While white people and others of privilege are far more likely to trust one another, black people must fight for that trust and rarely earn it except in specific circumstances: "Accordingly, the most easily tolerated black person in the white space is often one who is 'in his place'—that is, one who is working as a janitor or a service person or one who has been vouched for by white people in good standing."[3]

I mentioned previously in my example that queer people in queer spaces need to entertain cishet attendees in order to receive fair treatment and money. Anderson states the same is true for black people interacting with white people and others of privilege, specifically in regards to earning credibility in their own spaces: "Strikingly, a black person's deficit of credibility may be minimized or tentatively overcome by a performance, a negotiation, or what some blacks derisively refer to as a 'dance,' through which individual blacks are required to show that the ghetto stereotypes do not apply to them; in effect, they perform to be accepted."

This is why nobody of privilege is owed a place in a minority community's space. You might be invited to an event or read about it in a book or watch videos about it online, but those are merely windows into that world until such time as that community welcomes you further. And even then . . . even after you've gone past the gates, you must always remember that you are being honored with the gift of that culture's history without ever having to carry the burden of its visible identity.

Studies like Anderson's and others tell us that the more privileges you possess—especially race/skin privilege—the more likely you are to be assumed to be trustworthy, moral, honest, and knowledgeable. So when opportunities are created to teach or publish or speak, they are more likely to go to white people even if the topic is about BIPOC culture. Thus, there is a gate to respective BIPOC spiritual traditions and to BIPOC spaces in general, and the keepers of that gate are—and should be—the BIPOC communities themselves.

Minorities Aren't Monoliths

One last thing: A lot of people with privilege—of which I'm certainly one—get defensive when the idea of limiting one's entitlement is brought up. Or, as Franklin Leonard tweeted in October 2015, "When you're accustomed to privilege, equality feels like oppression." Very often that defense looks like trotting out the nearest person they know from the marginalized group in question to prove that they cannot be racist or sexist or homophobic or what have you because look at this one gay person they know. (Also known as the "my one black/gay/Latinx friend" defense.)

Pointing to one person who said you're OK/you're not racist/they weren't offended by what you said thereby puts the burden of an entire group of people on the shoulders of one person who may or may not be comfortable being honest in that moment.

In the inverse, this looks like a person with privilege going to their "one X friend" and requesting they perform the labor of explaining racism/homophobia/transphobia/xenophobia, et cetera. They might ask a transgender or nonbinary person probing questions about genitals or see a horrible news story about police brutality and then ask their one black friend to explain racism to them.

This happens in the spiritual community as well.

There is a difference between "my one X friend from Y community said it was OK for me to practice Z" and "members of the Y community by and large are asking for this practice to not be used by those from outside their community." No minority is a monolith. Conversations about what practices, traditions, and which sacred tools should and shouldn't be used by those from outside the respective community are happening and are ongoing. It is no less confirmation bias to seek out a singular opinion from within a given group for an inroad into a closed community. Such as, just because your one gay friend said they've never experienced homophobia in the workplace doesn't mean homophobia doesn't exist in the workplace. It can mean anything from they've never actually experienced homophobia in the workplace to they experienced homophobia but haven't fully processed it or recognized it as homophobia to they have definitely experienced homophobia but don't feel comfortable talking to you about it.

Speaking for myself and coming to this type of conversation as a gay man, I've seen people—straight people who would call themselves allies of the LGBTQ+ community—say that they can use some homophobic slurs "because my queer friend said it was OK." Now, the boundaries that exist within any relationship between two people are their business, and if those two people have decided this is a way they can respectfully speak to each other I'm not here to police that. What I will tell you is that just because it's OK between two people doesn't mean it's OK with others and that saying it out loud in front of other people doesn't come without consequences. LGBTQ+ people might have all sorts of reactions to hearing a cisgender/heterosexual person using certain terms or behaving in certain ways, including processing internal trauma or deepening a mistrust of people from outside their community.

If one person from an oppressed community gives you permission to engage with their culture in a particular way, that should not be mistaken for unfettered access or permission on a wide scale, as one person does not speak for the community as a whole. It's important to tread lightly and respectfully and listen to as many voices from within the respective community as possible before determining whether it is right for you to take a certain action or claim certain titles. The conversation should continuously be centered back on the voices from within the community itself and never made about you, your comfort level, or your one X friend who said it was OK.

Appreciation or Appropriation?

"This sandwich is my spirit animal."

"She really drank the Kool-Aid after getting a promotion."

"OMG, the barista flirted with me and then gave me a free Frappuccino. Must be my good karma."

Our everyday vernacular is filled with turns of phrase most of us use without thinking of their origins. Some of them, while out of place, are less overtly harmful than others. Some have really, really dark origins. (Seriously, look up the origins of "drink the Kool-Aid.") Others are straight-up racism repackaged as a folksy saying. Because so many people say these without a shred of ill intent or, indeed, any knowledge of these phrases' harmful origins, we don't dig deeper or ask ourselves whether we should be using such phrases in the first place.

Back in 2012, Andrew Bentley wrote an article for Partnership With Native Americans, a nonprofit group working with poverty-stricken reservations, in which he said the following:

> To the point, what is troubling about the use of "off the reservation" and other phrases like it is that they are freely used without any thought to literal meaning and how that is connected to casual usage.... They become a part of the common vernacular. Freely they move from mind to mind, mouth to mouth. Maybe the meaning of these sorts of phrases never should have been the issue. Maybe living lives without thinking about what we say and do is of greater concern.[4]

While I greatly enjoy philology, this isn't a section about unpacking all the different types of words and phrases we use that have horrifying backstories. I'm using these examples up front to illustrate the fact that we all engage in borrowing from or referring to various cultures every day without much thought. You do it. Your parents do it. Their parents did it. Everyone you know does it. Dolly Parton calls it "innocent ignorance," which is why she changed the name of her Dixie Stampede—a dinner-theater event in Pigeon Forge, Tennessee—to simply Dolly Parton's Stampede after learning that "Dixie" is a harmful term with hundreds of years of racism attached to it. There's no problem inherently with an innocent mistake. The harm comes from learning about the problematic history and continuing or defending its use anyway.

It's part of our culture, this borrowing and repurposing of terms and ideas, that is so immanent simply bringing up the topic feels like a challenge, an accusation. People get really defensive when you say, "Did you know where that phrase comes from?" Mostly because it may not have been said with malice, and we don't like feeling called out if we didn't *intend* harm. It's all very, "I'm sorry, Officer. I didn't mean to hit that sweet old man as he walked slowly across the road to get to the charity orphanage for underprivileged puppies, and if I didn't mean it you can't arrest me, right?" (Also, because I'm nothing if not a pedant, yes, killing an old man, even if you didn't mean to, is a crime. It's called involuntary manslaughter.)

Witchcraft is filled with appropriation. Utterly filled with it. I cannot swing a wand in a witchy shop without hitting a book that, at least in part, recommends an appropriated practice from an oppressed, colonized, or enslaved culture. The reason is that many of these practices were blithely borrowed so long ago that we no longer think of them as having any specific origin, or, if we do, we have the "Thanksgiving Play" mentality about it. You know how in elementary school you always learned the origins of the USA's Thanksgiving holiday as this delightful story about Native Americans and Pilgrims learning to become friends over corn and it wasn't until twenty years later you learned that's not even a little bit how it happened? (Yet, still, when you think of the first Thanksgiving, your brain immediately populates a pleasant scene with hand puppets and corn and you have to fight to shift your thinking. Or . . . is that just me?)

There are many, many examples we could unpack here, but two practices in particular cause significant debate within the magical community: smudging with white sage and Reiki. The conversation surrounding these issues is reflective of many other types of conversations, so rather than creating an exhaustive list, I will focus on these issues.

The burning of white sage to cleanse a person or space of negative energy is so common and accepted by mainstream culture that you can literally purchase bundles of white sage at grocery stores like Whole Foods, clothing stores like Anthropologie, and an endless supply of online retailers on sites such as Etsy. People who utterly reject the notion of performing any type of witchcraft will still actively recommend the burning of sage. I remember I once had a district manager in a previous retail job recommend burning sage in the store after an intense holiday season.

I've said before that our ever-increasing access to information has led us to confuse access with permission. White sage is a prime example of how proliferation and availability have allowed many of us to partake of the practice without having to interact with the culture of ownership or learn the history and context surrounding it. This has led to a lot of debate surrounding the use of white sage, as it's an appropriated practice from Native American cultures. Due to its rise in popularity and subsequent overharvesting, many Native activists state that their people experience great difficulty in obtaining white sage for ritual use. When Natives harvest the plant, they do so in a sustainable way that allows for its regrowth and propagation. Many companies that sell white sage for profit, however, often destroy the plant entirely.

In addition, the method of simply burning a bundle of white sage and waving the smoke around yourself or your space decontextualizes the practice from its more intricate roots in a smudging ritual, which is traditionally undertaken to cleanse the soul rather than your surroundings. Further, the use of white sage and other Native American practices and ideas—such as the concept of spirit animals or the wearing of feathered headdresses at music festivals—by non-Native people is problematic because it was illegal for Native Americans as a people to practice their spiritual traditions in the United States until the American Indian Religious Freedom Act was enacted on August 11, 1978.

In a July 2019 interview with the magazine *Bustle*, Ruth Hopkins, a Dakota/Lakota Sioux writer said, "It was illegal for Natives to practice their religion until 1978 in the U.S., and many were jailed and killed just for keeping our ways alive, including my great-great-grandfather."[5] This is context many of us might not be aware of as we aren't normally asked to think about it, and doing so now might place you in a state of discomfort. That's OK. It's normal. It's valuable. But don't stay in discomfort. Don't run from it. Work through it and use it as an opportunity to ask better questions of yourself and those providing you instruction, to parse out *why* white sage, and to find alternatives if appropriate.

I am not here to be the Practice Police, especially because I do not belong to the culture whose practice is being repackaged and commodified. What I am hoping to accomplish here is to get you to pause for a moment before you buy your next bundle of sage at the grocery store and think deeply about why you're doing it. Is it because you want to include smoke cleansing in your practice? If so, since you're at the grocery store anyway, you could head over to the produce section and pick up some fresh rosemary, bundle it together, and burn it instead. There are a number of other plants that can be used to smoke cleanse, and a number of other ways of cleansing instead of smoke. However, there are Native-owned businesses that sell ethically sourced white sage, and your dollars would go directly to supporting the community. If you're burning sage because you simply like it, think critically about whether simply liking something is enough of a reason to engage with it directly. (Is it a gate of permission or a window to appreciate from afar?) There are plenty of things I like that are not necessarily for me. Whatever you do, I hope that you'll center the voices of the culture of ownership and take your direction from them.

Part of the language of magical interpersonal conversation is the request for energy. You've seen it. The vague social media post "You guys... I don't want to talk about it, but I'm going through it and could use some energy... please send energy... but don't ask me what's going on... but please send energy." (Anyone else get the feeling those folks *really* want you to ask them what's going on? I digress.) However, ever more present in those conversations is the request for a form of energetic healing known as Reiki.

Reiki is an energy healing practice originating from Japan that was brought to the United States in the early to mid-1900s. Its roots are in Shintoism, an indigenous Japanese animistic religion. You might have heard the term "Reiki Master" bandied about or seen requests from your friends on social media asking for "Reiki healing" from whoever might stumble across their post. I was privileged to interview Marika Clymer, an Ainu, Japanese, and American Reiki practitioner and decolonization activist, and these are some of the issues she sees surrounding Reiki as practiced in Western cultures:

1. It's overwhelmingly practiced by white practitioners who contribute to the erasure of Japanese culture and tradition by decontextualizing Reiki from its traditional practice and mixing it with other belief systems such as Buddhism, Hinduism, and even Christianity.

2. These same white practitioners then sell the colonized practice to other white practitioners or, worse, back to the members of the culture from which the practice originated who have lost touch with its roots due to immigration, assimilation, and discrimination.

3. Western Reiki introduced the concept of "attunement" to create a concept of lineage and a way to capitalize on gatekeeping the practice. This concept does not exist in traditional Reiki healing as practiced by the culture of ownership. However, you, too, can become a "Reiki Master" for under $100 online or over a weekend at a Holiday Inn near you! Clymer states, "In traditional Japanese Reiki, anyone can practice. Reiki energy is an expression of Ichirei, or the 'One Spirit.' Healing is accessible and innate to everybody [without requiring attunement]."

4. As with many other colonized healing practices, white, Western practitioners have cherry-picked beliefs and practices from numerous cultures to create a system that is palatable to Western audiences. Clymer provided the example of substituting the seven-chakra system of Hinduism for the more complex energy point mapping from traditional Japanese energy healing as the concept of chakras are more widely known to Western consumers.

5. No matter how well-intended the practitioner, it should be remembered that Japanese people in the United States have a long history of oppression and forced assimilation into white culture. They were put into internment camps in the 1940s and continue to be an underserved racial minority in this country.

Again, I am not a member of the culture of ownership, and I cannot sit here and write these words and pretend like I sit in some ivory tower of perfect scholarship or unproblematic practice. I've bought and burned white sage, lain in a crystal grid to align my chakras, and dabbled in all sorts of other things along the way. The point, instead, that I am hoping to make is that when we learn better, we should do better. Just because these practices have been wrapped up in New Age thinking, Pagan practice, and witchcraft for years doesn't mean they cannot be examined, critiqued, and a new generation of practitioners decide whether their use should continue.

So much of this discourse is wrapped up in the notion of entitlement. Or, rather, that there are some people—typically people favored with many prized societal privileges such as race and class—who believe they are entitled to take, adapt, repackage, and even profit from other cultures. This type of dabbling tends to be focused on cultures considered exotic to Western audiences. Véronique Altglas, lecturer in sociology at Queen's University Belfast, discusses this notion of "religious exoticism," noting that this mining of yoga, meditation, kabbalah, and Sufism didn't lead to mass conversions to Buddhism, Hinduism, Judaism, or Islam. "Instead," she says, "these traditions are often explored as 'bits and pieces' that individuals combine in seemingly eclectic assortments of beliefs and practices." She argues there is a reason for this, that the belief systems chosen for appropriation share commonalities such as their being "ancient . . . mysterious and vibrant alternatives to a disenchanted West." The idea being that it isn't simply the beliefs that are appealing, but the aesthetics of the culture itself.

Altglas makes a few main points: first, that appropriation of specific practices without embracing the religion as a whole is colonization from the inside out, exhibiting an enduring "entitlement to the culture and knowledge of others." Also, these practices are often watered down in order to be seen as "universal sources of wisdom" that "[downplay] the significance of rituals and core tenets." Many practitioners of these decontextualized teachings express not only no intention to practice Hinduism or Judaism, for example, but an actual discomfort with the respective Hindu or Jewish origins.

Most salient, however, is Altglas's assertion that cherry-picking from seemingly exotic belief systems is due to the security of the one doing the cherry-picking. "'Spiritual seekers' are mostly middle-class individuals for whom being flexible, 'positive,' able to manage reactions, cope with stress, and develop harmonious relationships with others constitute a valuable type of emotional capital transferable in their social and professional environment." Many other scholars and activists have made this point as well, and it bears repeating that taking from other cultures piecemeal is an act of privilege by those who treat these practices as spiritual goods to be bought, sold, traded, and repackaged by those with the financial, social, and mental security to do so.[6]

✫

Appropriation isn't relegated to the selling of goods and services. It is also prevalent in the assumption of ideas and customs. We've all seen it: without fail, every Halloween there is at least one celebrity who decides to wear another culture as a costume. However, it is possible to Appreciate a culture and not Appropriate it. There is a good deal of overlap and gray area where good intentions mean something. One example might be a public event, such as events for Day of the Dead or Diwali, where members of the public are invited to attend and experience parts of the culture from which the celebration originates. Appreciation can take the form of learning to make certain foods, dressing in certain clothes, wearing certain hairstyles, and even participating in some or all of a religious ritual.

In an interview, the multiracial British restaurateur Stevie Thomas remarked that "the difference [between appropriation and appreciation] is what happens next. You can appreciate the music, the lifestyle, the love of the people—but appropriating is where you take the influences you see and completely copy them for your own gain."[7] The kind of appropriation Thomas is talking about here can be seen when white celebrities who appreciate the fashion of black or brown designers turn around and put out a line of clothing that mimics or steals the designs, repackages them, markets them using their whiteness and privilege, and profits. Or, in our community, the white practitioner who appreciates the making of certain types of poppets or oils or the worship of certain deities but then turns around, repackages them, markets them using their own whiteness and privilege, and profits.

The key difference often is who has the power in the situation. Who is centered? Who is profiting? If you are going to an event put on by members of that culture or you're invited to a ritual celebration, the power and the profit still firmly lie with the respective culture in question. The food vendors and face painters and hair stylists and clothiers from within that community are profiting. They're being centered in a space of their own making, and they are inviting you in to appreciate their culture. This is a good thing. Remember my earlier discussion of in-group/out-group dynamics. The more exposed you are to an out-group, the more likely you are to humanize them, to see them as equal and equally valid, to respect them and even fight for their rights and visibility.

The issue where appreciation veers into appropriation is when you cherry-pick pieces of a culture without regard for whether it honors the culture at hand or simply imitates it. These might be situations like wearing a bindi on your forehead as a fashion statement or painting your face like a *calavera* at Halloween. These actions decontextualize that part of the culture from which they originate, stripping it of its significance and importance.

Actions like these can also showcase serious imbalances of power and privilege in society. For example: Whereas it might be a fun and temporary style choice for a white person to imitate a traditionally black hairstyle, for many black people, black women especially, their hair is severely regulated. Schools, employers, and other settings deem many traditional black hairstyles as unprofessional or inappropriate, forcing BIPOC with varying hair types to homogenize their bodies into a simulacrum of whiteness to be accepted.

This goes back to something I said earlier. For the person in the marginalized community, they cannot take their identity off after the parade is over.

Listen, I know this can be a lot to take in. I'm suddenly asking you to perform a lot of calculations and ask a lot of questions when all you wanted to do was practice some magic. Things just got a lot more complicated for you, and if you're not used to navigating these waters let me provide you one last example I think might help: Blue Bell ice cream.

In 2015 there was a listeria outbreak linked to Blue Bell brand ice-cream products, which meant that for the first time in the company's 108-year history, they recalled products and shut down production. Now, if you live anywhere in the world outside the southern United States, you probably don't remotely understand how big of a deal this was. However, if you're my mother, this was basically a sign of the end times. Memes were posted by my friends and family in Texas that went something like "I don't think Northerners realize that we aren't simply down a brand of ice cream. We don't buy other brands of ice cream. Having no Blue Bell means we are out of ice cream!"

It was almost four years before Blue Bell returned to shelves in all of its previous markets, and still I see friends and family posting about how difficult it is to obtain at times. Absolutely nothing turns someone's brain into a supercomputer processing thousands of points of possibilities and outcomes to determine whether they should take an action like being told something they like to eat might kill them. And yet, no matter who you are, no matter how little you cared about how your ice cream was made or stored or shipped before, the moment you find out eating a pint of it might kill you, seeing that label in the store makes your brain ask questions such as:

- How much do I need ice cream?
- How much do I need *this brand* of ice cream?
- Would another brand of ice cream achieve the same end goal?
- Do I trust the news source telling me about the terrible disease?
- Is it possible that information was wrong?
- Have I suddenly become an expert on foodborne pathogens in the last thirty seconds?
- Should I assume the risk and do it anyway?
- Would my great-grandmother rise from her grave to haunt me if I chose another brand?
- Do I know a good exorcist?

See? If you can determine whether you should eat possibly lethal ice cream in a few seconds in a grocery store aisle, you can decide whether a given action is appropriation or appreciation. If you don't know the answer, it's probably best to not take the action but use that as a sign you should do more research. Remember, doing more research *should not* take the form of asking your BIPOC or queer or disabled or (insert marginalized group here) friend to tell you the answer. That places an undue burden on them and forces them to perform emotional labor to explain to you the intricacies of their culture. Sure, asking an OwnVoices[8] friend can be a fine way to engage with the topic further, but it should be done after you have undertaken your own research and only with their permission, as they are well within their rights to tell you no.

The good news is that magic exists in all cultures, is available for all people, and there isn't a single correct way of doing it. If you are inspired by something you learn about that exists in a closed practice or living culture, use that as fuel to seek out a way of accomplishing a similar end result without wading into the murky territory of entitlement or colonization. You do not have to use the same plants, crystals, methods, worship the same gods, to make effective magic. You can remove your own obstacles, protect yourself and your family, turn events in your favor, attract a lover, and do everything else in a way that works for you.

If you're still feeling adrift, try asking yourself these questions:

1. From which culture or group did this practice originate? (If the answer to this question doesn't immediately spring to mind, it might be a good clue up front that you should do some more research.)
2. Does that group experience oppression? If so, how?
3. Is this the only way to perform this type of magic?
4. Are you likely to get praise or benefit in some way from this practice that someone from within that community might not?
5. Would your use of this practice, tool, or terminology make someone from that community uncomfortable?
6. What makes it possible for you to engage with that practice in the first place? (Did you buy it at the grocery store? Did you have the financial means to travel the world to experience it firsthand? Did you read about it online?)

If the answer to any of these is "Yes" or "I don't know" or "because I'm financially and/or socially privileged," take a step back. Pause. Ask some more questions, and sometimes . . . maybe just find an alternative practice or method of accomplishing your goal.

The Dave of It All

Remember Dave? The guy from my Comparative Religious Philosophy course? The thing about Dave is that, despite being a student, he wasn't open to learning. Really learning. True learning is an uncomfortable process that requires you to break down your preconceived notions, your implicit biases, and move away from your comfort zone. It might be easier to be like Dave, but your world will be duller for it. (And you could very well contribute to real harm to other human beings.) You have to be willing to be wrong and to use that as a basis for introspection and growth. You have to welcome the possibility that other points of view and spiritual paths are just as valid as yours, and that sometimes you aren't welcome in all spaces and that not all practices are yours for the taking. You also need to remember that "No" is a complete sentence and sometimes you are not owed an explanation beyond it.

In short, don't be like Dave.

CHAPTER 8

CAN I MAKE SH*T UP?

When I think of magic, I almost always hear a *thunk* in my head. It's the sound of a very large, very old, very heavy book being dropped onto a table. It's bound in leather and might have pretty metal or gemstone adornments. Bonus points if you see little clouds of dust rising in the light-dappled air. No matter who you are, at one point in your life you loved a movie or TV show or children's book where someone pulled out The Book. From *Hocus Pocus* to *The Vampire Diaries*, the image of the ancient book of spells is indelible in culture. Often you'll see in various forms of media that rely on the big book o' magic as a plot device that spells from inside The Book work while spells not written in The Book don't.

Where did this book come from? Who wrote it? Why does their magic work so dang well?

The real answers, of course, are: A prop department. The screenwriter. Because of the plot.

There are these things called logical fallacies, which is a fancy name for flawed reasoning or a bad argument. One example of a logical fallacy that many know is the black-or-white fallacy, where you present two possibilities as the only possibilities when in reality many others exist. (Example: you either love the movie *Legally Blonde* or you are a monster who cannot be trusted.) There is another type of fallacy called appeal to age or, as it's more commonly known, "it's been around a long time, so it must be better." That's the fallacy at play here. On paper it's something most of us balk at. ("Well, Susan, I don't care how luxurious the ancient Thracians' hair was, I'm going to stick with my shampoo and conditioner.") However, in practice it's one of humanity's most consistent flaws in thinking.

It's built into our brains. We trust what we know because it hasn't killed us yet. "We've always done it this way." "Better the devil you know." "Why do we eat these particular fruits? Because when we discovered them and tried them out, they didn't kill us. Why don't we eat those berries over there? Because we tend to die quite painfully when we do." Logic like this is used to support everything from passing down secret family recipes to wage disparity.

The idea of the big, ancient book o' magic containing all the secrets to unlocking "real" magic, the magic you see in movies, the magic that "works," is incredibly appealing. It's something that's replicated often. You'll see witchy authors put out massive compendiums of spells and rituals in an attempt to satiate that *thunk* craving we all have. Even perusing the spells I've included in the back of this book might have you wondering, *Did . . . did he just make all this up?* We have this thing somewhere in our brains that's open to appeals to age or appeals to authority—another logical fallacy—believing that because the spell is old or written by someone with a book deal it's inherently better, more magical, more real. And, while there's something to be said for an experienced practitioner field-testing spells and passing along what works for them, it really raises the question:

Can you do that? Can you just . . . make up spells?

Yes.

Yes, you can.

A Little of This . . . a Little of That

Something I never saw a lot of growing up was a recipe book. My paternal great-grandmother was the matriarch of our family, and it was from her that all knowledge of cooking and baking flowed. My grandmother's chocolate chip cookies. My father's biscuits and gravy. My great-aunt's green beans. They all came from the mind and hand of my great-grandmother. Almost nothing was written down because she knew what worked from a lifetime of cooking for the family. Of course, the knowledge had to come from somewhere, right?

Once you've read your tenth witchy book of spells, you'll start realizing that a lot of ideas are repeated. This isn't a criticism of the genre; it's a reminder that practitioners rely on tried and true methods of manifesting magic that have worked for many years and for many people. (You might recall I talked about magical practitioners being a bit like scientists in that they observe and reproduce based on what has worked in the past for themselves and others, adapting as needed.) It's like baking. We've figured out how to make a chocolate cake by now, and the basics of what makes chocolate cake truly a chocolate cake are the same. But that doesn't mean that there's only one way of making chocolate cake, or that it can't be improved upon or, for example, personalized to your preferred level of sweetness. Or maybe you have to make some changes because you live at a high altitude or need to avoid a deleterious effect brought on by a particular ingredient. The same is true with magic.

There are the standbys we all know and love, and they're great! The good ol' "coat a candle in oil, roll it in a bunch of herbs, and light it on fire," anyone? It only takes one time of watching this become a giant pillar of fire that nearly burns your house down before you learn to ease up on the oil. But it doesn't mean you have to do it that way, especially once you've seen enough people tell you how the herbs and oil caught on fire and nearly burned their house down.

Need to spice up your sex life? A little cinnamon or rosemary could help. Make it into an oil and anoint your clothing before meeting up with that special someone. (Though watch getting it directly on your skin, as cinnamon oil can irritate.) Or rub the oil onto a candle and light it. Crush it up and mold it into a wax figure. Put it in a sachet and stick it under your pillow. Have an allergy to cinnamon? Don't like the smell of rosemary? Lavender could be for you. Or, if you're someone who doesn't really like smells at all, changing up your wardrobe to add a certain color can work equally well.

You get the idea. Once you learn the mechanics of magic, making a plan to add a little magic into your life to achieve a desired result becomes a really fun, playful exercise. But, of course, you have to unlock the "why" behind the "what" first. This was a lesson I learned the hard way once upon a time after a childhood Christmas when Santa brought me an Easy-Bake Oven. I told you my great-grandmother never cracked open a recipe book and that the habit continued through my family. Between watching the fairies in *Sleeping Beauty* haphazardly make a birthday cake and firmly believing I had my family's culinary talent baked (ha) into my very essence, I set about mixing together flour and sugar and milk and other things to make a baked goodie in my new oven. Guess what I made.

A mess.

Let me tell you what doesn't smell good is doughy gunk burned onto a lightbulb trapped inside a plastic box. The one and only lesson I distinctly remember taking away from being around my granny in the kitchen was this: sometimes you need to add a little extra. Looking back, my question should very much have been, "A little extra what?" But I didn't ask. I charged ahead thinking "a little extra" was a rule that could probably apply to anything and be fine. So I added extra milk. Extra powdery ingredients from within the Easy-Bake Oven kit. Extra salt, I think. Who knows? All I remember was that it came out wet, burned, and inedible. If I'd known the "why" behind the "what," I'd have known that extra wet ingredients added to pretty much any baked item need to be balanced with either additional dry ingredients or a longer bake time at a lower temperature.

Experimentation is possible and encouraged, though you want to make sure you're going to end up with magic and not with . . . the spiritual equivalent of Easy-Bake Oven gruel.

So, what are the rules? What's the trick to the "why" behind the "what"?

Science, Magic, and Misunderstanding

In my example earlier of spicing things up in the bedroom with magic, "spice" is actually the operative word. You'll find that many plants with warm scents or hot flavor profiles tend to be associated with sex, attraction, motivation, and activity in general. Why? Well, a lot of reasons (most of which we'll explore in chapter 13 when I talk about herbs). Books on magic typically devote a number of pages to something called correspondences. In magic, a correspondence is a type of metaphysical property associated with a given magical subject. These can range from easily accessible to unobtainable, from tangible to mythical or even hypothetical.

The most common correspondences and associations tend to be for more mundane items or things we interact with or view on a daily basis. Colors, scents, rocks, plants, household tools, and even some heavenly bodies. For example:

- Rose quartz promotes love.
- Mint helps clear your thoughts.
- Oak can bolster your strength.
- Brooms sweep out the bad and sweep in the good.

Sometimes, though, you'll flip through books of crystal or plant magic and find some pretty big claims and correspondences that seem to come out of nowhere. If you're like me, or if you've read this book and have learned to ask good questions, you might wonder how some of these correspondences came to be. The best illustration of this phenomenon I know is the stone lepidolite.

If you look up the stone in a book of correspondences or search around the internet a bit, you'll see associations such as "clears electromagnetic pollution" and "associated with the zodiac sign of Libra" and "aids in the relief of tension." You'll see websites call it a peace stone or grandmother stone and find comments claiming that it has a calming, nurturing nature. Now, I can't speak to the arbitrary way some people come up with astrological signs for rocks, but I can tell you that there's at least a bit of basis for one of these claims, but you wouldn't know it simply from reading the majority of correspondence entries.

In the book *Love Is in the Earth* by Melody, one of those massive books that pretty much everyone who makes lists of "must-have witchy books" includes in said list, you are told that lepidolite "vibrates to the number 8," relieves stress, restructures your RNA/DNA, and even brings stability to tectonic plates. You're also told it's great for digestion, the relaxation of wrinkles, stabilizing blood flow, and that it can be used in both the mineral form and as an elixir (which is when you place the mineral in a container filled with water, leave it for a period of time, and then drink the water).[1] What you are not told is that the stone contains lithium.

Yes, lepidolite contains lithium. A lot of it. In fact, lepidolite is the most abundant lithium-bearing mineral on the planet, which has a number of uses from bomb fuel to making oven-safe glassware. However, what you probably know lithium from is its medical use in the treatment of bipolar disorder. (Or an Evanescence song if you're an elder millennial like me and went through a very moody phase in the early '00s.) Since its discovery in the mid-1800s, it has been used in medical research to treat a number of symptoms, but these days doctors typically prescribe it in an oral tablet to treat certain mental illnesses. Furthermore, lepidolite also contains the alkali metals cesium and rubidium, both of which have explosive reactions when exposed to water and can cause burns due to the moisture in your skin. (Translation: that elixir you wanted to try might not be the best idea.)

Now, the way lithium, cesium, and rubidium are extracted from lepidolite involves the stone being broken down by acid and crushed (among other processes), so while it may not cause harmful reactions with simple handling, this is still important context to know, and lepidolite is a stone that should be handled with care if handled at all. For example, say you're putting a stone that is soluble in acid in your water and any part of it—even a small bit—breaks off and you swallow it and it travels to your stomach . . . which is filled with acid . . . that's probably not something you want. Rare? Sure. But not risk-free. This reminds me of a phrase I'll likely say later in the book: it's fine until it's not fine, and then it's *really* not fine.

The inclusion of lithium is rectified in other popular books such as *Cunningham's Encyclopedia of Crystal, Gem & Metal Magic* by Scott Cunningham, which states, "Lepidolite is a purplish type of mica rich in lithium," but doesn't go further into what lithium is or why its inclusion in the mineral might influence the stone's list of correspondences and associated uses. Cunningham's entry backs off some of the more direct claims of crystal healing and instead recommends placing it near your headboard to promote a restful sleep or to hold it in your hand while breathing deeply to soothe anger.[2] *The Crystal Bible* by Judy Hall also includes a mention of lithium in the lepidolite entry but again foregoes any mention of why that is important in the context of the associations and claims. Though it should be noted that Hall's entry explicitly states that lepidolite—in addition to some of the healing claims found in Melody's entry—"relieves exhaustion, epilepsy, and Alzheimer's."[3] Which . . . feels like a pretty big claim to make and one that might need to be vetted by a qualified doctor, but I digress. Blessedly, neither of these entries recommends ingesting the stone in any way.

Now, I'm as woo-woo as the next witch, and I am known to carry rocks with me when I want an interview to go well or if I am nervous about traveling. I might make pea soup if I want to improve my financial situation or sweep my house if the energy feels a bit stale. It could be a Dumbo's feather situation, in which my belief in the thing aids in my ability to achieve an outcome, or it could be magic. Either way, the result is the same. (Remember what Pratchett said about it still being magic even though you know how it works?)

That being said, doctors do not tell people to wear bottles of lithium around their necks to mitigate symptoms of bipolar disorder, nor do they tell people to meditate with a handful of tablets to correct the movement of tectonic plates. (I'm sorry . . . I'm going to be thinking about that one for a long time.) It is important to understand that the origin of certain associations has less to do with the metaphysical and far more to do with very real physical effects observed when interacting with the respective mineral, plant, oil, et cetera. That's my real point here: Many associations and correspondences have some kind of basis in real-world observation, but the link between that original, observable phenomenon (i.e., lepidolite contains lithium, which is used to treat depression) and the correspondence you found in your metaphysical crystal book (lepidolite is associated with stress reduction) is severed. The context and nuance is lost, and it is up to the reader to figure out where that correspondence came from. Was it a bit of folklore? An odd historical detail? A piece of scientific research that's been watered down? Something else?

Parsing that out can be difficult at first glance, but technology helps. A quick web search of the subject you are researching will help fill in some of the mundane gaps in information contained in the witchy book you're referencing. Also, as a general rule of thumb (and while I really thought it went without saying, it apparently needs to be said): please consult a licensed, practicing, credentialed medical doctor before drinking rock juice. Many minerals and metals can interact with your body in harmful ways, especially if you're on certain types of medications, and being witchy shouldn't come at the cost of your health. Same goes for consuming or in any way putting into your body herbs, crystals, oils, infusions, teas, or other magical substances.

It should also be remembered that books containing magical correspondences are to be viewed through a specific lens. Legally, the authors have to toe a line between providing information about the folk usage of a plant or mineral and prescribing medical advice outright. Unfortunately, when toeing this line, there are times when important bits are left out, as we saw earlier. I'll talk about this more later when I discuss creating a good mental filter. For now, let's refocus on correspondences that work.

The Senses of Correspondence

When you are first dabbling in magic, you'll quickly realize that most magical correspondences end up corresponding with at least one of the classical five senses. The more you ask "why" does something work the way the book tells you it does, the more you might find that it's tied up in the way our bodies experience the world around us. *Why* does rose quartz resonate with "love" energy? Is it because of the trace amounts of titanium, iron, or manganese that give it its pinkish hue and imbue it with supernatural properties? Or is it because pink is a pleasant color that many humans in the Western world associate with love and youthful romance?

While entire books, or series of books, could be written on each of the five senses, the way our bodies use them to interact with the world, and the way the outside world influences our psychology and behavior through those senses, I'm going to focus on a few standout examples that I think will prepare you to parse out possible origins of correspondence as you continue your research.

SIGHT

It is important to remember when reading your next witchy book that the correspondences listed next to a given color are true for the author of the book you're reading and not an immutable law of the universe. It is important to remember this because you might find that using certain colors as prescribed by the respective book might have either no effect at all or the opposite of the intended effect. Why? What's the basis or support for the use of color in magic? You may find some people hinting at studies alleging that certain colors alter human behavior in specific ways. This is a pseudoscience called chromotherapy, and it has not been proven in peer-reviewed study. In fact, quite the opposite.

For example: Baker-Miller pink. This color was invented by Alexander Schauss, who claimed it could lower heart rate, pulse, and respiration immediately following a workout. In 1979 it was painted on walls in a correctional facility in Seattle, Washington, and Schauss purported that it reduced violence and aggression in the inmates. All good, right? Pink = calming. A new correspondence backed up by science. When the same experiment was repeated at a Santa Clara, California, jail, however, they found that violence and aggression actually increased. Why? Could be a number of reasons. Men feeling emasculated or humiliated by a color seen as feminine. Embarrassment. Knowing you're being studied affects the outcome of the study. Either way, each of us reacts to color differently for reasons as varied as the people themselves. Green is often cited as a color to choose when doing magic involving money, mostly because the dollar in the United States is a shade of green. Does this association hold true if the currency in your country is, say, red? Maybe not. Maybe your prosperity color is yellow, because it makes you think of the mineral gold. Or perhaps your prosperity is the color of the blue water in Hawaii, because one day you want to have enough wealth to go there.

It isn't that color cannot have an effect on us, it is that they do not have the same universal effect on us. My friend might think of gray as a very calming color while I might choose a bright green. Neither of us is wrong. Instead of focusing on the correspondence provided in the book, create your own rainbow of associations.

TOUCH

I mentioned earlier that oak is associated with strength. It could very well be because it has some type of metaphysical property that humans can tap into, or it could be that we have observed it is incredibly dense over the thousands of years of humans working with oak. Unlike many other trees, oak is also resistant to insects and fungus because of its high tannin content. So, when you think of oak, you think of a very strong wood that is reliable for use in construction and capable of withstanding attack. Those might be properties you'd like for yourself or a loved one, so baking with acorn flour or carving a likeness from the oak wood could be a way to magically use the tree's natural properties to imbue a situation with toughness.

Creating a correspondence based on touch, or the way a given natural object feels, its physical state of being, will be most effective if it is based on your own interaction with it. When you hold the stone or plant or cloth (or whatever) in your hand, how does it make you feel? When you wish to make a charm to protect yourself in winter, what types of things feel like safety specifically in that season? Flannel comes to mind for me. Maybe the start of your charm could be to wrap something in flannel that you carry with you, or even simply wearing a flannel with your intention imbued into it.

TASTE AND SMELL

I'm grouping these together, because they work together. While taste as a stand-alone sense simply distinguishes between sweet, salty, sour, bitter, and savory (or umami), our perception of food is greatly enhanced with the addition of scent. Anyone who has ever had a cold will tell you that food doesn't quite taste the same if your sense of smell is limited. It is a condition of our evolution as creatures who once had to hunt and find food that we developed what is known as olfactory memory or, as I like to call it, the reason eating apple butter makes me cry. No other sense is tied as closely to memory as smell, and because smell and taste are so closely intertwined, the foods we eat and the scents we sniff have a powerful magic all their own.

This connection between memory, emotion, taste, and smell is often applied to magic, likely in ways you've already experienced. Ever come home from a terrible day at work or school and decided to bake some cookies (or, in my case, order a pizza)? Something about that warm, welcoming smell can immediately alter your mood. That something is because your brain associates those smells with multiple positive memories accumulated over your lifetime, and each time you come in contact with that combination of scent and taste your brain starts a chain reaction to calm you down. Likewise, our brains can associate certain smells or tastes as a warning. The smell of smoke or the taste of something sour when you know a food should be sweet can alert you that something has gone wrong. Not only that, your brain reacts to protect you. The smell of smoke might make you more aware of your surroundings, seeking out the source of the fire, while the sour taste of milk forces your body to spit it out.

Correspondences are used to focus our intention and give it a vehicle to carry out our magical desires. The mechanics of correspondences, however, are far more mundane than most witchy people will probably admit out loud. Our experience of the world around us begins and ends in our bodies and brains, and the way we relate to that world is therefore infinite and infinitely personal. That interaction, I believe, is a source of magic. It's a way to draw upon a power existing within us to perceive the world around us as one way and to endeavor to change it in a way that fits our needs. There is a place for charts of correspondences, of course. They can be a great jumping-off point for your own research. Do you have a problem without a narrow term? Using correspondence charts from various authors can help you define those terms and give you recommendations to begin spell work.

As the great poets say, though, your mileage may vary.

If you're trying to, say, stop gossip and the only thing the correspondence chart recommends is an herb you can't easily access (seriously, why is finding slippery elm so dang hard?), forget the correspondence chart. You're trying to stop gossip. So what does that mean to you? Being left alone? Feeling safe? Having people only speak the truth about you? Not speak about you at all? Want to seal their lips or send your gossipers packing? What foods say those things to you? What scents? Is there a fabric you feel secure in? A color you could wear or choose for a candle? This is where the "work" of "spell work" comes in. When doing a spell for something, knowing what you want to happen is important, and that knowledge will help you in determining what mechanics you'll employ. Or, in other words, what spell you'll make up to do the thing.

You Can't Make This Up

There are, of course, some limits. You can't just make anything up. You have to understand when magic isn't appropriate or, at least, shouldn't be your first solution. In matters of physical or mental health, personal safety, or other serious matters, magic can certainly be something you do alongside mundane actions, but it should not be the first or only thing you do. If you are reading a book on witchcraft and it is telling you to combat depression or abuse or cancer or any number of serious, real-world issues with symbols and spells instead of expressly telling you to seek professional intervention, put that book down.

In addition, if you are reading a book on the magic of plants, crystals, oils, or other witchy ephemera and it tells you to burn something, consume something, or apply something to your body in any way, please ensure you have thoroughly researched each ingredient before doing so. Witchy folks get so caught up in the idea of magic that we sometimes forget our words have real-world consequences. Like my example earlier about lepidolite being recommended as an elixir for digestion in an entry that ignores the fact that the rock contains multiple metals that should not be consumed without a doctor's oversight and could go boom if they interact with water . . . or your skin. You will find quite a bit of overlap in the witchy world with magical folks prescribing mystical remedies for all sorts of problems, because it feels a bit like we're stepping into the world of the witch of myth and folklore.

I, too, would like to one day be the mysterious figure in a cottage in the woods pulling a bottle of mysterious contents from a shelf while telling a young seeker to take two drops in their morning tea to find true love. But I live in the real world and filling our spells with toxic mushrooms or burning plants that give off toxic chemicals in their smoke is dangerous. Pagans don't have peer review, which means that unlike the scientific community, we aren't required to verify our claims or ensure our claims can be replicated before publication. This is fine until it's not. This is why I have said repeatedly in this book and elsewhere that magic should not be the only solution to a problem. It may be a meaningful accompaniment to real-world action, but it cannot and should not ever take the place of talking to a medical doctor, psychologist, attorney, social worker, or person with any other job title who doesn't sound like a whole lot of fun to talk to about your problems but is far better positioned to solve them.

Make It Your Own

The good news, of course, is that magic doesn't have to be hard. Now, there's a place for complex magic and ritual. I've done it. I do it. It's fun, but it can be wildly intimidating when you're first starting out. Most of the time spells and rituals are simple actions using simple, accessible materials. Improvisation is the soul of a good spell. If you're stuck trying to find an ingredient or tool, search your hobbies.

We create correspondences based on how we experience the world, how we observe, and we interact with it both physically and spiritually. This falls short of constituting evincible scientific data in that our correspondences and associations and experiences are personal. They work for *us*, and while they might work for others as well, they could just as easily not. And you know what? That's totally OK. That's why we continue to explore, to experiment, to try new things, and not get let down if the magic from the book didn't work exactly as it was written.

If you're an artist, maybe your spell is a painting. (Just don't go all Dorian Gray on us, please.) Painting a picture of your end goal or simply a palette of colors that make you feel a certain way can be mighty effective spell craft. I promise you that your spell will be no less effective than the one in the book if your whole heart and intention are behind it. I should know. I've made up lots of spells, including the ones in the back of this book.

So make it up. Make it your own. Just remember as you go about your witchy journey, do so with appreciation, respect, and a sense of adventure. Be an ethical dabbler. Oh, and, you know . . . don't drink toxic rock juice.

PART

3

SPIRITUAL
COMMUNITY

You're allowed to believe in a god. You're allowed to believe unicorns live in your shoes for all I care. But the day you start telling me how to wear my shoes so I don't upset the unicorns, I have a problem with you. The day you start involving the unicorns in making decisions for this country, I have a BIG problem with you.

— Matthew Shultz

Spiritual exploration is a deeply personal endeavor. We're reading. We're drooling over rocks. We're in our homes and backyards talking to ourselves hoping that our neighbors don't wonder why we're chanting at a cactus at 3:00 am.

But we aren't actually alone.

There is a whole community of people around the world who are also seeking and growing and learning and making magic. While most practitioners are content to quietly make it part of their everyday routine, some of them teach classes. Others open shops and sell wares. Still more use their skills professionally as psychics or mediums or healers.

You might seek these people out, hoping for a teacher to guide you or to obtain divinatory services. And no matter whether it happens in-person or online there are some things that might be helpful to know as you start to participate more fully in the Pagan and magical community. There are terms that come up, claims made, and ways of filtering information that are good to know either before you start your journey or to be used as a check-in if you're already on your way.

I like to think of these next chapters as the kind of thing everyone else seemed to already know when I was first starting out, but I could never find in any of the books I was reading. So, here they are in hopes that if you're new to this path they can serve as a guide, and if you've been on this path awhile they can serve as reassurance.

CHAPTER 9

SPOTTING *a* FRAUD

I mentioned in a previous chapter that, while it doesn't happen all the time, people lie. That's not a fun thing to think about, but it's the truth. As I discussed previously, people lie for all sorts of reasons. Some lie to gain power or influence, some for fame, and some lie because they're hoping to take your money. Knowing this in advance can save you time, money, and years of therapy. Take heart, however, because the good news is that there are far more genuine, earnest folks in the community than there are bad actors. This chapter helps you spot a fraud long before they can weasel their way into your life or your pocketbook.

Exploiting Gullibility

My first year of college I had a psychology professor who was also in charge of the on-campus clinic, where the graduate-level students did their supervised clinical training. Towards the end of the semester, he told us that part of what they did during the supervised training was teach students how to create personality profiles based on each patient in order to better meet their specific needs. He then took out a stack of brightly colored paper, telling us that he'd carefully analyzed our interactions, essay tests, clothing, demeanor, and other key indicators and, as a way of enticing us to join the psychology program, created personality profiles for each of us. He passed out said pieces of bright-colored paper, making a big show of ensuring each of us had the correct slip of paper. They had our names on them and were folded, and we were encouraged not to share with others so as not to create an environment of pressure for those who didn't want to share. He said we could take the pieces of paper with us and read them privately at home on our own time. He took it all quite seriously.

I opened my slip of paper and read it immediately, of course. People love nothing more than reading about themselves. It contained a paragraph that said things that clearly applied to me. I'll list a few of the statements below. See if any apply to you:

- At times you are extroverted, sociable, while at other times you are introverted, wary, reserved.
- You pride yourself as an independent thinker and do not accept others' statements without satisfactory proof.
- Disciplined and self-controlled outside, you tend to be worrisome and insecure inside.
- You have a tendency to be critical of yourself.
- At times you have serious doubts as to whether you have made the right decision or done the right thing.

I. Felt. Seen. It was like my psychology professor had snuck around in the dark recesses of my brain and pulled out things I'd always felt about myself but never said out loud. I *was* insecure inside while portraying a disciplined exterior. That's so true!

Then a classmate and I switched letters, because we were so excited to read all about each other. And . . . you guys . . . it was the same paragraph. It was all the same words in the exact same order with the sole exception that the paper was a different color and the name was different. How could that possibly be true? What I'd read had felt so personal, so relatable, so accurate, that I couldn't fathom it being true to someone else. At least, not every word of it. That was when my professor got everyone's attention and explained that this had all been an example of the Barnum effect.

The Barnum effect was so named by the psychologist Paul Meehl after P. T. Barnum (yes . . . the guy from *The Greatest Showman*), who famously would give psychological tests to patrons for money. Those patrons then came away believing that Barnum showcased a high degree of accuracy. The effect itself is a phenomenon where people believe that vague generalizations that could apply to anyone specifically apply to them when presented in the context of tools such as personality tests and astrology charts. This effect is also known by some as the Forer effect, due to the applied research of Bertram Forer.

Bertram R. Forer, psychologist and professor, studied the phenomenon in 1948 by having his psychology students take a personality test and, a week later, providing every student the same set of responses. Most of the respondents claimed the responses were highly accurate, with the average response being a 4.3 out of 5 where 0 is very poor and 5 is excellent. Forer attributes the success to the Pollyanna principle, or positivity bias, wherein we "use or accept positive words of feedback more frequently than negative words of feedback."[1] In other words, if we're told vague yet mostly positive things allegedly based on our personality, we're likely to believe them and believe they're specific to us. The less kind way of restating that is to say that people are gullible and easy to manipulate or trick, especially in instances where we want to believe the information. And who doesn't want to believe a long list of nice things about themselves?

Many researchers have replicated the Forer experiment, making little adjustments here and there, and they have consistently found the Forer effect to be true regardless of factors such as gender or age as long as certain general criteria are met:

- The statements should be mostly positive. While there isn't a specific ratio of positive to negative traits that must be met, it's more likely the recipient will agree with the overall assessment if it makes them look good.
- The subject is more likely to believe in the assessment if it is labeled "for you." In other words, if you tell someone that the assessment is specific to them, they'll believe it no matter how vague or even incorrect the assessment might be.
- The statements should be vague enough that the subject can read their own meaning into them (such

as qualifying a statement by saying "at times" or "you have a tendency to," which gives the subject a way of agreeing with a statement they might not otherwise agree with).[2]

Lots of people in lots of professions exploit the Barnum effect. Salespeople, psychics, financial advisors, astrologists, politicians, and even some psychotherapists all exploit the Barnum effect to some degree. As in most areas of life, there's a spectrum of ill intent applied here, and oftentimes these techniques are trained into us in our workplaces. (If you've ever worked a retail job, you've probably had some type of generalized sales pitch drilled into your head.) So, the basic act of employing a Barnum statement isn't on its surface harmful, but when used in certain contexts it can be a warning sign, especially when those statements are passed off as a display of actual psychic ability. The magical community is, unfortunately, not without its fair share of people who exploit our intrinsic good natures, and it's important to know when you're dealing with those situations.

Cold Readings, Horoscopes, and Self-Serving Bias

Some entertainers clamoring to get famous (or get your money) pass themselves off as magicians, psychics, mediums, or fortune-tellers. These people practice a technique called cold reading, which employs a combination of vague statements (or Barnum statements), probing questions, and a practiced eye for picking up nonverbal cues to make a person believe the cold reader is providing incredibly accurate psychic readings. A cold reader gets buy-in from the participant up front, which immediately puts them in a psychological state to be receptive to what is said and to read into any messages for personal applicability. Basically, once you've said, "Yes, I'll participate," your brain starts wanting whatever the psychic says to be real and to apply to you.

You've seen these on television: "I'm getting a message for someone in the audience with a connection to someone who has passed whose name begins with the letter *t*." If nobody immediately takes it, the reader might change it to a series of letters that look similar. "It could also be a *j* or *f*. Is there anyone in the audience with a connection to someone on the other side whose name contains a *j* or *f* or *t*?" Suddenly the likelihood that this doesn't apply to anyone diminishes exponentially, mostly because everyone knows a John or Frank or Tom or someone else with a name beginning with those letters. Cold readers often use generic, popular names to appear to get a hit from someone in the audience, when really they're playing the odds.

You'll also notice when listening to those practicing cold reading that they are quick to hop on to any hint that the information is hitting true to you and equally quick to abandon a line of questioning that is going nowhere. Doing so keeps the subject in the space of positive reinforcement, which you just learned is a key to employing the Barnum effect. That's why, if you ever see psychics (or the like) on television or other media and they're talking 90 miles a minute, it's a good indicator that the person is practicing cold reading.

Maybe it's not a name. Maybe the psychic is talking to you about your departed grandmother and says, "She's holding something very special to you. She says you wouldn't leave home without it when you were little." Because you've agreed to the reading and because you're in the throes of the Barnum effect, you'll offer up, "Oh, that must be my teddy bear Ralph. I lost him a long time ago, but I wouldn't go anywhere without him when I was little." Every child had something that, at one time or other, they couldn't leave home without. Children form all sorts of attachments to things. Sometimes it's a stuffed bear, sometimes it's a piece of your mom's jewelry, and sometimes it's a pair of crab legs you keep hidden under your bed because you think they're toys and nobody realizes until they've started to stink. (My little brother was gross, y'all.)

The key with these types of readings is to say something generally applicable to most people and get you, the subject, to provide the information. By the end of the supposed reading, most people walk away convinced that the fraudulent psychic displayed immense otherworldly gifts. There are all sorts of variations on the technique, and I encourage you to watch videos or read further articles about the ways in which this technique has grown more sophisticated over the years. This style of vague, mystical statements eliciting belief in metaphysical gifts or access to supernatural information isn't relegated to the verbal patter of a TV psychic.

Multiple studies have been done regarding the way in which some purported astrologists and other professional practitioners give their own readings. These days you can pay anywhere from nothing to literally thousands of dollars to get an astrological, channeled, tarot, or other type of reading online. Oftentimes you pay your money and get the reading emailed to you in a time frame that can range from a few minutes to a few days. When it comes to these types of readings, fraudulent practitioners will keep their emails in the vein of Barnum statements, typically aligned with commonly accepted personality traits as ascribed to what is known as your birth chart. (You know . . . you're a Taurus sun, Virgo moon, and Sagittarius rising?)

In 1971 the psychologist Bernie I. Silverman, professor and researcher at Michigan State University, ran an experiment where he took the personality traits typically attributed to the twelve sun signs and removed the signs, leaving only the list of traits. Subjects were asked to choose which set of traits applied to them, and wouldn't you know it, almost nobody chose the traits typically attributed to their sun sign. However, when the sun sign names were added back to the trait lists, subjects became far more likely to choose the set matching their birth sign.[3]

Further findings were published in the *Journal of Consulting and Clinical Psychology* in 1977 by C. R. Snyder, R. J. Shenkel, and C. R. Lowery, who asked three groups of participants for increasingly personally identifiable information. In the first group, no personal information was provided. In the second, a birth month was provided. The participants in the final group gave their full birth dates. The participants from the third group were more likely to state that the individualized horoscope provided to them was accurate. The kicker was that all three groups had been provided the same set of personality traits.[4]

No matter the method of reading, the subject is far less likely to believe that it is applicable to them—and therefore less likely to believe in the alleged proficiency of the psychic—if the traits listed or messages provided are negative. In 2002 Dany J. MacDonald and Lionel G. Standing published a study examining what is known as "self-serving bias," especially as it relates to the Barnum effect. The short version of their findings is that the more positive or socially desirable the reading, the more likely the subject was to believe it was accurate. Not only that, the researchers found that the inclusion of too many negative traits will actually cancel out the Barnum effect and give the subject the impression that that information is incorrect and, therefore, the reader was not truly gifted with whatever respective gift they are alleging.[5]

This is why the disingenuous astrologer or psychic or what have you will provide you a glowing reading. Are you a kindly kindergarten teacher who volunteers to rehabilitate sick and injured kittens on the weekends in between donating blood and baking cakes for your elderly neighbors? "If you'll give me your birthday and exact time of birth, you can get a super awesome reading telling you how awesome you are!" Or perhaps you're a nefarious serial killer who spends time drowning sacks of kittens after icing down your sidewalk so all your elderly neighbors slip and fall? "If you'll give me your exact birth date and time, you will also get a super awesome reading telling you how awesome you are!"

You're probably sitting there thinking, *Jeez, this guy doesn't seem to believe in psychics, yet he wrote this whole book on witchcraft. Seems pretty sus.* I get why you'd think that. And I do not want to send the message that *all* psychics or mediums or tarot readers or astrologers or rune tossers or some other style of practitioner you meet in the wild is a fraud. I do not believe that to be the case. What I'm hoping to arm you with here are tools to understand how to spot a fraud when you meet one in order to save you considerable heartache. Or, perhaps, let me state this another way....

Real Psychics Make You Mad

The practitioner who is sincerely going about their work in good faith in order to provide you with a genuine metaphysical service is not likely to pepper innumerable positive aphorisms in the reading to keep you on the hook. Instead, they'll straight up tell you what they see, whether it's good, bad, or indifferent. In addition, they're a lot more likely to tell you when they don't see something, whereas the disingenuous fraudster will always purport to tap into some spirit or guide or energy to provide you with the experience of a reading.

In all my years of interacting with witchy folks in and around the community, the people I've met who provided the best readings were those who could look at their divinatory tools, look at me, narrow their eyes, and read me for absolute filth. (Sorry, if you don't speak drag queen, "to read" means to incisively expose a person's flaws.)

I got to witness a very uncomfortable moment once when someone I used to know requested a tarot reading for her birthday. Then, in a room filled with this person's friends and current boyfriend, the reader asked, "Do you want me to be honest?" to which the young woman replied, "Of course." (Sidenote: This is never true. Nobody actually wants the truth, unless the truth is that you're winning the lottery next Tuesday and every Tuesday thereafter.) The reader then told the young woman that her relationship was fraught with deceit and that it would shortly end. She laughed this off, and yet, within the next few weeks, the boyfriend had dumped the young woman and was threatening to kill her dog. Turns out, he'd been lying about quite a lot of things—including dating many other women and possibly a man (I never got all the specifics about that last part)—and didn't take kindly to having the truth revealed.

To take it out of the realm of magic for a moment, a TV psychotherapist will say a bunch of general things to get you to believe they understand you and your situation and will likely make you cry in front of millions of viewers. One big reveal, one emotional outburst, and voilà, your problems are solved. A legitimate therapist, however, will quietly, genially, methodically open you up over a period of weeks or months and work with you as you wade through your old stories, emotional baggage, relationships, et cetera. It's a slow process and it can be far more painful to go through, but it is usually better for people in the long run. Legitimate therapists won't tell you what you want to hear, but they will ultimately guide you to what you need to understand about yourself and the ways in which you interact with the world.

Practitioners who care about doing a good job will endeavor to be honest with you, whether that means telling you something you want to hear or not. Most of the professional practitioners I've talked to say that it'd be far easier to do the cold-reading thing, because that builds up a much larger repeat customer base much faster. Genuine practitioners also will be less likely to urge you to come back to them. They'll provide a good service, and, sure, they hope you'll return for more good services (we all have to eat), but they will never dangle hidden information or tell you that you must come see them again next week or something terrible will happen to you. People like hearing good things about themselves, and when they pay money to a reader they want to get the experience they saw on television. They don't usually recognize that the people on television, attempting to impress millions of people and keep up a certain image, are likely far less genuine than the humble card reader in front of them.

Finding a Professional

Since I'm talking about good, ethical practitioners I thought it would be helpful if you had a few tips about how to start a search for one in the first place. Sure, you might be prepared at this point to spot when someone is being less than forthright, but what if you want to be proactive? For this, I reached out to Cassandra Snow, a professional tarot reader and author on the subject. Snow gave me a few simple guidelines for how you can seek out a genuine practitioner:

- Seek out a metaphysical store in your area that offers reading services and ask them about their vetting process. Now, I know you might think you live in too remote or too conservative an area to have a metaphysical store, but I promise you a quick internet search will show you that you likely have several within driving distance. Listen for clues about whether the readers are vetted and how (more about what to listen for in a minute), and check them against what you know about unethical practitioners. If they get cagey or defensive when you ask follow-up questions, you can simply thank them for their time and head to the next store on the list.
- Seek out readers on social media. Doing this helps you get to know the reader a bit from a distance before clicking into their online shop and scheduling a session. You'll be able to hear how they talk about their tools—such as cards, dice, or runes—and

whether they come from a point of view with which you connect. If you like them, you can try them out by jumping when their spots open, or, if they're not taking new clients, ask them for a recommendation. Even famous readers with huge social media followings can help guide you because though they may not be open for new clients (or may be out of your price range) you can see who *they* like and follow using that as a tacit recommendation. Though you might get lucky and they could respond to your email or direct message with a referral. Snow promises that most professional readers are happy to provide a referral, as they simply want you to have a good experience.

- Go to psychic fairs. Snow said this one might be a bit controversial as these aren't well liked by the community, and because of that controversy frauds don't typically show up at them. If you're not sure what will resonate with you, hopping around to different readers can be a good crash course. This is one of the pricier ways to find a trusted reader, as people at fairs don't typically hand out readings for free. You are expected to pay, but in that setting they usually have a cheap and fast option—such as $5 for a five-minute reading—where you could at least get a taste for their style and method.

- Ask a trusted friend. Referrals are always the best way of finding a genuine, ethical professional. This is true in pretty much every industry, and seeking out divinatory services is no different. If you're in a situation where you're the only one in your friend group who is openly exploring their witchy side, this one might not be applicable, but these days getting a card reading or astrological chart interpretation is becoming much more common.

Before we depart the subject of spotting a fraud, I'd like to provide you an incomplete list of lessons I've learned from being in and around the magical community for a couple decades.

Big Witchy Warning Signs

Along your witchcraft journey, you're going to encounter all sorts of people claiming to be authority figures or masters or experts of some kind. Some you'll seek out, some you'll stumble upon by chance, and some will slide into your DMs. Perhaps you're hoping to find a teacher or spiritual mentor to help navigate the witchy waters in person. Maybe you'd like to learn a specific skill or tradition from a person who is already a master. Because we're a decentralized spiritual group, it can be difficult to determine whether the person in front of you 1) is actually the expert they claim to be or 2) intends you harm.

Harm can look like a lot of things. It can look like ripping you off financially. It can look like stalking. It can look like using you as a means to boost their own ego or influence. Yes, it can mean physical violence or sexual assault as well. I've spent a good long time in this community, and I've seen all types. Not only that, I've talked to hundreds of people all over the world who have had similar interactions with supposed leaders who turned out to be creeps, leeches, time wasters, or straight-up criminals. In the spirit of hoping you don't go through what I, and many others, have gone through, I've put together a brief list of signs to look out for when interacting with others in the magical community. While some of these signs might end up being harmless in a specific context, these are generally good indicators that something might be wrong and you should perform a more critical analysis before you go any further with them. In no particular order, here is my (incomplete and ever-growing) list of Big Witchy Warning Signs.

YOU ARE CURSED

When I ask others what is the number one way you can tell a spiritual person is a phony, overwhelmingly the top response is "tell me I'm cursed." If someone tells you that you're cursed and you do not have a longtime, trusted relationship with this person, it is a very good indicator that this person is a fraud. While witches and other Pagan folks do believe in curses, a practitioner with good intentions would not typically offer up that type of information, especially without having met you or spent any quality time with you.

APPEAL TO LINEAGE

If someone starts telling you that they're descended from a long line of witches or shares that they're a certain degree priestess in the Something Important tradition that can be traced back to Gerald Gardner's teapot, it might be a good indicator that they're trying to keep you from looking deeper at their credentials or that they are using lineage as an excuse for not having any real expertise in the subject at hand. Most of the initiated witches I've met don't really list their degrees of initiation (it's gauche), and people who actually are experts in a certain area will usually tell you that instead of who their great-great-grandpappy was. This can also take the form of dragging out alleged ancestry (bonus points if they have their DNA results handy), past lives, or some connection to a particularly magical homeland—real or imagined—such as ancient Greece, ancient Egypt, Atlantis, et cetera. Oh! And if someone starts telling you their great-grandmother was burned at the stake in Salem, run. Nobody was burned at any stakes in Salem.

A Note on Lineage: There's a space in which lineage can be used to vouch for the validity of a teacher or practitioner. Because we are decentralized, lineage can be used by some sects of Wicca—such as Gardnerians—and other traditions to separate good from bad actors. This is often not done publicly (so it doesn't appear as a boast) but rather as an invitation to speak privately followed up by the providing of names and contact information of those who can vouch for the person's years of study and identity.

DISPLAYS OF POWER

Applied kinesiology. Walking on broken glass or hot coals. The use of certain tools or technology. Stage illusions passed off as magical power.

Plenty of spiritual people will try to trick you into believing they are incredibly powerful through the use of long-debunked parlor tricks that, if you haven't seen them before, can look quite impressive. After you have oohed and aahed over them, however, do a quick internet search for the trick at hand and see if it's actually evidence of awesome cosmic power or perhaps just a fun trick to play on a friend.

UNSOLICITED ADVICE

Whether they're sliding into your DMs on social media, approaching you in a witchy shop, or you've simply had the bad luck to be in the wrong place at the wrong time, this person typically has an urgent message for you from a spirit, ghost, or other entity that must be shared with you *right now*.

Unsolicited advice is almost always paired with one of the other warning signs and, just like outside the witching world, is never wanted. Nobody likes going out shopping for a new crystal or enjoying some music at a Pagan Pride day and suddenly having to deal with urgent news from the beyond or, worse yet, a stranger's opinion about whether they should or shouldn't pick up that stone or wear those types of clothes or whatever.

CULT OF PERSONALITY

While this term is typically applied to actual cult leaders, I'm using the term here for someone who, while they may not have an actual cult, probably wouldn't mind being in charge of one. These people purport to be masters of pretty much any and all subjects under the Pagan, occult, or esoteric umbrella, no matter how improbable that might be. These people are very likely to boast about how many followers they have on a social media platform or other area, and they get incredibly defensive when presented with critique. While they may clothe themselves in the garb of scientific language, they abhor the scientific method, misuse scientific equipment or misrepresent scientific findings, or even outright deny science if it does not fit their agenda. If the person in front of you simply cannot help but tell you how amazing they are at every turn, it's a good indicator that there's probably a better teacher out there for you elsewhere.

DEMANDS FOR MONEY OR TIME

I have said it before, and I'll keep saying it until it sinks in: there is nothing wrong with charging money for spiritual services. Everyone has to eat, and if you're exerting time, energy, and resources to provide a service, you have the right to request compensation for that. However, charging exorbitant fees for a service that the purported spiritualists claim only they can perform or for a very inexpensive item that they claim has immense magical powers imbued in it is a big indicator of fraud. For example: hundreds of dollars for a very common crystal or simple beaded bracelet might be a big warning sign.

This can also look like convincing you that they have important or secret knowledge you need while keeping it behind a steep paywall. It might not be money the person is after but, rather, your time. They might demand more and more of your time, requiring you to sacrifice work, family, school, or some other important area of life to spend more time in service with them.

OVERLY VAGUE OR
HYPERSPECIFIC LANGUAGE

These are the kinds of statements parodied in film, on television, and in all sorts of other media. While these can be Barnum statements, they can also simply be random phrases, even riddles, that aren't meant to be generally applicable; rather, they're meant to give the person an air of mystery and mysticism. Alternatively, incredibly specific language can be used to make it appear the person has access to immense psychic or intuitive insight. When said with confidence by a master of cold reading, hyperspecific language is a way of getting you to believe that they have information you don't and you should continue to give them your time, money, et cetera, lest you miss out on finding out exactly what will happen next Tuesday at 3:12 pm.

BLINDING YOU WITH SCIENCE

Or pseudoscience in this case. Similar to the last point, if the person in question is spitting out a lot of technical jargon, details, or information without explaining why it's important, relevant, or contextualizing it, this is called blinding you with science. It's a term indicating that someone is attempting to confuse you and complicate their point by spitting out a word salad that's overwhelming enough to make you think they know a lot about a topic when they may not. You can see this in many areas of Pagan study, but an easy example is astrology, because it comes with lots of technical jargon and specialized terms the average person might not fully understand. You might hear someone list out a long series of phrases such as "The New Moon is in Capricorn while Venus is square Saturn and Jupiter with Mars conjunct Pluto. You need to pay attention to your seventh-house placements, because . . . [*gestures vaguely around*]." This is simply information without definition or context and tells the person being read nothing while making it seem that the person saying it is an expert. If someone is simply spouting off information but not grounding those spiritual details with real-world context—such as, "Your moon placement might indicate a predisposition to lethargy, but you're also surviving a pandemic, so in either case it might warrant a talk with your therapist or trusted friend"—the person might not be the expert they want you to think they are.

THE ONE WAY

If anyone, anywhere tells you that their way is the only way of doing something, simply smile and thank them for their time. It isn't true. Ever. There is no one right way to practice magic, no one right way to access the divine, and no one right way to be a witch, or Pagan, or occultist, or whatever other magical label you're seeking. Moreover, there is no one system of belief that can solve all problems, reveal all answers, or perfect our lives.

SOLICITING SEX

A very good indicator the person speaking to you does not have your best interests in mind is that they, at any time, suggest or solicit sex. This can look like a lot of things. It can look like sex with them, such as if they make it sound like the gods want you to have sex, that sex is part of initiation, or that sex is a requirement for a deeper magical understanding. It can look like shaming you for not wanting to participate in sex happening at certain events, such as festivals or other magical gatherings. If they call you a prude or demand that you go outside your comfort zone of body autonomy or in any way sexualize your spiritual journey, that is a big warning sign to get away.

ISOLATIONIST TACTICS

If the person in question tells you not to talk to people who have left their group or other students who have taken their classes, it's usually a sign that the person doesn't have the best intentions. If the person tries to isolate you from friends or family, from other people in your life—either magical or mundane—that's also a pretty good sign to turn tail and run. You should note that not all isolationist tactics are obvious, and often they build on one another over time.

★

So many of these warning signs overlap with one another. For example, it's commonplace for someone you either barely know or have never spoken to to send you an urgent message saying they have received a message from Spirit that you are cursed, but for $500 they can remove it. (That's why "You Are Cursed" was number one on the list.) Sometimes these warning signs are subtle. Sometimes they don't feel like warning signs at first but helpful suggestions or juicy gossip. Keeping good notes or telling a trusted friend about your experience can help you keep track of whether the things being asked of you or behaviors exhibited by the person in question are benign personality traits or warning signs. If the warning sign merits, you may need to involve someone with the authority to intervene. The last thing you want is to allow that warning sign to go unexamined only to find out later real and lasting harm was done to someone else.

Where Money Is Concerned

Fraudulent psychics and the like are not only obfuscating the legitimate practicing of divination or mediumship, but to put it bluntly, they're thieves trying to separate you from your money. If someone is claiming to guide you along your spiritual path, open up your latent superpowers, rid you of a malevolent spirit, or reconnect you with your dead grandmother while also parting you from large sums of your money, that is bad news. Far too many news stories come out each year of fraudulent practitioners tricking people out of their livelihoods and even their homes by preying on fear, gullibility, and good-faith belief.

New seekers need to be told up front, outright, and often that there are thieves and predators both in this community and masquerading as part of this community, and it's the naive seeker who gets taken.

This is not to say that money should never be exchanged for spiritual services. There is some discussion in the Pagan and magical communities that says one cannot ever charge money for teaching or spiritual services, and I firmly disagree. You'll most often find these same people running websites with pirated books and stolen artwork operating under the auspices of the faux austere belief that information should be free to justify committing a crime. For what it's worth, information can be obtained freely...from a library. If someone is performing a service, even spiritual services, and their body, time, experience, and resources are being used, they deserve to be compensated.

Spiritual teachers and professional psychics exist who act in good faith when it comes to their clients or students. They charge a fair rate and are honest with you when it comes to the expectation of results. They will not make wild or improbable claims about their abilities, nor will they try to keep you on the hook week after week for more money. Good-faith spiritual actors might even turn down an offer of money after realizing you don't need a magical practitioner, but perhaps you need to speak to your doctor or a therapist.

A Note about Experts

Experts, teachers, mentors, elders. We need them. They're a vital part of building a lasting community. And while you should keep in mind that there's practically no information regarding the history or use of magic that cannot be found for free online or at a library, assuming you can learn anything on your own is a little like saying "there's nothing about plumbing you can't find online." It doesn't mean it's a good idea to go about doing everything you see online or in a book or on a blog without the oversight or training of an expert. There is undeniable value in guidance from the people who've gone before you.

That said, keep in mind that not everyone who has been in the community a long time or sets themselves up as an expert is worthy of your time, attention, or patronage. Be smart. Trust your instincts. Tell other people where you're going and who you're interacting with. Keep notes. Check credentials. (Remember how I talked about lineage sometimes being used as a way to verify someone? Remember to flag keywords. For example: If they're "licensed," how so? With whom? Can they verify? Et cetera.) Ask questions. Research the answers.

If anything stinks at any time, you have absolutely nothing stopping you from walking away. It might feel painful or scary, but I promise you that your health, well-being, mental and physical security, and future self will all thank you.

CHAPTER 10

DEVELOPING *a* FILTER

Until now I haven't really extolled a lot of Pagan theology, virtues, tenets of belief, or other specific esoteric knowledge. This is due in large part to the fact that the focus of this book isn't about teaching you Paganism or witchcraft but, rather, about how to learn about Pagan traditions and witchcraft on your own. How to be a prudent seeker. How to perform good research, recognize warning signs, and curate this knowledge into a sustainable, meaningful, magical practice once you've gotten it.

With that in mind, I would be remiss if I didn't include a chapter about "developing a filter." This is a principle I've talked about on my podcast since the beginning of the show back in 2009 (though by no means is it a concept I invented), and for good reason: even after you've navigated the waters of expectation versus reality, cultural appropriation, respected your gates and windows, and avoided the obviously fraudulent, there is still a lot of information for us magically minded folks to take in.

One normally talks about filters like this in the sense of social filters—the little voice that reminds you to watch what you say and helps you determine whether what you want to say should be said by you in that time and place. It's based on a collection of your own lived experiences, the experiences of others, and learning from mistakes you've made up until that respective point in your life. (Like . . . you really only make the "so when is the baby due?" mistake once.)

The filter I'm talking about in this chapter, though, isn't just about what you put out into the world but also what you allow into your mind. Basically, think of this like your good ol' uncle Fire Lyte sitting you down for a nice BuzzFeed listicle–style session of good advice and life lessons. Why? To build on what we learned in the last chapter. Instead of focusing on bad actors, however, I am going to focus on the actual information you're researching and how that translates into actions you may wish to take in and around the magical community. How do you determine whether the information you're reading or hearing is providing you with genuine knowledge or a skewed perspective? How do you know whether or not your action is required in a particular setting? Not having a quality filter might lead you to believing bad information is genuine or taking an action when it isn't warranted.

I'm dividing this up by a phrase originally written by Éliphas Lévi, nineteenth-century occultist and poet, which has been adopted by a number of different sects under the Pagan umbrella from Thelemites to Wiccans and all sorts in between:

To Know, To Dare, To Will, To Keep Silent.

Sometimes called the Witches' Pyramid or the Pagan Virtues or the Four Powers—among other names—it is part of a longer writing by Lévi and has since been interpreted and reinterpreted in a number of ways. Here I will be using the Witches' Pyramid as a helpful framework for navigating your learning and interaction with the world of witchcraft. I will be using the terms as follows:

- To Know—pertaining to your mind, emotions, thoughts, knowledge, et cetera
- To Dare—pertaining to your actions, trying new things
- To Will—pertaining to your determination to push boundaries or challenge convention
- To Keep Silent—knowing when to speak and when to keep your own counsel

So ... you know ... when you're writing your book review, you could leave out the part where in chapter 10 he mentions Éliphas Lévi, but then it's not about kabbalah. Or your historical understanding of the Witches' Pyramid. Just the framework. OK? OK.

We are often told after the fact that the information we learned about a given subject was insufficient or wrong, and that can lead to feeling like our time was wasted. Worse, it can leave us feeling foolish for having not spotted obvious signs of bad information. In addition, the more we learn and the deeper we become engaged with new ways of viewing the world, the more we might be tempted to take action. To publish, to teach, to volunteer, et cetera. Knowing whether it's right to act now is a skill that can take years to master, and it typically comes with lots of fumbles along the way. (Trust me. I know. Jumping in headfirst without really considering whether I should is like . . . my thing.) I hope these lessons and advice will save you some of the more embarrassing or painful first steps you might otherwise experience as you continue further on your path.

To Know

The first place to start is with your own mind, since it controls the information you take in and how you weigh it, measure it, and determine if it is a good foundation from which to grow. If you can start off spotting misleading information or poorly supported arguments early, you will be in a much better place to begin your spiritual journey.

When creating a filter for your mind for what you perceive and accept as good information, there are a few things to watch out for that might clue you in that what you're reading or listening to isn't worth your time.

MISLEADING KEYWORDS

Remember, there are people who want to persuade you, to paint themselves in a positive light, and to sell you things. To that end, they often say something that isn't technically wrong, but neither is it the full story. Some great examples of this are found in advertisements and social media bios. For example: If someone tells you a product is "award-winning" and it's something like laundry detergent, you should probably ask, "What kinds of awards do laundry detergent win?" and then go look that up for free on the internet. You might find that the term is technically true, but the claim is misleading. When Sudsy's Laundry Detergent puts out a statement saying, "Try Our Award-Winning Laundry Detergent," the implied claim is that Sudsy's was so great at cleaning clothes that someone gave them an award for being best at clothes cleaning. But say you want to dig into the claim with a quick internet search and you find out that the only award Sudsy received was for "Products That Are Secretly Battery Acid." You should maybe not absorb that particular bit of information supplied by Sudsy as the entire truth. Look for descriptive words, specific claims, dates, awards, names of celebrities who allegedly promote the ideas, et cetera. Research those. Figure out if the keyword matches the implied claim.

LACK OF SUPPORT

Alarm bells should sound when an entire argument hinges on a single blog, web article, YouTube video, or other source. (Looking at you, niche Wikipedia page.) But you try to do your due diligence, so you click on that source, and it's just another solitary blog without citations or another YouTube video making similar claims. Try to validate the information elsewhere. If someone is telling you that 9 million women were burned at the stake for witchcraft, see if you can validate that information by reading some history journals where the information has been peer-reviewed. While some claims might make it into a witchy book or onto a blog without any vetting, they are far less likely to get through the gates of academia without rigorous inquiry.

ANCIENT WISDOM

In the witchcraft community, it's very easy to fall prey to the logical fallacy called appeal to ancient wisdom. It's this idea that people a long time ago knew something we didn't or did something a certain way, and because they lived a long time ago it must be true or, at least, contain a greater understanding of the universe than we currently have now. Books on magic are rife with this fallacy. (Like, "The ancient Druids used to . . ." or "Women in ancient Greece used to . . .".) A formula that should send up immediate red flags tends to look like "for hundreds of years, X Thing was used to cure Y Malady." A simple internet search might show you that this is an example of a misunderstanding caused because people of the day didn't have the technology or knowledge we have now. Context like this is important.

If you see a claim being made and it's rooted in ancient wisdom alone, it's a good thing to be caught in that filter of yours. Sure, people a long time ago might've been flying in the astral plane drinking and talking to animals, but they also drank poisonous rock juice and thought thirty-five was old age. Be inspired by history, but place it in the proper context.

NOVEL IDEAS

The flip side of appeal to ancient wisdom is appeal to novelty. Our society craves progress and sees change as inherently good. "This software upgrade will fix my phone's problems." "This electric car will fix global warming." "This change in government will solve our nation's ills." These days a trendy bit of information—bad or good—can go viral in a matter of hours. If the internet's algorithm likes what you say or how you say it, your content can be seen by millions of people in an incredibly short time span. This can be great in some instances. Think of a worthy charitable cause suddenly getting visibility and needed funds or massive social movements that upend unjust systems. Where it can falter is when it is spreading misinformation. The year 2020 saw the COVID-19 pandemic sweep the globe in what felt like a matter of days, and, understandably, people who were scared and desperate to cling to any amount of hope were sharing dangerous medical advice, supposed cures, and a host of other frankly bad information. No matter the subject, our brains are almost hardwired to believe that whatever is new, whatever everyone else is talking about, must be true and better than any older information.

Unfortunately, newer technologies, institutions, and ideas are more fragile, as they are untested. In the witchcraft community, this type of fallacy can take hold as well. You'll see trends in practices spread rapidly, revivals of ideas based on a handful of people's misinterpretations or cultural appropriation, or simply a very big idea turned into bumper sticker spirituality and parroted by hundreds of social media content creators. Because so many people are talking about it and it's new to you, it will feel like a good idea, like good information, but before you absorb it make sure to vet it.

The crux of the matter when it comes to filtering ideas or practices is context. "Sure, this was said, but *why* was it said?" "Sure, the ancients did this, but *why* did they do that? Was it out of necessity? Was it the best they had at the time? Do we have something better now?" Sure, everyone is talking about X, but does that mean it's inherently better than an existing idea?

The best way to bolster your To Know filter is to place value in researching your spiritual life in nonspiritual ways. The more you know about history, philosophy, art, other religions, sociology, and psychology the less likely you are to allow bad logic or faulty ideas to get through your filter and permeate your thinking. I know. I know. Witchy books are *very fun*, but very few of them are fact-checked and, again, there is no peer review for Paganism. Translation: just because it's in black and white or said by a creator you like doesn't mean it's accurate.

To Dare

My husband and I thought we could install our new dishwasher ourselves because we already had a dishwasher, and surely it was only a matter of unplugging the old one from whatever it was plugged into and plugging in the new one. No big deal, right?

A couple hundred dollars, multiple arguments, pleas to various deities, and one very elaborate pipe fitting later, we'd spent a week trying to do it ourselves. When certain pipes or hoses didn't connect to the other pipes or hoses in ways we thought they should, we went to the home repair store, asked questions we didn't really understand, got answers we definitely didn't understand, bought more widgets and gizmos and whatsits, and brought them home hoping they'd solve the issue. What we ended up doing was spending far more money than we would have if we'd simply paid for a professional to install the dishwasher in the first place, and we still had leaking pipes and a dishwasher that didn't quite fit correctly into the spot. And yes, we still had to pay for a plumber to come in, undo everything we'd done, and redo it all correctly.

Knowing when and how to act might seem like less of a topic to discuss in the setting of seeking a magical life and more aligned with, say, military strategy or Black Friday shopping in one of those massive indoor malls. (Those might be the same thing, come to think of it.) But it can be incredibly important to understand that there is a time to act, a time to abstain, and a time to realize some actions might never be for you.

READ THE WHOLE BOOK

A quick audit of many popular witchy books will show you that there is an emphasis on including spells, rituals, and other activities for you to do. In a book of 150–200 pages, you might find 40–60 pages of information and 100+ pages on praxis. I mean, I get it. You probably didn't come to the witchcraft section of your bookstore to pick up a book on theory. You came because Bradley broke up with you, and you want to turn him into a toad or as near as you can get for $9.99 on a Friday night.

As heavily weighted as the book might be on spells and as tempted as you might be to flip to the "Love" section and start lighting candles, I very much encourage you to read the entire book for the author's context and guidance. There might be important information about the system of magic being used, cultural context you should understand, or perhaps even important ideas and theories you should consider before starting. It's sort of like diving into a home repair thinking you can reference the instructions as you go along, getting stuck, and then realizing you needed to read the warnings, package content details, and required tools thoroughly before starting on step one of the repair.

There might be feelings that come up during your working that reading the early chapters could have prepared you for. Perhaps there might be ways of raising energy that the author recommends to go along with their style of magic. There's nothing quite as dull as lighting a couple dozen candles, getting all worked up to do some magic, getting halfway through, and realizing, *Oh shit, I don't know what the author means when they say "call the corners," and now I have to go look it up.* Nothing like stopping to grab a dictionary or google a term or going back and reading chapter 3 to take you right out of the mood for magic.

EVEN BETTER . . . READ TEN BOOKS

OK, so there's this idea in Wicca and some other Pagan traditions that you should study for a year and a day before going through any type of formal spiritual dedication or initiation. Sure, you can practice some forms of magic and engage in certain rituals, but you're encouraged to dedicate a substantial amount of time to studying before being given the green light to go deeper. I swear I won't be that extreme with my advice on the practice of magic, not that I think it's a wholly terrible idea, mind you. I'm not going to tell you that you need to study magic in a purely theoretical context before you do your first spell. What I will tell you is that getting the perspective and understanding of multiple practitioners would be an invaluable basis from which to begin practicing magic.

I'll continue with the metaphor of home repair here. Sure, minor fixes like replacing a lightbulb or assembling flat-packed furniture might not need a ton of prior knowledge or additional research. Where the real trouble comes is when you begin doing something you *think* is a simple repair but suddenly isn't. Before flipping open the book and assuming that no matter what arises you'll be spiritually and magically prepared to handle it, doing lots of reading, practicing, and learning of theories and systems will help you be the most successful witch you can be. At the very least, you'll know when to call the handyman.

Reading many different books, listening to different podcasts, watching videos, et cetera, is all a great way to help introduce you to *why* things are done the way they are. That way, when you're performing a spell and you don't have an ingredient on hand or the weather prohibits you from casting in a particular location, you'll have a solid understanding of the mechanics behind the magic in the book and can either make changes when possible or choose a different working if it is infeasible.

The lesson: learn as much as you can before you act.

KEEP YOUR HANDS IN YOUR POCKETS

When my mother took us shopping as children, if the store sold breakable objects she'd tell my brother and me to put our hands in our pockets before we went in. It was a caution, a little mental trick to teach a young child that not absolutely everything needed to be handled and that, if you were going to handle something, to do it with intention and care. It worked. I'll be honest, I still automatically do it to this day when walking in a store with lots of very breakable things, but these days it's because I would be the one mortified, trying to figure out if I can afford whatever thing I just bumped off a shelf.

Everyone, I hate to be the bearer of bad news (who am I kidding? No, I don't), but not every situation calls for a magical solution. I know. I know. *I know.*

That is not what you picked up a book on witchcraft to hear. We all secretly hope that one day we'll pick up a book on witchcraft to be told that for every mundane problem from finding a parking space to dealing with gossipy coworkers there is a magical solution. If you do much scrolling through various forms of witchcraft-focused social media, you'll find plenty of people who espouse this idea. Except the more of this you see, the more you realize it starts to go a bit overboard.

Jim wouldn't stop talking in the break room, so I wrote his name down and put him in my shoe. Sally forgot my birthday, so I stuck her name in a vinegar jar. Derek used a pejorative when speaking about me, and I'm spending my Thursday night making a poppet of him and burning it.

As someone who has dealt with anxiety and depression since before I knew what either of those words meant, let me be the first to tell you that Jean-Paul Sartre said it best when he said, "Hell is other people." However, magic shouldn't be a substitute for what many mothers in the South might call good home training. Not every social slight merits a curse or, really, any form of magical action. Sometimes the best way forward is to engage in social discourse. If someone is talking too much in the break room, bring headphones. If Sally forgot your birthday, please realize people make human mistakes and that very likely you won't remember this a year from now. If Derek said something terrible to you, well . . . OK, yeah. Sure. Maybe sew his lips shut.

But, see, this is what I'm talking about. Daring to engage socially versus magically will help you understand when to expend your energy and time and resources and when to reserve them. Social media might make you *think* that everyone is casting spells all day every day, but social media doesn't tell you whether all those spells were effective . . . or even if they were actually performed at all. (People lie.) Remember what I talked about previously regarding effective magic and that right combination of intention and need and energy. You simply are not as likely to be in the right headspace for effective magic if you're doing it every time you experience a minor inconvenience.

Choosing the correct action is sometimes the most daring thing we can do. Understanding the difference between whether you should let a situation run its course without your interference, whether you should take mundane action, and whether it's time to bust out the cauldron and get to chanting is an important skill.

Not every situation requires *your* intervention. If the situation does not directly affect you and you have not been asked to intervene, don't. Keep your hands in your pockets. Just because it's magic you do in the privacy of your bedroom doesn't mean that it's any less an intrusion than if you were to interrupt a conversation in which you have no stakes to give one party a piece of your mind. Not every situation requires magical action, but when it does, perform it with intention.

THIS ISN'T FOR YOU

The great thing about the internet is that more knowledge is available at our fingertips than ever before in human history. The unfortunate bit is that people have confused access with permission. I've talked about this elsewhere, so I will not belabor the point, but during your research of witchcraft and esoteric practices you will undoubtedly come across information stemming from closed systems and oppressed cultures.

You should not feel that every culture's practices are available for you to use or to be cherry-picked for inclusion in your own practice. Sometimes the information is a gate inviting you in and at other times it is a window allowing you to learn from a respectful distance. In addition, there will be times that conversations happen *about* those cultures or practices. If you are someone from outside the respective community, your job is to listen, and your privilege is best used to move the spotlight to center the voices of that community.

To Will

So you've got a solid foundation for deciding what information to accept, when to pause and verify, and what to outright reject. You have a functional understanding of when to act magically and when to act mundanely and when to do neither. But what about moments when you want or need to challenge conventional wisdom on your own? What if during your research and amassing of different voices and perspectives you find information that should be corrected or, better yet, you've found an area where you think you could deepen the knowledge base or contribute a furthering of conventional praxis? How do you recognize the opportunity to push boundaries?

First, let me dispel this notion that there's something possessed by bloggers, podcasters, vloggers, authors, or other witchy content creators that you don't have. When I began my podcast I had a laptop with a built-in microphone and a little voice inside that told me what I had to contribute was valuable and worthy. I've seen authors who got book deals less than a year after starting their spiritual journey, and I've seen people with decades of experience never choose to write about any of it. The only thing separating you from most of the names printed on book covers in the witchy section of the bookstore is that they strung forty thousand words together and you didn't.

I say this because I don't want you to wait for permission to push boundaries, to try new things, to call out wrong information or harmful practices. Everyone is entitled to their voice and a right to share their perspective and you're part of everyone. Our community is less than a century old, and if we want to not only survive but also thrive we would be utterly fooling ourselves to believe that the body of knowledge and established lineup of publicly available perspectives represents the entirety of magical knowledge.

That said, there are times when you should recognize you might not be the right person right now to push those particular boundaries. This was a lesson I learned the hard way publicly, repeatedly, and often. I started my podcast at a very young age, and, being in my early twenties with the immense social privileges afforded a cisgender white guy, I did a lot of explaining to people far more experienced and knowledgeable than me about various topics how very wrong they were about those various topics. As you can imagine, the person who was wrong more often than not was . . . well . . . me.

I committed the fallacy of believing that my research and life experience until that point had resulted in a concrete answer that should apply to the community at large when, in reality, it had merely served as a waypoint along my own spiritual journey. All of this said, I have three bits of advice on using your will to push boundaries and advance Pagan discourse.

"WHY" IS MORE USEFUL THAN "WHAT"

If you've noticed ahistorical information or a claim made that doesn't quite align with accepted science, the best way to further discourse that

I have found is to ask "Why?" Gather your research, state what you've found, then ask the reader/the community *why* the belief exists. More than that, be prepared to receive an answer. (If your blog goes viral, be prepared to receive *lots* of answers.) Be open and receptive to feedback, and, more important, be open to being wrong. There might be a very good reason *why* certain beliefs have come about and survived or, at the very least, some entertaining origins. However, if your information is compelling or your ideas are particularly innovative, asking "Why?" might very well incite a conversation about whether established convention should continue.

ONLY EXPERTS ARE EXPERTS

Unfettered access to the world's information has not only given us a sense of permission to center ourselves in situations where it may not be warranted or appropriate but also created an entire generation of armchair experts on a number of subjects in the witching world. You will find a lot of made-up or misappropriated terms that seem to confer legitimacy on someone's claims that they are an "expert" in realms like history or theology. Sometimes just having a slick web presence conveys a level of unfounded expertise. Please know that there is a difference between understanding the magical roots and folk use for things such as plants and minerals and being a geologist or medical doctor. If you take a great interest in the metaphysical use of such things, there are plenty of avenues to further discourse without overreaching. No matter the intention, offering medical advice or providing a less-than-robust expert understanding in some of these areas can lead to real harm.

KILL YOUR DARLINGS

This is a phrase used in writing circles derived from advice by Arthur Quiller-Couch in 1914 (who used the more graphic statement "Murder your darlings") meaning that sometimes to serve the work best you must sacrifice the part of it you love the most. In other words, don't be so precious that you cannot tear apart what doesn't work. If something seems too sacred to poke at, grab the biggest stick you can find and poke it. Remember, the scientific method works by systematically testing a hypothesis to see if it fails, not building up evidence for its veracity. (That would be confirmation bias.) There are a lot of rules of magic and Pagan spirituality that are thrown around as though they are immutable laws of the universe. Sometimes they're even called laws even though they're just witchy ideas— like the law of attraction. Do not be afraid to question them out loud and often. Both you and the community at large will be better for it.

It's up to each generation of magical practitioners and spiritual seekers to further the body of knowledge and understanding, not simply preserve traditions and mystical maxims. Since you're now on your journey of seeking witchcraft, you're part of the next generation of witches whose job it is to challenge, to push, to prod, and to make the community better for your having done so.

To Keep Silent

One of the best lessons one can learn is when to understand that your action is not required. As a dear friend might say, oftentimes it can boil down to the following bit of good advice: First ask: "Does this need to be said? Does this need to be said by *me*? Does this need to be said by me *right now*?"

Sometimes you will come across discourse online or in person and feel a desire to engage, especially if the topic is controversial. Nobody loves a hot take more than the person giving it. While I realize this kind of thing doesn't mean much in black and white, please let me tell you from experience that unless you're directly asked or directly involved there's no point in jumping into an ongoing, often heated, conversation. Very often people do not listen to hear what the other person is saying; they are silently waiting their turn to talk. These are two very different things.

More than advice on avoiding someone else's drama, however, it should be said that there are times when it is simply not appropriate for you to speak. For example: If you are speaking about a culture that is not yours, and you're setting yourself up as an expert when there are OwnVoices experts you can point to, reevaluate, and recenter the discourse back on the community in question. There's a term for one who believes they're jumping in to rescue someone, whether they asked for it or not: "white knight." If you're an ally to a member of an oppressed group, you may have found yourself in a situation where you thought you were speaking in defense of someone only to later find out that you were being a white knight. This typically looks like a self-aggrandizing attempt to show off how amazing you are at being an ally or how much knowledge you have about a given marginalized group.

This can apply to and overlap with the previously discussed areas as well. For example, if you're not a geologist, don't pretend to be. It takes humility, but it's OK and *necessary* to admit that you are not an expert on a given topic. I've read a lot of books on magical rocks and magical plants and magical oils and magical foods. However, I also know my limitations and realize I'm not an expert in any one of those areas. It takes a big person to realize that sometimes the best way to add positively to the discourse is to simply direct a seeker to an existing book or teacher or source that explains the topic well and tell them why you enjoyed it.

In the spiritual community, there are many areas where it is a fine line to walk between knowing whether you're furthering discourse, using your privilege in defense of a marginalized group or person, or simply being a white knight. Remember, keep the spotlight centered firmly on the group in question. Keep silent except to use your privileges or visibility to continue to refer back to the voices who own the topic. If a conversation is occurring about a topic you'd like to know more about, but it's in a realm belonging to a group of which you are not part, say very little and keep your ears open. Take notes. Use that To Know filter and research what is said. If you're uncomfortable with what is being said, sit in that discomfort and unpack it later.

Forming the Pyramid

So you have the groundwork for some solid skills in terms of how to tell if someone has your best interests, whether information is well supported, and how to determine when or whether to act. Putting it all together means that you'll become an informed, capable spiritual seeker able to not only research well but also advocate for yourself and others should the need arise. In the next chapter, we're going to put those skills to the test all at once in a scenario that is unique to the Pagan community: Unverified Personal Gnosis.

CHAPTER 11

UPG . . . WHAT NOW?

My husband believes in ghosts. I mean . . . I believe in ghosts, too, but my husband is all the way obsessed with ghosts. Ghost sightings. Ghost-hunting shows. Haunted houses. Personal stories. If you ever meet him out in the wild, tell him your ghost experience. He will be your new best friend. What's more, over our years together he has regularly reported multiple encounters with ghosts. Everything from deceased relatives visiting him to a house we used to live in being haunted. When I wasn't home he'd hear footsteps along the floor upstairs and the sound of cabinet doors being opened and shut.

My belief in ghosts is more agnostic. I believe in the *possibility* of ghosts. I've had experiences that left me wondering whether I'd interacted with the beyond or possibly been freaked out at a trick my brain was playing with me. He has his experience, and I have mine. I cannot honestly say that I've seen a ghost or heard the disembodied spectral voice of one. I'm not alone, either. You wouldn't know it from the utterly incredible volume of TV shows and YouTube channels and podcasts and other sundry media about them, but it's uncommon to see a ghost. According to the Pew Research Center, only 18 percent of adults claim to have seen or been in the presence of a ghost.

I know. I'm disappointing. Join the club of people who think that. (My parents are the founders and co-presidents.) You want the guy writing your book on witchcraft to tell you he talks to the dead constantly, that I have brunch with my deceased great-grandmother every Sunday morning and stay up late Friday nights watching horror movies with a girl who drowned tragically in a nearby pond on prom night fifty years ago. I get it. The people who write these books are supposed to be *all in* on every aspect of the witchy and weird. But, like most people, they simply are not. I, like many other creators of some form of magical media, have a spectrum of belief, and those beliefs are usually backed up by experience.

Why do I believe in magic? Because I believe I've seen it work, not just in my life but in the lives of others. Why does my husband believe in ghosts? Because he believes he's seen them, felt them, been in their presence. Here's the good news: Neither of us is wrong. We just have different UPG.

Defining Terms

UPG, or Unverified [sometimes called Unsubstantiated] Personal Gnosis, is a term mostly used by the witch and Pagan communities. There is a chance you could have read about it in other books, but its home is mostly on social media where people cite their UPG as a kind of source to support their information or claim. UPG places a greater value on the individual's spiritual experience as basis for belief rather than, say, a given spiritual community or set of dogmatic practices. Because UPG relies on self-validation and personal experience, it is rarely supported by objective, corroborating evidence.

To continue with the example of ghosts, there are people—my husband included—who believe they've not only seen the ghost of a loved one but also received messages from them, conversed with them. These messages can be incredibly affirming for the recipients. Some people report receiving forgiveness or acceptance from those beyond the grave.

The book *Faery Tale* by Signe Pike is about the author's journey around the world exploring UPG regarding faeries (spelled this way to denote she is seeking real faeries rather than fairies from a storybook). The TV docuseries *Hellier* makes a whole meal out of intersecting UPG in an attempt to understand the "high strangeness" occurring in and around a cave system in Kentucky.

UPG in a very generic sense is simply the act of believing you've had an experience that you cannot objectively prove you had. However, that UPG can become the cornerstone of a person's spiritual worldview. You've probably heard someone say, "God told me to . . . ," or, "I feel called to. . . ." You might have been somewhere that "vibrated with energy." If you've ever known someone needed you before receiving a text or phone call, you've had a run-in with UPG. And if you've lurked in witchy corners of the internet for any period of time, you'll see that the types of claims attributed to UPG are endless.

Having a UPG is, in and of itself, a fairly common occurrence and it's one that transcends religion, race, or socioeconomic background. In this context, however, it shares a linguistic kinship with another term that originated in 2005 from Stephen Colbert: "truthiness." It means that a truth can be something you feel to be true and not necessarily something validated by evidentiary support. While Colbert typically uses the term in a social or political context, the two ideas share common ground.

The Way Things Are Done

Belief in the spiritual and magical is the bedrock of UPG. Many founders of spiritual traditions created them out of some type of UPG experience— hearing a deity's voice or interpreting a sign seen out in the world. More than that, someone else's UPG tends to govern the ways in which witchcraft is performed, how deities are worshipped, or the proper way to interact with the natural world. This type of governance is, again, not at all relegated to Pagans or witches (think Moses on a mountaintop or Buddha attaining enlightenment), but we're the ones who seem to have adopted this specific term for it.

Communing with and passing along messages from the divine (or Spirit or deity or supernatural beings or whatever label you'd like to assign) is a thing we've been doing a very long time, and there have been many millions, if not billions of people around the world who believe they've had their lives enriched by these experiences over the course of human history. There is a necessary and beautiful space for that, so don't worry, we'll get there. First, though, I feel it is important to talk about the slippery slope of declarations of UPG and allowing them to create yet another gate to keep. (You thought we were done with gatekeeping? Foolish mortal.)

What you quickly find on your journey into witchcraft is that, no matter what the book says, if you go back far enough the origin of "The

Way Things Are Done" tends to be some form of UPG. Why is amethyst used to combat drunkenness? UPG. Why is the direction of east associated with air? UPG. Why should you plant lavender by your garden gate? UPG. (And also because Alice Hoffman said so and you do whatever Alice Hoffman says. I don't make the rules. She does. UPG.) In other words, nobody found a user manual for the universe and copied out the rules that run all the things. UPG as the origin for The Way Things Are Done makes it really difficult to question whether that way is the best way or the only way or even a legitimate way at all.

For example: You're going to a meetup for the first sabbat (witch's holiday) of the calendar year, Imbolc (beginning of February), and you think it would be fun and festive to bring some oranges as both food and offering. This greatly displeases Sandra, the group's leader, who says that oranges are a summer fruit and shouldn't be used in spring festivals. Putting aside the fact that citrus is actually in season in winter, you say, "It's . . . just oranges," but Sandra then tells you that the goddess Hecate herself bestowed upon her a message that all citrus fruits are verboten from any sabbat offering until summer. You really don't want to get on Hecate's bad side and most definitely want to avoid Sandra's wrath, so you dump the oranges in the garbage and try to be as helpful as possible for the rest of the evening. But you're left with questions:

- Why does Hecate care so much about oranges?
- Is it possible that Hecate doesn't care about oranges?
- What if Hecate does care about oranges and I've offended a goddess?
- Could Sandra be making all this up because *she* doesn't like oranges?
- How do I verify what Sandra said?

I realize this seems like an incredibly silly example, but it doesn't take much scratching of the magical surface to realize that it's not exactly that far from people's lived experience. Whether I'm speaking at a Pagan Pride Day or hosting my podcast or someone comes up to me at a witchy shop or bookstore, everyone has a story to share of how someone else's claims of UPG affected their life. There's a range, of course. Some are small and harmless things like "Fairies in my backyard told me to leave them freshly picked wildflowers every full moon." Some are bigger: "When you see deceased loved ones in your dreams, that is actually their spirit returning to speak with you." Then, of course, there are the harmful ones: "I am a channel for the god Loki, and it is his will that we have sex."

The beliefs and practices of the witch and Pagan communities are decentralized, meaning there's no rulebook or person in charge, no one source to check and verify that the information you're being told is correct. Therefore, we rely on community elders, books, and other created media to guide us on the hows and whys. Due to this we enter this seeker's path open and trusting. That state of being is not itself harmful, but it does make us susceptible to harm. Why? Well, people are fallible. They take advantage and bend the truth and use your good-faith belief for their gain. Sometimes they pass along harmful UPG because it was how *they* were taught and they took the lesson at face value. Sometimes, as we remember from my earlier discussion, people simply don't want to be wrong. They've been doing things a certain way for so long that any other way can feel like an accusation, a finger pointed. Nobody likes feeling that way.

In other words—and I cannot believe I am quoting Ronald Reagan here—trust but verify. UPG can be used as an excuse to defend bad behavior of all varieties, from cultural appropriation, to manipulating someone, to something as simple as refusing to perform further research. I mean, I get it. If you believed an eternal being revealed some great truth about the world to you, you'd probably assume that eternal being knows what they're talking about. Except our minds are strange places and they can play tricks on us, which is why it's a good idea to verify your experiences with other people who have had similar experiences, history, folklore, and—in some cases—even your doctor. Gaining a fuller understanding of your UPG can be a powerful way to enrich and guide your magical path, but some people use their UPG as a way to invalidate the experiences of others. And that's where you need to tread lightly.

Dead Rats and Shared Experiences

Have you ever heard of near-death experiences (NDEs)? Someone gets in a car accident or run over by a couple dozen shopping carts and reports back later that they saw what happens after you die. Accounts of NDEs vary wildly. Some people report seeing deceased relatives and pearly gates, while others report a light at the end of a tunnel. (My husband had an NDE and reported that the afterlife was an endless expanse of comforting darkness. Not even a Starbucks. Just . . . darkness.)

A few years ago, National Public Radio had a story about a doctor named Jimo Borjigin of the University of Michigan in Ann Arbor. She and her team studied NDEs in hopes of determining exactly what is happening inside the brain at the time of death and whether that has any impact on the NDE itself. The research team studied the brains of nine lab rats as they were being euthanized. Researchers discovered what appears to be a momentary increase in electrical activity in the brain associated with consciousness. Although the experiment relied on animals, the results could apply to humans, too, the researchers said.

Borjigin wanted to understand these experiences, believing that if people can remember them there must be some kind of evidence for them in the brain. Fortunately, you can't go around killing people just to watch their brains die on computer monitors. (Though when they did it on *Black Mirror* it was a superromantic love story, so . . . you know . . . maybe in the right context?) Killing rats to watch how their brains blip across a screen, though, that's totally fine. Apparently. *Science.*

Now, when it comes to people and NDEs, Borjigin says:

> Many of them have out-of-body experiences. It includes feelings of peace and quiet, always seem to have a dark tunnel and bright light. And they also seem to meet their deceased relatives. Many of them think it's a—it's evidence they actually went to heaven, perhaps even spoke with God.[1]

Patients often report that what they experienced in those moments after their heart stopped felt more real than reality, so real that it's often life-altering. But Borjigin thinks that what they're experiencing are sort of like superintense dreams. When you dream, there's a lot of activity in one part of your brain and the other part is trying to figure out what's going on. Borjigin hypothesizes something similar is happening with

NDEs.[2] One part of the brain is trying to make sense of what's happening as another part kicks into a hyperactive state to try to survive.

Borjigin says that she and her team found a massive, measurable burst in conscious activity after the heart stops for at least thirty seconds. NPR's reporting was quick to point out a problem with qualifying it as "conscious activity," saying that scientists aren't even really sure what that is. The question of "what is consciousness" or "the conscious mind" is something that has stumped philosophers and doctors alike for centuries, and that's a whole different rabbit down a very different hole for a very different book. In this instance, the researcher is looking for evidence that NDEs are caused by biological processes. It's an attempt to understand the spiritual by examining the physical, and another example of how science and spirit can work together to help us better understand ourselves and our world.

NDEs often change people's lives. They can have a deep, profound impact on the very basis of how a person views themselves, their choices, and the world around them because of that "more real than reality" feeling. But you don't need to cheat death to achieve the same life-altering result.

People in cultures all over the world report these types of experiences achieved through meditation, the consumption of certain drugs, religious rituals, and other spontaneous occurrences. Plenty of people in the magical community have experiences that transform their relationship to deity, to witchcraft, and to the world around them. What's important about the difference in how we interact with these UPGs inside the magical community is that, for some, the experience isn't relegated to just one person's life but also used to transform everyone else's behavior.

If you see fairies dancing in your garden every full moon, it doesn't mean that fairies only dance on the full moon or that they only dance in your garden. It simply means that this is your experience. It is unfortunately common, however, to see discussions inside the community where someone's UPG is used as a cudgel to invalidate another's UPG. To say "fairies *couldn't* have appeared in your garden last Tuesday, because it wasn't a full moon." Other examples can range from the benign ("you *cannot* use amethyst to promote physical activity because it's a calming stone") to the problematic ("Thor *couldn't* have appeared to you, because

he only appears to white people with a genetic link to Germanic tribes").
(Yes, that last one is a thing people say.)

The thing about all of this is that we don't *really* know what any of it
means, so invalidating any experience based on your own experience is a
logical fallacy (the anecdotal fallacy). What we know is that rats have a lot
of stuff happening in their brains as they die. We know people the world
over have reported a number of differing accounts of the same gods,
spirits, the afterlife, magic, and all sorts of witchy and weird things in between. Heck, even the Bible has four books reporting the same events in
four completely different ways. It doesn't make any of it any less valid
of an experience for the person having it. If anything, UPG should be a
springboard for introspection and further research.

You don't see many people attempting to invalidate someone's NDE
based on someone else's NDE. (Though I'm sure it's happened somewhere.) That might be because we're all very busy being grateful that the
person is still alive and therefore not terribly concerned that one person sees a light while another sees their grandparents and still another
doesn't see anything. We take it all as a collection of experiences of the
infinite beyond. Magical UPG should be like that.

An interesting point to note is that individuals who report having an
NDE also report no longer fearing death. My husband is one of those people. He handles death far better than I do. There is a lesson here for other
types of UPG. Focus on the ways in which your personal experience can
bolster your practice.

The Stakes of Unexamined Gnosis

By this point you should know that I'm a "bad news first" kind of person.
So, when I discuss UPG, I feel it's important to mention first and foremost that unexamined UPG can become a source of anything from gatekeeping others' practice based on personal belief (the "you need to wear
your shoes in a certain way so you don't harm the unicorns" argument)
to fear and paranoia. It's that latter part that can lead to real and lasting trauma. From alien abductions to shadow entities to false memories
to believing you're under a curse to possession to conspiracy theories, a
little bit of unexplained gnosis can quickly derail a spiritual seeker and

send them in a direction of being afraid of the spiritual or into a spiral of misinformation. I've said before in this book, and I'll continue to say it, that if your spiritual journey leads you to a place of fear, that's a good indicator that some further examination is necessary. Many experiences and conspiracy theories have mundane explanations, and I realize that's not the fun answer people want to hear.

What people often want to hear when they say, "I saw a dark entity in my bedroom staring at me as I tried to sleep," is, "Oh my gosh, that's horrifying! That definitely happened, and I've heard of it happening to lots of other people. Here's how you make a protective amulet against bedroom demons." We've been afraid of things that go bump in the night as long as we've existed as a species. When you express that fear, it's natural and normal to want that validated and to arm yourself against it for the next time. And, yes, while taking a protective spiritual measure might make good sense both magically and psychologically, it's also worth your peace of mind to explore mundane explanations. Dark entities in bedrooms can be attributed to anything from dreams to sleep paralysis to a pile of laundry. (Few things will motivate you to fold and put away your clothes like thinking they're a death crone beckoning you into the great beyond at 2:00 am.)

This is a lesson most of our parents tried to teach us when we were little and afraid that there were monsters in our closet or hiding under our bed. They turned on the lights. They opened the doors and stood with you. They got down and examined that space between your mattress and the floor with you. They invited you to check for yourself, to see with your own eyes that there were no monsters, and eventually you could sleep soundly.

One of the most prominent examples of UPG finding an explanation is the phenomenon called hag riding. Also called a night hag or old hag or one of dozens of other names from cultures around the world. The experiences reported typically take the form of a person declaring that a supernatural entity was in their bedroom—sometimes sitting on their chest or at the foot of their bed—preventing them from moving. This can understandably cause fear, terror, and panic. (How would you feel if you woke up believing there was something in the room while you were unable to flee? It sounds horrifying.)

It's called hag riding because of the belief in recent centuries that a "hag" or "witch" (sometimes used interchangeably, sometimes not) was the root cause of the phenomenon, that the hag was literally sitting on a person keeping them from moving or fighting back. Some even report to have seen the face of an old hag, thus the name. The phenomenon was used as evidence in court cases against suspected witches, and for those experiencing the paralysis it became incontrovertible proof of malevolent witches seeking to do them harm.[3]

Eventually, this phenomenon was researched and understood as a by-product of sleep paralysis, which is a condition that occurs typically when a person is either just waking up or falling asleep. The person is aware of their surroundings but unable to move or speak, and they might even have visual, auditory, or tactile hallucinations—such as seeing the face of a hag or demon. There are a lot of theories and studies about the why behind the what of this phenomenon, but the point here is that it has a mundane explanation. It's a trick of the brain, and while it might be scary at first, the more you examine it, unpack it, research it, and understand it, the less of a chance it will continue to cause you fear. How do we do that, though?

Unpacking Your UPG

Critically examine the observations you're making as you try new things, open yourself up to mystical experiences, and invite magic into your life is a crucial part of your spiritual journey. Whether you believe that you heard the voice of a deceased relative, interacted with a deity or spirit, had a prophetic dream about work, saw a book fly across the room, or simply felt weird in a particular location, working through the experience is important for both your mental health and spiritual understanding. A bit of context, a dash of research, and some good old-fashioned honest conversation with a trusted friend or teacher can help you parse out whether the thing in your bedroom was a demon or maybe you should tweak your sleep habits.

The following are my top tips and life lessons when it comes to understanding UPG.

ACKNOWLEDGE IT HAPPENED

No matter how weird or brief the experience may sound, don't dismiss it. Did a chill run down your spine that felt like more than a chill? Did you see a departed loved one? Did you have an experience of déjà vu and then seem to know what was about to happen next? It's easy to write these things off, because, as I talked about previously, we are more concerned with *how people think about us* than *how we think about ourselves.* If you believe it happened, acknowledge that experience. Don't concern yourself immediately with whether it was "real." If it happened, it happened.

WRITE IT DOWN

Your notes app on your phone. A small journal you always keep with you. A diary by your bedside. Your book of shadows—or book of mirrors if that's your thing. Write it down, but don't at all feel like it needs to be shared with anyone else. This is your tool to help you 1) acknowledge your experience and how it felt in the moment and 2) see if certain kinds of experiences seem to pop up regularly for you. If so, they'll help you answer the important questions of how, when, why, where, and what. Do you see certain things around the equinoxes? Do you have that déjà vu early in the morning? On Tuesdays only? Don't just write down the experience itself, though. How did the experience make you feel? What had you eaten that day? Were you on any medication? Had you had anything particularly bad or good happen to you that day? What time of day was it? Unpacking your experiences later will be a lot easier if you can remember whether you could see clearly at the time or not.

REVISIT THE EXPERIENCE

After some time has passed, go back through your notes and mentally review the UPG. I recommend doing this during the day after a restful night's sleep and without a lot of electronic distractions. Spend time with your thoughts. Walk back through the experience start to finish. If you've been journaling for some time, try to go back through similar experiences and note any similarities or differences. If this was an experience at a physical location and you have the means, attempt to actually revisit the place during the day, especially if your UPG happened at night. Make notes of any feelings, conditions, or other matters of importance that jump out to you about either the location, your emotional or physical state, or whatever else feels significant.

ASK A LOT OF QUESTIONS

This is the part where you revisit those all-important *W* questions, which will sometimes be fun and exciting and at other times feel like you're slapping yourself in the face for reasons you can't quite name. What happened? When did it happen? Why did it happen? Could something else have happened other than what you thought happened? For example: You were gazing at moving water and suddenly saw the face of a loved one. You acknowledged it, wrote it down, spent time examining it, and even revisited the spot where it happened. Is it possible you saw the face of someone you loved, or is it possible you experienced pareidolia—a condition where the human mind tries to take patterns and rearrange them into familiar shapes, like seeing faces in clouds? Was the sound you heard and the creepy feeling you felt because you were surrounded by ghosts, or was it because it was 2:00 am and you were in a dark building without much light?

Remember, when scientists come up with a hypothesis, they don't set about trying to prove it but, rather, to disprove it. They find ways to tear apart the hypothesis, so that if it holds true after testing they know they can draw the conclusion that the hypothesis was correct. (Or, as Sherlock Holmes famously said, "When you have eliminated the impossible, whatever remains, *however improbable*, must be the truth.") I invite you to be similarly rigorous with your experience. The goal isn't to invalidate your feelings or the power of the experience. Your goal is to think critically, so that when you come out the other side of it you can stand firm in your belief.

TELL SOMEONE YOU TRUST

This part is scary. I know. Nobody wants to be judged or called crazy for talking about hearing voices or feeling something a bit out of the ordinary. But let me assure you that there is practically nothing people like talking about more than their own "weird experiences." My incredibly conservative parents who fully believe witchcraft is part of Satan's toolbox will still talk about Great-Aunt Luna, who could see the future sometimes, or a particularly impactful visit to a tarot reader. Now is not the time to go off and talk to strangers on the internet about your UPG. Start small. Remember, this is about your journey, not impressing people online. Telling others is a wonderful way to help you affirm your experience, learn about someone else's experience—whether similar or not—and even help talk through parts that might have unsettled you.

★

We treat so much of witchcraft and spirituality with a sense of fear: fear that it is all some breakable thing, that you could do it wrong and not be able to do it again, that none of that is true. You're not going to break anything, and if you're setting out to seek magic and any part of it makes you feel fearful, you should stop and process that. Your spiritual journey isn't always going to be easy, but it shouldn't be filled with fear and uncertainty. Even if you're hunting ghosts or dispelling curses, you shouldn't feel fear. Fear comes from the unknown, and if you've truly done your internal work to understand and unpack your UPG, you can interact with the spiritual world with respect.

Now, there's a part of unpacking your UPG that begs the question: Could it be both? Could you have felt a certain way because of a physical stimulus, but perhaps that physical stimulus put you into a state of being that allowed you to experience something supernatural? Yes. Sure. Absolutely.

Maybe you find that you are a bit more receptive to precognitive messages after you've eaten very spicy food. Perhaps being in a dark place helps you tune out distractions and open up to spiritual communication. This can be a great way to start developing your own practice. Write these things down as well. Ever seen *Stranger Things*? Seven certainly can access her powers in her daily life, but it's a lot easier for her to perform certain tasks while sitting in front of a television blindfolded and playing white noise. (That's a ridiculously specific set of circumstances, but who knows . . . maybe you'll find you need to be wearing red on the full moon if you want an accurate tarot reading.)

Talking UPG

I want to briefly dive a bit deeper on the ways in which we talk about UPG as a spiritual community. It is important to be careful about the ways in which we frame our UPG so that we clearly communicate the experience and that the experience is understood by those we are telling. We should do this for a number of reasons. First and foremost, we want to foster an honest dialogue in the witchy community, and ensuring we are practicing good communication skills is the first step towards that. Second, with so much of the community interacting online these days, quality communication means that two people can feel confident they are having the same conversation with each other.

Really, you don't want to spend several hours with Person A talking about brewing calming tea for mental and spiritual relaxation and Person B thinking the conversation is about haunted teapots.

While I understand that neologisms exist and that hyperliteralism is itself a barrier to true communication, it is still important to be as accurate to the experience as possible when you're relaying your UPG. Did a book "leap" off a shelf, or did a book "fall" off a shelf? Did you audibly hear the voice of a deity, or was it "as though" a deity spoke to you? Did sparks fly from your fingers as you chanted, or did you feel tingling in your hands? Save the hyperbole for a BuzzFeed headline. The point of sharing a UPG should not be to get clicks or to appear to be a Super Witch. If you're reading this and you've been on your spiritual journey for a long time, you will likely be nodding your head vociferously at this section and remembering back to your early days of trying to parse out whether the person online *literally* meant a demon appeared to them or *figuratively* meant a demon appeared to them.

In addition, be careful about any implied claims your statements make. While you might not intend a statement to be read one way, it can nevertheless be interpreted by a reader as meaning something wildly different from the experience you had and intended to share.

For example: Let's imagine reading the statement, "I was diagnosed with cancer five years ago. I wore a labradorite bracelet, and it really helped me. Now I'm cancer-free!" Sure, the statement doesn't say labradorite cured the person's cancer, but it also doesn't . . . *not* . . . say that, either. Statements like this are ambiguous and might lead some to believe that the stone mentioned cured your cancer. Remember, the difference between scientific data and magical observation is that the former is supported by observation, evidence, and replicable experimentation in a way that allows for falsifiability while the latter is based on personal observation and experimentation but doesn't meet the same level of falsifiability or scientific scrutiny. (And that's *totally OK*, because we're talking about spiritual beliefs. Those don't always need to be validated in a lab!) Correlation does not equate to causation, or, put another way, the rooster crowing isn't responsible for the sunrise even though they seem to happen at the same time.

If you're just stepping out on your witchy path, please let me assure you right now that so much of the—to borrow from Aladdin's genie— Phenomenal Cosmic Powers (or experiences) written about online are sensationalized. We witches all live on the same planet you do, with the same laws of physics and the same constraints on the natural world and our physical bodies. So, basically, if it sounds impossible and a quick Google search doesn't tell you something like, "Oh yeah, 12 percent of the population can actually fly thanks to this weird genetic trait," it's probably safe to assume that particular UPG is not an accurate portrayal of something that happened.

My Ghosts, Your Goblins

My husband believes in ghosts. He sees ghosts. He interacts with ghosts. I don't see them, but I believe my husband when he says he sees them. The most important thing we can do when interacting with the witchy world is be clear, accurate, and honest about our experiences. If someone is using UPG as a path towards getting their way or making themselves look superior or, gods forbid, attempting to manipulate others, see it for what it is and take appropriate actions to remove yourself or someone else from a bad situation when necessary. When you can honestly talk about UPG, examining it from all angles and testing it like a hypothesis, weeding out what can be disproven or isn't genuine, you will be able to see the magic all around you and know it is real.

★

I've spent this part of the book talking about spotting bad actors, learning to filter knowledge and actions, and unpacking spiritual experiences. The magical world is vast, and yet the community can feel like the smallest of towns. This book has a very large focus on community, mostly because many, many other books on witchcraft focus very heavily on everything else. Spells. Moon phases. Myths. Folklore. Proper wand-waving techniques. But we rarely talk about the community in black and white. Remember, your experience is your own, and nobody else gets to tell you that you're doing it wrong.

But now, finally, because you've been very good, and because this is a book about witchcraft, let's do magic.

PART

4

The TOOLS
of MODERN
WITCHCRAFT

I am sure there is Magic in everything, only we have
not sense enough to get hold of it and make it do things for us.

—Frances Hodgson Burnett

I've done a lot of talking in the previous three parts of this book about the culture of modern witchcraft and the ways witches are perceived not only by society at large but by one another as well. I've also talked about the myriad ways that magic and witchcraft are filled with appropriated practices, problematic information, and a level of cognitive dissonance when it comes to where you get your magical tools from.

Over the next few chapters, I'm going to share with you some of the ways I personally go about performing magic, working with plants and researching crystals, cleansing my home, protecting my loved ones, and generally casting a spell over my everyday life. This is the "fun part," as we in the magical community very formally refer to it. But before we go too far into different types of magic and techniques for employing them, I want to let you in on a few secrets of magic, at least as I understand them.

CHAPTER 12

MAKING MAGIC

My grandmother is an artist, a painter, and since I was very little I wanted to learn to paint as well as her. Unfortunately for me, I absolutely fall apart when trying to draw things like hands. I won't be drawing splash pages for Marvel anytime soon, because "superheroes can't keep their hands in their pockets all the time." (Whatever. One day *Pocket Man* will be a billion-dollar blockbuster movie.) She has a gift for realism that I'll likely never achieve. When I was little, she sat me down and gave me some basic lessons: *This is how to draw a circle. This is how to draw a line.* No matter what kind of artist you become—whether you're an abstract expressionist like Jasper Johns or a sculptor like Auguste Rodin—there are basic skills you learn early and carry with you forever. Yes, even if you're one of those painters like Mark Rothko who paint a whole canvas a single color.

The same is true in magical practice. No matter where your spiritual journey takes you, there are basic skills that will prepare you for more complex practices and rituals down the road. This chapter will focus on three: spells, cleansing, and divination. Why these three? They're what I—and other Pagan content creators—get asked about most often. *How do I cast a spell? How do I cleanse myself or my home? How do I learn divination?* Naturally, each of these could be their own book, and as usual I direct you to the "Resources" section at the back for more in-depth instruction on each of these. Right now, the focus is on the basics: *This is how to draw a circle. This is how to draw a line.* Why do we learn these basics first? Because once you learn them, you'll begin to see that everything is lines and circles. Once you understand *why,* you'll be able to more effectively understand *how* to construct your own practice.

Theories of Magic's Efficacy

There are a lot of theories about why magic is effective that range from armchair quantum physics to intervention on the part of spirits or gods to basic psychology. Now, I know that I said before that why is always a more useful question than what, so this might seem out of character, but bear with me. Likewise, I understand the rationale behind asking these questions. If magic is real and it really works, then why? Why does it work? That's a valid question. Unfortunately, I see a lot of beginner witches get either very confused or very disenchanted when they go too far down any given rabbit hole promising an answer to why.

The answers you'll find vary. "The practitioner is working with an as-yet-undefined energetic force immanent in all things." "The practitioner is employing spirits or deities to act on their behalf." "The practitioner is altering reality in accordance with their will." Going too far down any of these paths of reasoning with any sort of scientific perspective and a critical eye takes you out of the mindset of belief and puts you into a frame of mind where the belief must prove itself. We have to allow space in our hearts and minds to wonder, to marvel, and to believe for the sake of keeping a bit of magic alive for ourselves.

Remember the Force in *Star Wars*? What was it? The Force. Why did it work? It was the Force. It's a weird quirk of the universe and it's everywhere and for all people, but a few people seem to be a bit more in touch with it than others. That's it. That's all we needed. We could believe. But . . . remember when the Star Wars series introduced midi-chlorians in the prequels, deciding that decades after we'd all accepted that the Force was simply a part of the universe they needed to explain it after all? Did we really need that explanation?

Questions like these are begging for an answer to the question "Is magic real?" without fully considering the nature of what it means for something to be real. What is "real"? What would make magic "real" to you? Think about the movie *Dumbo* for a moment. If I give a big-eared elephant a feather and he jumps off a high-rise, he still ends up flying whether he holds the feather or not. The feather didn't do anything. Or did it? Could he have gotten over his fear of heights, his understanding that he was an elephant and elephants shouldn't be able to fly, *without* the feather? The feather could be magic or it could be placebo, but either way the result was real.

The placebo effect is a term that comes from medical trials where an observable improvement in symptoms occurs despite the subject receiving a nonactive treatment—a sugar pill in place of the actual drug, for example. Pain, depression, and, yes, even something spiritual like demonic possession have all at one time or another been shown to improve because of the placebo effect. The placebo effect is theorized to occur because we have taken actions that we believe will correct some problem in our lives, and thus our bodies kick-start the healing process. Professor Ted Kaptchuk of Harvard-affiliated Beth Israel Deaconess Medical Center studies the placebo effect and cautions against believing that the effect is itself some kind of curative magic: "Placebos may make you feel better, but they will not cure you. They have been shown to be most effective for conditions like pain management, stress-related insomnia, and cancer treatment side effects like fatigue and nausea."[1]

But Fire Lyte! you say. *I thought you made the argument that magic is real! Didn't we cover this in part 1? Are you now saying it's just placebo?* Well, for one thing, I feel it would be disingenuous if we had a conversation about the efficacy of magic without acknowledging the placebo effect as a distinct possibility alongside the more metaphysical explanations for magic. But more important, I mention all this because I want to reiterate that the limitation of magic is it *must* be possible. So you need to set your expectations appropriately. Just like a medical placebo might help alleviate symptoms, because there's no chemical interaction it's unlikely that the underlying cause of the illness will get resolved. That's why the magical actions recommended in this book involve both a magical and a mundane action in order that you can ensure you're treating the underlying issue while getting your magical assist.

Finally, you need to adjust your boundaries for what you consider "real." It could be the feather that makes you fly, or it could be that you had the capability all along and the feather didn't do anything. But you needed to believe in order to take the leap, to have the courage to try. So, perhaps, there was magic in the feather after all. Perhaps we can let the Force be a property of the universe that doesn't need more explanation than that. That's the liminal space where I sit, and there's plenty of room for you as well. Whether magic is "really" just a placebo or whether it's "really" a part of the universe or whether those are the same thing, it still works.

A Brief Note to Acknowledge That Witchcraft Looks Silly

It's very acceptable to feel silly while casting spells or performing rituals. Talking out loud to an empty room, commanding bad spirits to get out of your linen closet, can be an objectively funny sight. Embrace this lightheartedness in the same spirit as a romantic comedy movie. The best romcoms are the ones where very good actors take the job of being funny seriously. They embrace the ridiculous situations they find themselves in but turn on the emotion when the time comes. Casting spells can be the same way. Embrace the objective silliness of the act if that's how you feel, but be conscious and serious in your intent. In other words, take yourself and your craft seriously but never so seriously that you cannot laugh at yourself.

Embracing the Mundane

The kinds of rituals, spells, and other magical workings that I recommend might be a bit more pared down than you were hoping for. While you can certainly fill a room with candles and chant the names of a dozen deities in a ritual written in Latin while burning bundles of herbs that were difficult to find surrounded by a circle of rare gemstones, effective magic doesn't have to be that complex. Especially after the pandemic of 2020, people are reassessing where they should prioritize their time, energy, money, and space. So, while it can be incredibly fun to collect exotic sounding flora, spend a day setting up a complex cleansing spell for your home, or close your eyes and max out a credit card to obtain a massive crystal shipped from halfway around the world, the chapters that follow are going to prioritize simple practices and free or inexpensive methods to perform effective witchcraft.

In fact, while the traditional tools of the witch—the cauldron, the broom, et cetera—may feel ancient and mystical to us now, in reality these were the tools people (especially women) had around their home and used every day during a particular period of time in human history. We will explore this in greater detail in chapter 14, but if you don't have the tools recommended to perform a work of magic, do not go out and buy them unless you want to. You can absolutely substitute almost anything in a witchy book for something you have on hand. It is in that spirit of using what you have handy, what grows or is found near your home, and what you can achieve using the time available to you that these chapters were written. The magic comes from within you after all, not a jewel-encrusted knife or intricately wood-burned wand.

It's in this liminal space of belief and using what you have that I'm going to discuss the basic skills most magical practitioners use: basic spell crafting, cleansing, and divination. You won't need to run out to the store for anything new. If that feels like a bit of a letdown, I get it. I wanted to give all my money away to metaphysical shops when I was starting out at one point, too. But instead of going broke hoping to buy your way into "effective" magic, let me show you around what my friends refer to as Fire Lyte's School for Discount Witchery. Here you'll learn basic spell components, how to cleanse yourself and your space, and even get a primer on peering into possibility using divination.

BASIC SPELL CASTING

When I was a kid there was this TV show called *Second Noah*. Don't worry if you don't remember it or never heard of it. There won't be a pop quiz or anything. To this day I think I'm the only person who ever watched it. The only notable thing about it was that it was James Marsden's big break in Hollywood. (Shout-out to the original Cyclops.) The show was something like the Swiss Family Robinson meets *Seventh Heaven*. Conventionally attractive adults meet, get married, and proceed to adopt a whole bunch of kids and enough exotic animals to have their own zoo. Standard nineties family dramedy, right?

The singular memory I have of watching *Second Noah* was a scene where one of the characters is having a really bad day and Deirdre O'Connell's character, Shirley, tells them to write the problem down on a piece of paper, which she then puts in a jar that she seals and places in the freezer. The character feels better. Problem solved. Perhaps at one time or other you've received similar advice. Putting a problem "on ice" seems quick and easy—and it is—but it also perfectly illustrates all the elements of basic spell craft.

Or, to put it another way, Debbie Reynolds said it best in the movie *Halloweentown* when she said, "Magic is really very simple. All you have to do is want something and then let yourself have it!" The unique part of creating a spell is defining *how* you let yourself have it.

Most spells—and certainly the ones in this book—involve what is known as sympathetic magic, which is a kind of magic where an object or ritual mirrors the person or event you wish to influence. (Such as putting a situation in a freezer to cool it off.) James Frazer first used the term in his book *The Golden Bough* in 1890 and explained it like this:

> If we analyze the principles of thought on which magic is based, they will probably be found to resolve themselves into two: first, that like produces like, or that an effect resembles its cause; and, second, that things which have once been in contact with each other continue to act on each other at a distance after the physical contact has been severed. The former principle may be called the Law of Similarity, the latter the Law of Contact or Contagion. From the first of these principles, namely the Law of Similarity, the magician infers that he can produce any effect he desires merely by imitating it: from the second he infers that whatever he does to a material object will affect equally the person with whom the object was once in contact, whether it formed part of his body or not.[2]

To put it plainly, one can affect the material world by first creating something that represents the thing—such as a doll, a picture, or even simply a word or name on paper—and then manipulating that in a way that represents the change required. For example: Is there a lot of red tape preventing you from obtaining a goal—perhaps you have a lot of bureaucratic issues preventing you from receiving an inheritance? Get a red ribbon and a pair of scissors and ritually cut the red tape. Spells thrive in this space of metaphor and similarity because they help you focus your intent on your end result.

Let's stay with this red tape example for a minute, because it high-lights a few crucial things. First, this magic is possible: You *can* receive an inheritance. So far so good. It also exemplifies the basic formula for a spell:

- Identify your end goal. (Obtaining your inheritance.)
- Determine a sympathetic action corresponding to meeting your end goal. (Cutting the red tape.)
- Focus your intention (using symbols, spoken words, gestures, objects, et cetera. In this case, you could speak clearly your intention to cut the red tape and clear the obstacles preventing you from receiving your inheritance).
- Carry out the action with intention and focus. (The actual ritual cutting of the ribbon.)
- Repeat as necessary. (You could choose to perform this action daily/weekly until your goal is obtained alongside your mundane actions.)

Like the best recipes, this is simply a basic template for a spell. This isn't copied out of the universe's *Rulebook for How Everything Works* (not a book, but if you ever find it could you flip to my chapter and tell me why I am the way I am?). It can be added to, taken from, remixed, or done away with completely as you grow.

You'll want to keep notes. Remember, you're a spiritual scientist, and as you try new things you'll notice what works for you and what doesn't. In other words, you'll figure out how *you* make it rain, not how to make it rain anywhere all the time for anyone.

There are lots of applications for spells. People use them to modify the weather, seek a lover, assist with a job hunt, find a parking space, keep an unwanted person away, protect themselves or their loved ones, and even locate their lost car keys. There is no problem too large or too small that someone somewhere hasn't used magic to assist with solving.

BAAAAAAAAD MAGIC

I want to touch briefly on a point made at the beginning of this book, chiefly the notion of there being "good" and "bad" magic. Again, there is no such thing, just like there aren't good and bad forks. (Though I do believe it is a marker of adulthood to have strong opinions about the shape, weight, and design of cutlery, and I have been known to have a meltdown in Target when trying to buy new forks. But I digress.) Curses, hexes, and other terms relating to magic that is intended to either afflict someone or otherwise cause something to happen that they don't want to happen scare people. A lot of people speak of these spells as though they shouldn't be performed and say that if you do perform them terrible things will happen (insert thunder and lightning here). My perspective is this: if you believe your action is necessary, that's your business and not theirs. Use good judgment. This is where that filter I talked about in part 3 comes into play: you'll need to determine whether action of any kind is necessary and, if so, whether a mundane solution can be found or whether the solution involves both magical and mundane actions.

MAGICAL STAGE DIRECTION

Instead of thinking of magic in terms of good and bad, I tend to think of them like the three possible types of stage blocking: propel, impel, and repel. In theater, when an actor might receive stage direction based on how their character is reacting to either a line being said or an action taken by another actor, they will be told to either move forward, retreat, or stay where they are. Magical actions are the same.

★

Propel—magic intent on moving a person or situation forward. Examples include (but are not limited to):

- Prosperity
- Luck
- Love
- Weather (summoning desirable weather)
- Healing (alongside mundane actions and recovery)
- Comeuppance (speeding along the course of a person's actions so they catch up with them faster)

Impel—magic intent on keeping someone or a situation in place. Examples include:

- Binding
- Freezing

Repel—magic intent on keeping someone or a situation at a distance. Examples include:

- Banishing
- Law Keep Away
- Protection
- Weather (sending unwanted weather away)

None of these are inherently good or bad actions to take. Binding, for example, is simply preventing a person from taking a given action. It's just as possible to use this spell to support someone's best interests, much the way your parents stopped you from touching a hot stove before you fully understood that the stove could hurt you. Context, perspective, and need all go into determining whether an action is right for you to take, and, as always, those decisions are yours alone.

Cleansing

You ever have those days where no matter what your intentions were for how great that day was going to be, you still missed your alarm, hit every single red light on the way to work, forgot your lunch and your wallet at home, had to pretend that break room coffee was enough to sustain you throughout the day, finally get home only to remember that you were supposed to pick up groceries and have nothing to eat, and when you decide to just order a pizza and call it a day the delivery driver is an hour late? (Can you tell by now that this is from personal experience?) If you've ever been in an absolute funk, you might want to do a little spiritual spring cleaning. (Or summer cleaning or fall or winter, depending on what the weather is doing outside.)

And, judging by my inbox over the years, cleansing is a common concern for many dabblers. Even if you don't make it a regular part of your practice to cast spells or divine the future, there is the pervasive idea that bad stuff follows us home and sets up shop in all the dark, forgotten corners of our spaces. This bad stuff is thought by many to perpetuate negative cycles of behavior and cause bad luck, sleeplessness, bad dreams, and more.

The terms surrounding spiritual cleansing are bountiful: "energy," "clearing," "cleansing," "vibes," et cetera. The definitions of those terms, the literal actions and objective meanings they're supposedly tied to, are incredibly vague. Different cultures over the course of human history have laid blame in different places for ills requiring spiritual cleansing. Sometimes it's ghosts or bad spirits. Sometimes it's the ire of a god. Sometimes it's demons or the fae or some other figure of folklore that followed you home. Other times it's the jealousy of a neighbor or the ill wishes of an enemy. It might even be a witch casting a curse.

For all I know, it could also be a rough night's sleep preceded by months of food insecurity and financial instability. It could be social or psychological or situational. The thing is, whether it's an actual curse or a demon or simply "bad vibes," performing an act of spiritual cleansing has proven positive effects.

A growing number of psychologists want to more or less sanction the belief in possession by the mental health community. One possible and often successful treatment when someone believes they're possessed by a malevolent force is to allow that person to undergo an exorcism. It's successful because of the placebo effect. At least, that's what researchers say. (What, you thought they were going to say, "Yes, we found the demons and used our poking stick to poke at them and tell them to shoo while throwing water and shouting at them in Latin"?) Basically, the scientific explanation for the success of exorcisms is valid whether we agree on the objective reality of the cause, because we can agree on the objective reality of the result.

Whether it's "real" or not doesn't actually matter. What I mean is that whether there is an actual evil presence lurking in your spirit making terrible things happen to you or you simply think there is an evil presence lurking in your spirit making terrible things happen to you, the action of exorcism can often yield the same result.

So whether there are bad spirits or negative energy or the ire of a jealous god in your house—or possibly the weight of being a human existing in a flawed world has gotten to be a bit too much—taking an action to spiritually cleanse yourself and your space can be beneficial for you.

The basic steps of the cleansing methods provided are to first rid ourselves and/or our spaces of negative energy and then recharge ourselves and/or our spaces with a chosen energy. I'm going to use the classical five senses as a guide for different methods of cleansing, because you might not always need the same type every time. You may also find that certain types of cleansing are more effective for you than others. I'm the kind of person whose stress tends to melt away when I can visually see a tidy living or working space, so I tend to perform the cleansing methods found in "Sight" more often than other types. However, I will use each of these at different times. Read through each section, try them all, or adapt them into your practice as you see fit, and find a method that works for you.

SIGHT

Forgive me for sounding parental for a moment, but, personally, I'm far more likely to feel as though I am surrounded by negativity when my house is a mess. Perhaps this is something I should be paying a therapist to work through; however, I don't think I'm alone in saying that the piles of unwashed laundry I ignore are the perfect physical manifestation of my accumulated spiritual *ish*. Cleaning up is also an incredibly easy win that gives you the perfect psychological boost in mood and clears space for you to focus on doing something *else* for yourself. I am far more creative, willing to see friends or taking time for myself to read a book or watch a favorite movie stress free, if I've spent a little time picking up my space first.

This is actually backed up by science. Dr. Joseph R. Ferrari, professor of psychology at DePaul, researches the link between clutter, procrastination, and stress. He and his colleagues published a study in the journal *Current Psychology* in September 2017 that found that problems with clutter contributed to a significant decrease in satisfaction with life, especially as we age.[3] Now, I get it. We're busy. I fully support that, sometimes, after a long day—a long few days, let's be honest—or even during massive swings in your daily routine (such as . . . oh . . . a worldwide pandemic), keeping your home tidy isn't on the top of anyone's lists. Nor should it be. Our priorities oftentimes need to be elsewhere.

That said, one way of cleansing your home can be pausing your routine and intentionally decluttering your space. It doesn't have to be huge. It can be that chair in the corner where you throw all your dirty clothes at the end of the day or the table that you are pretty sure was once used to eat meals.

But you aren't just tidying your home. You're going to *magically* tidy your home. Spoiler alert: This doesn't mean that the clothes are going to walk themselves to the washing machine. What you'll actually be doing is a conscious assessment of the current state of either your physical self or physical space in order to understand the emotional and energetic state of both.

Magical cleansing of any type starts with awareness. Your goal is to look around you to get a clear sense of what, specifically, needs tidying up physically and energetically. Do you need to spend your time deep cleaning your entire house, or would washing your windows to let more light into your space do the trick? Ensuring your efforts are going toward only what needs to be done will not just save you time, but will keep you focused on your intention.

1. **Look at it!** Spend a moment in the middle of your space and really take it all in. When we go about our daily routine, we tend to get blind spots for all the areas we toss our clothes or kick off our shoes or let

those piles of miscellaneous papers pile up. Make sure you see it all, but ...

2. **Do *not* judge it!** Oh my various gods, the last thing you should do here or take away from this chapter is shaming yourself for the mess you have. We *all* have mess. All of us. Yours is just in front of you. Most of the people with neat, tidy homes on social media have their mess shoved out of sight of the camera. Use this brief moment to acknowledge all the spaces where life has piled itself up in your home. Then ...

3. **Name it!** Sure, you could use this opportunity to list the reasons why you've allowed things to pile up, but as I said before, "why" is always more useful than "what." You already know you're busy. You already know other things took priority. But why are you taking this intentional action right now? What are you getting rid of while you cleanse your space of clutter? Name it! Is it Stress? Is it Anxiety? Is it Workplace Gossip? This mess can be a representation of all the things you need to clean—physical, mental, and spiritual. Speak clearly and declaratively about what the mess represents and that your intention is to cleanse that energy from your space. And, of course ...

4. **Clean it!** Go through that pile of paper detritus! Get that laundry done! Sort through those toys! Remember, though, really dig in with your intention as well. You aren't just throwing out a pile of old mail; you're throwing Brenda's Gossip from the Break Room in the trash. Get thorough, too. Don't leave any crevice untouched. This isn't a regular tidying but a thorough cleansing. This is also the perfect opportunity to use your witchy implements! Grab your broom; bless your carpet sweeper; charm your Roomba. (More on household objects as magical tools in a later chapter.) Whatever you use to clean is

now a mystical tool of arcane magic. Sweep out the Anxiety, vacuum up the Stress, and when you get rid of it . . .

Bless It on the Way Out! I'm not suggesting that you give the dirt from your vacuum cleaner a hug or something. Rather, acknowledge that your actions have both decluttered your space and your mind, and send that energy back out in the world with the positive thought that it isn't in your home anymore. Feel free to add in words if that feels right to you. You can make this a formal spell or simply an acknowledgment that you're parting with an energy and feeling that has kept you from being at peace. Personally, I like the very Southern "you don't have to go home, but you can't stay here." Why? Because it's a bit of humor to help lighten the mood, my intent clearly matches my words, and it feels like I am politely but firmly shutting the door on the feeling that energy gave me.

Remember, you can cleanse any size space. I once felt an immense stress lift off me after clearing off a small table in the corner of my bedroom that had piled up several months' worth of old mail and receipts and other little paper things you dump and tell yourself you'll sort through one day. Do what you are able to do when it feels right to you. After you've intentionally cleared your space, go back to step one and really look at it before continuing on with your day. Celebrate the work you did.

Time to Recharge

I've found it to be true that after cleansing a space sometimes the energy feels a little blank. While the clutter and accompanying negative energy weren't positive, they were something, and the blankness left behind can feel a bit dull. So, I always recommend adding back something that helps bring an energy you want to invite. Since we're focused on sight, I recommend choosing something visual to recharge the space. Is it a crystal that gives you joy? A new succulent to add a bit of life? Is it a new throw pillow or simply moving an extra lamp into the room (even temporarily) to give extra light? This doesn't need to be anything you purchase and could easily be something you make or repurpose and give pride of place in your new space. Personally, I change my sheets. I choose a fresh set of white sheets and add a white duvet, because that's what works for me.

That's what turns the sight of my bedroom into a place of order and calm, a feeling that emanates through the rest of my home whether I've cleaned it or not.

I would also recommend choosing an energy type. Simply filling your space with "positive energy" doesn't work as well in my experience. Choose something specific. Invite "motivation" or "creativity" or "passion" into your space so that when you look at your object, you're reminded of it and the magic is renewed.

SMELL

Few things instantly invite me to unwind, relax, and energetically decompress like scent. The smell of coffee alone can be enough motivation to get me out of bed and to complete a task I've been putting off. The scent of certain flowers makes me feel peaceful or romantic. We've talked before how scent is tied to memory and smelling certain things can revive various feelings, bringing you back to a different time and place. You can also incorporate scent into cleansing rituals, not only focusing on remembering the past but also helping to direct your future.

If the air in your space feels stagnant, not only physically but energetically, first things first: cleanse it. Now, there are a lot of ways you can go about this, and there are plenty of rituals and methods used, but I've always found the simplest, cheapest, and best to be opening your windows. I realize that cracking a window to let some fresh air in doesn't feel witchy, but I've always found that the simplest actions can very easily be dressed up with magic.

First We Cleanse

Open Your Windows! When you do, say in a clear, declarative voice that you intend to remove the negative energy from your space with the aid of the air. If your work involves air spirits, certain deities, et cetera, you can call upon them as well to enter and clear your space of all that has been allowed to stagnate. An example might simply be, "I intend to cleanse this space of negative energy." You can make up a short rhyme if you choose or a more rhythmic chant that you repeat while you clean. The ritual, as are all these rituals, is yours to adapt however you see fit.

Grab a Broom! Come on, no witch is complete without a broom. Whether it's a handmade wooden besom made of blessed wood and sacred straw or it's the $10 aluminum number you got at your grocery store, grab it and sweep the air around you. Just like when you're cleaning your space, moving the broom through the air is thought to help stir the air not only physically but magically as well. If you don't have a broom or if it doesn't feel right, grab or make a fan. If all else fails, I've heard of mighty good results from witches who simply stood in a direction facing the open window or door and blew or whistled air in that direction. The point is to move the air. Once again, you can *speak your intent* and make it part of the magical process as well.

If it's very cold (or very hot) you might not want to leave the windows open for long. That's OK! The point is to get some fresh air in the space. If you're somewhere that the windows cannot open or the weather is truly prohibitive of opening them at all (seriously, I get it . . . when you live in Chicago and it's -80° F outside, the windows do not open. Ever. For any reason.), that's fine. Still speak your intent and move the air. The point is to stir it up so that it is no longer stagnant. Then we recharge. This can be done in a number of ways.

Recharge!

Make Some Smoke! Incense, burning a plant bundle (like rosemary), or even just lighting a match or three. Whatever way you go, smoke has long been used to cleanse objects and spaces of negative energy, harmful spirits, et cetera. For this purpose, I would forego the usual matrix of correspondences and spend time thinking about what scents both feel clean to you and inspire you in a way you need to be inspired right now. Are you wanting to fill your space with bright, motivating energy? Perhaps for you that means an incense that smells of lemon or coconut. Or, if the energy you need is calm and quiet, a bundle of lavender, rose, and other soft florals could do the trick. Figure out what works for you.

Note: If you have pets or have (or live with someone that has) breathing issues, be very careful when choosing smoke as a cleansing method. If you have pets, consult your veterinarian before engaging in the practice, as different kinds of pets are more sensitive than others. While my large dog might not be as bothered by a little incense, my bird shouldn't be in the same room as smoke. Be considerate of all the life under your roof before trying this. In addition, if you're choosing to use a plant bundle, research the plant in question. Some plants can give off toxic chemicals when burned.

Spray! This one is a lot of fun and is really easy to fit into whatever purpose you have. The only requirement is a spray bottle. This can be one of those large misting bottles you fill with cleaning solution to wipe down your counters, or it can be a tiny bottle that fits in your cosmetic bag. The size truly doesn't matter here. The mechanics of this process are simple. All you'll do is fill the bottle with a liquid and then mist your space with it. If you'd like, you can speak your intent clearly and declaratively. The components are where you can get really magical. You can use a cologne or perfume that reminds you of the type of energy you're hoping to inject into your space.

Or you can make your own! Add a few parts of plants or minerals that remind you of the energy you're wanting to put into your space into the bottle and fill it with water. Wait at least a day so that the plants can infuse into the water, and then spray your space. I usually use mint, as it's typically accessible at the grocery store and is a scent that helps me clear my head. You can, of course, take the entire process to the next witchy level. Maybe your water was left out under the light of a full or dark moon. Maybe you add a few chips of a tumbled stone to boost the process. The possibilities are as endless as the combinations of plants and minerals. (See chapter 13 for more ideas.)

Wax/Oil! Candles, wax burners, potpourri pots all have their place in magical cleansing. Just as you would with a spray bottle or smoke, you can simmer plants and stones in a potpourri pot or oil burner, or you can light a candle containing your cleansing scent. Wax burners offer a great alternative if open flame isn't something you want to risk.

Note: No matter how powerful you think you are, blow out your fire when you leave your home. Your house can still burn down even if you're a witch. Also, be careful around pets. I have a dear friend whose cat cannot seem to see a lit candle without setting his tail on fire. Keep fires up and out of reach of all babies, human and animal alike.

TASTE

Witches can get so focused on all the negative energy outside themselves that they forget about all the work inside as well. This cleansing method helps you take a moment to focus on your internal energy. Ever heard of a palate cleanser? It's a food or beverage that is generally considered to have a neutral flavor—not too spicy, salty, sweet, et cetera—and often has an acidic, absorbent, or effervescent quality that removes the taste and residue from previous food or drink and allows you to more accurately taste the next dish. If you've ever gone out for sushi, you've probably been served a side of pickled ginger you're meant to eat between tasting different types of sushi. Certain breads and sorbets are also used for the same effect.

Think of this as a magical palate cleanser. We aren't just experiencing the negative stressors of our surroundings; we also absorb that stress. This has a real impact on our well-being. You can cleanse yourself as well, and taste is a delicious way of doing that.

At the end of a long week, or any other time when I'm personally feeling sluggish, unmotivated, or generally down in the dumps energetically, it's time for a magical palate cleanser. Like a mundane palate cleanser, this can take the form of food or drink or both. Also, like our previous cleansing methods, I recommend doing this in two parts: cleanse first, then add in the energy you wish to replace.

Cleanse

Choose a food or beverage (think light snack, not full meal) that cleanses your palate. You might select an apple, a slice of unbuttered toast, or even a small salad. If you're choosing a beverage, you might choose sparkling water, a bit of mango, or mint tea. This is an opportunity to speak your intent clearly and declaratively that you are cleansing yourself of negative energy from the inside out. Eat consciously, chewing or drinking slowly and deliberately.

Recharge

Here is where comfort foods and drinks come in handy. Speak your intention clearly and declaratively. Then eat or drink something that makes you feel good. Perhaps choose flavors that make you feel more bold, confident, happy, strong, et cetera. For example: Really good hot cocoa in winter makes me feel warm, but not just in temperature. There's a feeling that comes over me, settling my nerves and recalling better times. I might drink hot cocoa after cleansing myself if I want to inspire steadfastness and perseverance, knowing that if I do what I need to do now I will make it through tough times.

TOUCH

While I'm talking about cleansing of self from the inside out, let's work on the outside of you, too. Very few things feel as refreshing to me as a little self-care and bodily attention. While my recommendations do mention bathing, you may adapt the recommendations to be done in any form of dress that is comfortable to you.

Cleanse

Before you bathe, take a moment to sit consciously with your body. Close your eyes and run through each part top to bottom. How is your scalp feeling? The base of your neck? Your shoulders? Consciously reach out and understand how the parts of your body are feeling that you don't think about often. Your shins. Your knees. The backs of your arms. The soles of your feet. Are you sore? Are you carrying stress in some areas? Does anything feel tight or dry or uncomfortable? Spend a moment getting back in touch with the vehicle that carries your consciousness through life. Then speak your intent clearly.

Next, you will bathe (or, if either comfort level or the situation does not allow, you can simply wash your hands, splashing water on your face and neck as well) while focusing on your body, massaging areas of tightness and consciously willing the negativity and stress you've carried to be washed away. There are a wealth of body scrubs and soaps and herbal blends out there on the market to aid you in your cleansing endeavors. However, I think we tend to forget that we have everything we need without spending much money. If you'd like to add in an additional cleansing element before you reach for the soap, I've found that a salt scrub does wonders and is typically inexpensive and available in most stores. In addition, salt is thought to be metaphysically as well as physically cleansing. If you'd like to use a scented salt scrub, choose something that smells cleansing and calming to you. Eucalyptus or mint works for me, but perhaps you associate the smell of lemon or patchouli with cleansing. Remember, we'll add in additional scents in our recharge portion, so you don't need anything too strong. Once you've spiritually cleansed, you can continue bathing as usual.

Recharge

Choose a lotion, skin-safe essential oil, or perfume scent you associate with the energy you wish to carry with you. Perhaps you washed away insecurity and wish to replace it with confidence. On the flip side, perhaps you washed away the stress of societal expectations and wish to replace it with an energy of contentment. Personally, I know that much of the stress and negativity I carry in my body is from needing to be different people in different settings and the prolonged stretches of time between when I can feel at ease. Speak the intention that you wish to replace the negative energy with this new energy and consciously apply it to yourself as you see fit.

SOUND

We live in a noisy world. One of the adjustments I made when my husband and I moved from rural Texas to Chicago was to just how much noise there was constantly. However, even now when visiting my family I realize that we don't escape the noise; we simply carry it with us. I am probably guiltier than most of being overly plugged in. If I don't have my headphones with me, I simply don't quite know what to do with myself. As much as the world's background noise can be a source of comfort at times, there are days when it is a bit overwhelming. We can and should take time to cleanse our spaces and ourselves with sound as well.

Cleanse

Speak your intention clearly and directly that you wish to cleanse yourself and your space. Then turn off or silence as many electronic devices as you can. Now, the next steps can look different depending on your comfort level. If you appreciate the silence, you may spend several minutes with your eyes closed consciously processing the now empty soundscape surrounding you allowing what thoughts or sounds that might make themselves known to you to pass through. However, I'm not someone who deals well with sitting in silence with my eyes closed for any extended period of time, so I've adapted to enjoying lo-fi playlists available for free on video and audio streaming services such as YouTube or Spotify. These are typically instrumental playlists of background music meant to help you relax. If you choose to play music, keep the volume low and pleasant.

If music isn't your speed, but you wish to cleanse with sound, there are a couple of options that are fairly old-school. You might choose to ring a bell, gong, chime, or other manual instrument. If you have a tuning fork, that works, too. One final option for ridding yourself or your space of negativity might have started off as a bit of an internet joke, but it works. If you really need to chase out a nasty energy or spirit, banging pots and pans while yelling out lots of curse words is quite effective and very fun. (And, hey, who am I to say what is calming to you? I know plenty of people who unwind to the extremely loud, complex soundscape of heavy metal.) Your experience is your own, of course. The point is to use sound to chase away the negative *ish* in your space.

Recharge

Turn the volume up and put on your favorite playlist. Have a dance party if you wish. I have different songs and playlists that put me in different moods or enhance a mood I might already be in. Just like comfort foods can help you ease into a setting, so can sound and music. This isn't just your favorite pop song, however. You may have used your cleansing time to rid yourself of the feelings of being busy or pulled in too many directions, so your recharge music might simply be the sound of rain or a trickling creek. If you have the ability, you may wish to get out in nature to hear these or similar sounds. Focus on figuring out what energy you wish to replace the background noise in your life with and consciously choose that. Remember that you can speak your intent as well before or during the process of adding that new sound to your ears.

★

There are a myriad brilliant authors and voices out there that can teach you new and interesting methods of spiritual and personal cleansing. I highly encourage you to use this as a springboard for further research and figure out what works best for you. In all likelihood you might find that different methods work for you at different times. Some days I might feel best after a conscious cleansing in the shower while others I might need to change up what I'm seeing or hearing to—as my dad might say—get my mind right. Don't be afraid to experiment, and certainly don't be afraid to combine or leave out certain kinds of cleansing. Do what feels best to you, your body, and your space in the moment. The one thing I hope you take away from this chapter is that you do not need to spend any money at all to perform effective spiritual cleansing. All you need is a bit of time, conscious thought, and things you already have in your own home.

DIVINATION

If there is one thing beyond plants hanging in the window and crystals lining a shelf that indicates you might be dealing with a witch, it is the deck of cards, sack of runes, or other tool of divination. When people think of divination, they think of fortune-telling, peering through the mists of time and space and predicting how events will unfold in days to come. We'd all like to know a bit about our future, right? There's nothing certain in life, so if we could have someone tell us what will happen or what to watch out for, we can modify our actions to ensure we meet with the best possible outcome.

OK, So What's in the Crystal Ball?

Will you be able to navigate the sea of life's possibilities and accurately predict outcomes for yourself and others every time you throw your dice or pull a card? No. (Sorry, I keep forgetting when I'm supposed to yell, "Spoiler alert!") I mean, really, if the answer were yes, everyone who learned a type of divination would make it a habit of winning the lottery.

At the very least, anyone practicing divination with enough skill should be able to avoid heartbreak, anticipate bad news, or herald disaster. Every time. Without fail. Yet that isn't happening, so we must cope with the reality that divination is a skill with limitations. I've interviewed a lot of professional practitioners of some form of divinatory skill over the years, and almost all of them have told me that the majority of their job is being a good listener. They and their magic become a sounding board for people who want someone to talk to. In fact, a few of them are even licensed professional counselors.

Embracing this, there is still quite a bit you can get out of practicing divination. Whether you're wanting to pick up some tips for self-reflection or to put your skills to work in the service of others, there is absolutely something you can get out of this ancient practice.

Based both on personal experience and my interviews with a number of professional practitioners over the years, most people approach divination for one of three key purposes:

Self-reflection—using divination as a tool to process emotions, situations, or help you come to terms with underlying thoughts. One might use this type to help suss out how you're feeling about a situation at work or to process fears or excitement about an upcoming event.

Revealing the truth—building on self-reflection, this is going outside yourself, your emotions, et cetera, to reveal truths about a past or present situation you did not already know. A common use of this type of divination is "what is preventing me from achieving X?" in which the reading would help you identify what roadblocks are in your way that you may not know about keeping you from attaining your goal.

Predicting the future—this one is a bit tricky, and there are a lot of professional readers who will tell you up front they don't provide predictive readings. Those who do will provide their own caveats such as "this is what will happen if nothing changes" but then acknowledge that the act of receiving the reading inherently affects events going forward. Suffice to say, this one flummoxes a lot of people, and plenty of readers (professional and otherwise) don't do it, and you aren't any lesser of a practitioner if you choose not to.

I believe it's important to contextualize that predictive readings are not like what you see in media, which is why some people walk away from these readings feeling that they didn't get an authentic experience. As with the other types of divination, the tools you're working with help you through interpreted symbols that allow you to unpack gut feelings, memories, et cetera. In predictive divination you are still using symbols and interpretation, but unlike the other forms, you're having to guess about things to come rather than using them to contextualize events that have already occurred. Yes, I said "guess," because that's what we're doing. We are using our intuition—our gut feeling—and our skills of interpretation to guess at what the cards, runes, tea leaves, et cetera, might be telling us. Sometimes things are only clear in retrospect, and sometimes we simply get the interpretation wrong.

Choose a Starting Point

No matter what kind of reading you're doing, they all start with the same place: you need something to read. There are entire books, entire series of books even, dedicated to the different methods of divination humankind has employed over the centuries. I'm not going to go into all of that, since . . . well . . . frankly, that would make this a much longer book. Instead of focusing on the various types of reading materials—cards, bird sightings, cloud patterns—I want to discuss how to improve your understanding for what it is you're actually reading: symbols.

Whether you're dripping wax into a bowl of water, analyzing a dream, or watching for patterns in a forest canopy, the most common unifying feature of the various methods of divination is the interpretation of symbols. There are a number of ways you can do this, but if you're looking for a starting point, I recommend starting by learning the basics of tarot. Even if it doesn't end up being your go-to divination method, the lessons you can learn through tarot will apply to your study of other methods. I think of it like learning an instrument. I grew up playing the French horn, but because I knew the basics of playing a brass instrument I could eventually play the trumpet and baritone equally well. Same thing with strings. Once you learn the violin, there isn't much difference from playing the cello.

My first tarot teacher told me she could just as easily read a stack of inkblots or a stack of product labels (like label cutouts of Joy or Tide, et cetera) as she could tarot cards, because it was less about knowing the exact definition of each card and more about recognizing a symbol and confidently interpreting it. As you start on your course to being an adept diviner, keep some of these tips in mind:

> **Get to know the cards!** Spend time examining the artwork. Pull a card every day and look at it. What do you see? How does it make you feel? Why does it make you feel that way? Are there colors that set a mood, objects or symbols that remind you of something from your own life experience? A detail on a cup or a hand position or the posture of a figure in the scene? Look at everything and figure out how the card feels to you.

> **Read the book!** Every deck comes with a book. Read it in full. It is tempting to use the book as a reference tool, looking up cards as you come to them, but most tarot decks tell a kind of story if you read about the deck all at once, which can assist greatly in understanding how the various symbols that make up the card—and by extension the deck—are employed.

Remember my catchphrase that "'why' is always more useful than 'what'"? That applies here, too. Why were those the colors chosen for the Swords? Why is the Empress seated or standing? How do they relate to other cards in the deck? Figure out how the author of that deck and the artist who drew it (sometimes they're the same person, sometimes not) feel about the card in question and how it relates to the other cards in the deck. Also, compare how the author feels about the card with how it makes *you* feel. Neither is more or less valid than the other. These are *your* cards that *you'll* be interpreting, after all.

Practice! This one feels fairly obvious, right? But it needs to be said, because even the most experienced practitioners—myself included—forget that part of being a "practitioner" is "practice." I recommend taking time every day to pull a card and sit with it. The natural urge is to ask a question every day, but until you get really comfortable with what each card looks like, the symbols used, et cetera, I would simply pull a card and process how it makes you feel. Then progress to asking questions that help you process your emotional state. In other words, ask questions you already know the answers to ("How am I feeling today?" or "Why am I sad?"), while using the symbols on the card to help provide color to the situation. They could help inspire you to pursue something good, avoid something bad, or simply dive deeper into an understanding of yourself.

Take notes! Let's say you ask, "What is bringing me joy lately?" and pull the Hermit. This is typically a card depicting a cloaked, hooded figure embracing solitude. Each deck is different, so yours might depict anything from a man holding a lantern to a woman putting her computer away. Take note of how it makes you feel and any symbols that stand out. Jot down a few notes next to each symbol about your first impressions of why those symbols stand out and what you associate with them. What you might find is that the same solemn figure you'd have interpreted one way feels completely different when the question is "What is bringing me joy lately?" Suddenly it is a card of embracing alone time, getting in touch with your own needs, and practicing self-care. Then, tomorrow, look back at your notes and see whether those same symbols and interpretations feel correct. Keep taking notes and hone your skill at spotting symbols, interpreting them based on the situation presented, and reflecting back.

Seek many sources! Read books, listen to podcasts, watch video courses, all from different voices. Find those that resonate with you. Try new and different methods. Every teacher is different and no way is necessarily wrong, but there will be plenty of methods that aren't a good fit for you. That's fine and valid. If it is not cost prohibitive for you to do so, try taking a class. They're available individually and in groups. Don't feel bad if you realize that a particular teacher's methods don't make sense to you right now or simply don't work for you. That's fine. There are others. Find yours.

There are two things that must be stressed above all when you're working in divination. First, divination methods should always be employed in concert with practical solutions such as journaling, talking to a trusted friend or family member, or seeking therapy if that is available to you. Divination can be one of many tools you employ for self-reflection and guidance, but it isn't a substitute for any of them. Likewise, you shouldn't make major life decisions based solely on divination. Divination might help you figure out how you're feeling about the possibility of, say, a big move or reveal conditions about your current situation you hadn't considered before, but it cannot tell you for certain exactly what will happen if you take one choice over the other.

As always, *you* are the magic, and you are the ultimate authority over your own life, not a deck of cards, sack of runes, or cup of tea leaves.

★

There are endless ways to employ magic, and the kind of magic you end up using most in your daily life might surprise you. Perhaps you will make magic in the kitchen and imbue a mug of hot cocoa with a protection charm to keep your loved ones safe in winter. Your life might need a bit more protection, so your energy might go towards keeping others out of your business. Whatever you do, remember that the most effective magic is personal, simple, and fits in with your life on your terms.

CHAPTER 13

NATURE'S MAGIC

Gazing out your window, you verify that the moon is still full, then turn your attention back to the simmering pot quietly bubbling over an open fire on your stove. You double-check your notes from the pages of a leather-bound book. *Ah yes*, you think to yourself as you grab a small collection of dried herbs that had been blessed under the light of last month's full moon. You dump them into the pot and take in the new aroma, a magical blend of sweet florals and musky grasses. Then, holding a polished wand of willow wood in one hand and a glittering crystal in your other, you mutter a rhyme that fixes your intent upon the brew and manifests your witchy will upon the world around you.

This is the witchy aesthetic everyone who has ever entered the magical aisle of the bookstore aspires to achieve in some form or other. It's the aesthetic that Instagram and other social media outlets will have you believe exists in the home of every practicing witch. Crystals, herbs, oils, brews, all overflowing from shelves and cabinets and drawers. These are the hallmarks of witchcraft, and the Witch's Council (not a real thing) would revoke my license to practice magic if I did not include at least one chapter on working with crystals and plants in my book on witchcraft.

And don't get me wrong, they're great. But there are a number of common misconceptions one might have after reading other books on the respective subjects. I touched upon some of them previously, but it is important to remind you that correspondences and associations are often in reference to a combination of folklore or a historical use (medical or magical) that has since been either debunked or placed in a different context thanks to updated science and a better understanding of history. If nothing else, they're likely a reflection of UPG. Since many of these qualifiers are often left out, readers can come away with the feeling that a book on magical herbs or healing crystals suffices to begin brewing remedies and prescribing mystical Band-Aids to life's ailments, both physical and otherwise. This can lead to unintended harm, not because you're likely to rhyme the wrong words and thereby turn the head cheerleader into a pineapple, but because you may be inclined to use plants and crystals in ways that are not advisable by doctors (or geologists).

I'm hoping that this chapter can serve, not necessarily to cover the entirety of the magic of the natural world, but to be an introduction on what to look out for and how to read some of those other books. I will, of course, offer my own ideas for working with each of these natural tools as well because I cannot help myself. That said, let's get started with that most glittering of witch objects....

Crystals

So shiny. So pretty. So many. So expensive. Witches typically come in two camps: plant parents or crystal goblins. (I swear the latter is a term of endearment.) If it is shiny and came from underground and you wish to hoard them in quantities so great you'd make Smaug envious of your hoard, you're likely a crystal goblin. Social media has done a lot of good in helping to spread knowledge about crystals—like that not every specimen on your shelf is actually a crystal (though I'm using the term "crystal" in this chapter for literary convenience)—but also glossed over some information. The following are some ways of working with crystals, ways not to work with them, and tidbits that might be handy to know before you head out on your next rock-shopping trip.

WHAT TO DO WITH CRYSTALS

You've likely seen the charts on social media or lists of correspondences in books. *Use Rose Quartz for love. Use Amethyst for peace and to cure drunkenness. Use Serpentine for ... um ... maybe guarding against snakes? We'll get back to you.* By now you have gotten a pretty good lesson in this book that correspondences tend to be better when they're personal to you, so I won't belabor that point. When the chart says to "use" the stone, though, what does the writer mean? There are a number of ways that witches interact with crystals, gems, minerals, rocks, et cetera. The following are the most common ways I've seen them used in the community and the ways in which I use them as well.

Get to Know Your Crystal

Spend time with your rock. Look at it from all angles. Feel its texture. Look at it through different types of light. Does it fluoresce under a black light? Is it smooth? Was it formed that way or was it made smooth by human intervention? Where is it from? Was it grown in a lab? How long does it take to form? You can use multiple free online sources to start learning about your crystal—even Wikipedia can give you a solid start. We often gloss over learning about where and how our crystals came to be and find themselves in our possession and, instead, treat them like integers in a magical equation. However, I've found that a deeper understanding of the crystal in question can really illuminate how it might be useful in my work or perhaps why it is associated with certain correspondences. For example: Magnetite is associated with attraction because it has an actual, measurable magnetic field. Some witches will set an intention upon a piece of magnetite and then "feed" the stone a little bit every day by sprinkling iron fillings on it and watching the stone attract them.

Meditate with Your Crystal

Sit with your crystal in an environment where you can comfortably focus without distraction. If this is in a silent room, great. If this is in your living room with a cat on your lap and ASMR streaming in the background, also great. Whatever you do to get comfortable, do that. Then hold your crystal. Spend time with it in your hands with your eyes closed and with your eyes open. Make note of any particular feelings that arise while doing so. Does the stone make you feel particularly happy? Somber? Introspective? Joyful? Does it just feel like a rock in your hand? All of these are valid and should be recorded. Sometimes a crystal doesn't make you feel anything. Sometimes the feelings you get from a crystal change over time. Sometimes a crystal you didn't previously resonate with will surprise you by becoming a cherished tool later on. This is not a test and there are no right answers. You might feel a stone has a bright and exuberant energy to it, then look it up later and find that the correspondences listed are "peace and tranquility." Contradictory? Maybe, but what was true for the author of that book doesn't need to be true for you. In fact, your own history with the crystal (where you got it from or who gifted it to you) might very well influence the way it makes you feel. Those memories and emotions are powerful magic. If that particular crystal makes you feel lighter and more alive, that's likely the energy that will best serve your magic.

Make Magic with Your Crystal

Working with crystals magically can appear to be far more complex than it actually is. From the maintenance (charging them under a particular moon phase or time of day or under rarer conditions such as eclipses) to the implementation (crystal grids, gem elixirs) to simply the collecting of crystals (how many is too many, and do you need all of them to be an effective witch?), it can feel like you're behind in a race you didn't know you were running. The reality of working with crystals is that magic performed with them typically falls into one of two categories: passive or active.

Passive crystal magic is like a radiator in a home. Radiators are put in a room and radiate heat, slowly but surely warming up the space. Crystals can be used in the same way. You can keep a piece of amethyst on your nightstand to aid in peaceful, dream-filled sleep. You can place a piece of onyx at your desk at work to deter those who don't have your best interests in mind. In these examples the crystal radiates its unique, respective energy to infuse your space. You can also make this effect mobile. Another term you'll hear in witchy circles is "pocket rocks," which quite literally refers to carrying crystals on your person. This could be in your pocket or a small bag around your neck. If you're someone who wears a bra, it's also common to put your "pocket rocks" in your bra either in a small bag or loose. (Be careful of doing this with anything other than smooth, polished stones. Ouch.) Jewelry is another easy way to carry crystals with you.

Active crystal magic may not look too different from passive crystal magic, but the effect is slightly different. If I continue my example of heating a room, an active crystal might be more like a heater with a fan that blows the warm air in a specific direction. If it is a very cold day and you're trying to warm yourself up, a direct stream of warm air is more likely to satisfy that need faster than radiant heat. In other words, you're directing the energy of the crystal to more accurately hone in on the issue you'd like it to influence. You can do this by verbalizing your intent out loud (example: "As I carry this carnelian with me, let me be filled with the confidence to perform well in my staff meeting today") or nonverbally (example: meditating with a crystal and visualizing its energy forming a protective cage around you).

Both styles of crystal magic are powerful and require a bit of trial and error. Try them both on and see what is effective for you. And remember: you don't need to break the bank to find crystals for your practice.

WHAT NOT TO DO WITH CRYSTALS

Magic is fun, but no matter how powerful a witch you are there are still ways of interacting with crystals that aren't advisable (at least not unless you're a geologist or medical researcher or some other type of expert). While I understand this makes me a bit of a downer, I'm including this information because I want you to practice safe hex and sometimes that means knowing when not to do something. Some of the points listed are to clarify misinformation that regularly makes its rounds online. People who are already in the know understand that these are jokes or not meant to be taken completely seriously, but we rarely say that explicitly. And, as I've said before, if we don't say it out loud and often, it leads some to believe that these aren't jokes and are, instead, meant to be taken as legitimate recommendations.

Don't Eat Rocks

Yes, you say. *Of course*, you say. *Who would ever?* you say. And yet here we are. Social media and wellness bloggers have made consuming crystals in some form or other a very trendy thing to do over and over again. How? Putting crystals in your water bottle, for example. Or telling you to literally add them to food as it cooks in a stewpot. While there are some water bottles that have vessels inside them keeping the rocks away from your drinking water, these bottles tend to be quite pricy and more affordable options are typically made of cheaper material that breaks down sooner. For those who can't afford any of these methods, some people literally just plop a few stones into their drinking water and call it an elixir.

While dietitians and geologists tend to get into long debates over whether any of these things are detrimental to your health, the crux of the matter comes down to the following: crystals—even polished ones—are able to break, which presents the possibility of either choking or swallowing a shard of something that could cause injury to your body on its journey through your gastrointestinal tract. In addition, some crystals are water-soluble, which means they break down when exposed to water. (It's worth reminding you that even if a crystal isn't water-soluble, that doesn't mean it can't interact with your stomach acid and cause deleterious effects.) Even more crystals are porous or have rough textures that make them difficult to clean properly before you stick them in your drinking water or food. Depending on the kind of crystal, like my earlier example of lepidolite, there may be chemicals released by the rock you shouldn't ingest without supervision or medical guidance.

WHAT SHOULD I DO INSTEAD?

The intention and energy of the crystal is what matters here, not the physical touching of rock to food. If you'd like to infuse your food or drink with crystal energy, hold the crystal of choice next to the water bottle or above your food for a few moments before eating. Visualize the energy of the crystal becoming a laser or cloud (or whatever image your brain conjures up) and coming out of the crystal and into the consumable cuisine. Enjoy!

Don't Have Sex with Rocks

Yes, we're going there. You've seen them. We've all seen them. The crystal phalluses that you've giggled at like you're a twelve-year-old who found a dirty magazine in a box behind your dad's tools in the garage. You've seen the jokes online and probably wondered, *Do . . . do people actually . . . you know?* The answer is yes, some people do put rocks in their genitals. Geologists, toxicologists, various types of surgeons, and more than a few Pagan scientists have weighed in on the matter over the years, but there is no more perfect example of why not to do it than the great malachite discussion of February 2020. (For pictures, do an internet search for "malachite phallus" and . . . well . . .) A user posted a stalactite made of malachite to Tumblr. Because it was phallic in shape, it led the internet to do what the internet does and ask if it could indeed be used as a sex toy. BuzzFeed's science reporter Dan Vergano said it was probably safe as long as you washed it thoroughly to remove any malachite particles or dust.

For weeks the internet thought you could, indeed, have sex with the malachite safely. However, a food science expert who goes by the name Sarah and the username badscienceshenanigans corrected the record when she reminded the internet that it is simply not enough to consider the crystal itself, but you also have to think about how it interacts with the body. She noted that malachite is soluble in water and that both lubricants produced by the human body and many store-bought lubricants are also mostly water. In addition, if you're a person with a vagina, you likely know that the vagina is fairly acidic and filled with salts. All of these things speed up the dissolution of malachite, thereby exposing you to copper, which is a big component of pesticides and of malachite. The potential copper exposure is enough, actually, to kill off the good bacteria and fungi that keep a person's vagina healthy and free of yeast or *E. coli*. Bottom line? Intersectional science is important. You cannot just consider the crystal but also must think about your body's chemistry and the way it will react to that particular crystal.

And as if that were not enough (and why wouldn't it be), using things that are not designed to be sex toys can lead to their own complications. Namely, as was said previously, breaking apart inside you. Crystals are not as flexible as sex toys and are far more rigid. Some are water-soluble, and all of them can break. Moreover, many of the crystals people mistake for sex toys are not designed to enter the human body and can, for lack of a better term, "get lost in there," leading you to need a very urgent trip to the emergency room for an extraction. All this to say, it's just not worth it. There are plenty of other ways to use crystals in sex magic.

WHAT SHOULD I DO INSTEAD?

If you'd like to use crystals in sex magic, you can use them in a number of ways. Bless them beforehand and have them nearby during the act, on a nightstand for example. You or your partner can touch them to the outside of your body while speaking your intent. You can also wear jewelry made with the crystal.

Don't Abandon Your Rocks

This goes back to knowing more about how your crystal was formed and its respective properties. Some examples: If you own certain types of opal, it can actually dry out. Therefore, you should keep it in a small jar filled with water. (Note: Some are sold that way.) Stones like amethyst and citrine should not be left out in direct sunlight—such as on a windowsill—as their colors can fade, leaving you, eventually, with a clear quartz. Some crystals degrade when exposed to higher levels of humidity and need to be kept in a box with a desiccant packet. One of those is pyrite, which definitely shouldn't be left out in a humid environment, as it can actually degrade and produce sulfuric acid in certain conditions. All that to say, knowing a bit more about the makeup of your crystal, not just how it looks or its magical use, is important.

WHAT SHOULD I DO INSTEAD?

Keep your stones in an environment that is suitable for them, which comes from learning the science behind your stones.

BUYING CRYSTALS

It's shiny. It's tiny. It's shaped like your favorite animal. It's on sale for $2. It's going straight on your shelf at home, right? Not so fast. Did you see a source for the crystal? If you're at the grocery store and you're purchasing food, there's typically a location of where the food was made and packaged somewhere on the label. If you want to, you can use that information to find out more about the company, their practices, whether their employees are paid a living wage, and a whole lot more. With crystals, they're normally sitting out loose on a shelf or in a basket next to a label telling you what the crystal is. It's easy to make a quick purchase of a crystal, especially if the price is right, but there are some factors you might wish to consider before doing so.

Journalist Emily Atkin wrote a phenomenal piece for the magazine *The New Republic* in May 2018 titled "Do You Know Where Your Healing Crystals Come From?" If you haven't read it, I highly encourage you to do so. In it she details how the rise of crystal use in metaphysical circles and, over the last few years, as a tool of various wellness trends has meant an increased demand for them. However, what most people don't realize is that the crystals we purchase might originate from massive industrial mining operations and are actually by-products of the mining company's primary endeavor—mining something like gold or copper. If the company hits a vein of, say, jasper, then they'll dig that out and sell it as well. These large companies will ship the raw crystals off to trade shows where other companies purchase the crystals, clean them up, and resell them. Sometimes this change of hands happens multiple times, so that by the time that crystal winds up on the shelf at your local witchy shop or grocery store or Etsy shop, the retailer might not actually be able to tell you where the crystal came from (and even if they can tell you which country it's from, it is less likely they can tell you which *mine* it came from, which is the important bit).

Atkin's article provides a number of examples where online stores and distributors list all sorts of crystals specifically as healing crystals or possessing metaphysical properties. The problem is that they are sourced from countries or specific mines belonging to businesses that have long histories of labor violations and environmental destruction. Children as young as seven years old have been found to be working in mines in the Democratic Republic of the Congo—where a lot of tourmaline, amethyst, citrine, and smoky quartz is sourced—while jade mines in Myanmar have been linked to an increase in heroin use and HIV infection by the Kachin miners. Furthermore, many industrial mines, including some here in the United States, contaminate surface and groundwater by adding billions of gallons of acid and metals into the environment per year during their extraction efforts.[1]

The problem for a consumer is that it can be difficult to determine whether you're purchasing an ethically sourced crystal or one that was dug out of the ground by an underpaid child in a foreign country. Atkin's article showcased a number of owners of large online retailers of healing crystals who said they know where every one of their crystals came from, but none would disclose the specific mines, factories, or tumblers that were used in sourcing their crystals. Shop owners can be quite protective of this information. Even if the shop owner is actually sourcing from a reputable mine/factory/tumbler, they're reticent to disclose the information as they fear that might drive up competition. (Why buy from them if you can go a little higher up the production chain and buy more directly, right?)

In any case, if you're practicing a spiritual path that involves connecting consciously with the world around you—and since you're reading this book, there's a good chance you are—being mindful of where the tools of your craft come from should be part of that journey. To that end I spoke to Kathleen Borealis, a geologist and geophysicist who hosts the Pagan podcast *Borealis Meditation*, wherein she explains both the metaphysical applications and natural science surrounding crystals. She had a load of helpful tips that might aid you in building a more ethically conscious crystal collection. Here are some of her dos and don'ts:

Don't purchase your crystals from large, faceless retailers. Purveyors might use language like "ethically sourced" or provide you the country of origin making you think they have ethically sourced their crystals, but unless they're disclosing more than a vague geographical location it's best to steer clear. Also, "ethically sourced" is sort of like the word "natural" appearing on food packaging. It doesn't actually mean anything, since it doesn't indicate a universally recognized standard of sourcing. Where in food production, words like "organic" do imply that the makers have met a given standard, there aren't any such terms in the crystal industry at this time.

Do buy from rock hounds and other local crystal sources. Rock hounds are amateur geologists and collectors who pick rocks themselves either from local mines or by knowing where to look in the natural environment.

You don't have to worry about a massive mining operation poisoning the water supply when you're literally talking to the person who dug your quartz up out of a mountain with their two hands and a pickaxe. Internet searches will help you find gem and mineral shows in your area (I've lived in extremely rural East Texas and even we had several gem and mineral shows come through every year) where you can meet rock hounds. Their booths are usually filled with pictures of them at their respective sources, proudly showing you where your crystal came from. Better yet, most states have mines or other areas where you can go and dig yourself, and often you're allowed to take home whatever you find for free or for very little money. The internet is also a great place to help you find a dig-it-yourself area. Take some friends and make a day of it! Getting to know what is available in your area will help you better understand the land you live on and boost your spiritual connection to it.

Don't be drawn in by perfect points or shaped stones. Crystals do not grow underground in the shape of a seahorse or a perfect circle or a pointed obelisk. To get crystals that are perfectly pointed or shaped in some way requires there to first be a very large block of that crystal. Very large blocks like that more often than not come from industrial mines. A seller who procured the crystal themselves or sourced it ethically, then shaped it using their own skills, will likely be up front about that information, and it is highly unlikely that such a shaped crystal would be found for cheap.

Do buy ugly rocks. Crystal clusters with a bit of dirt still in their crevices. Imperfect points. They're the same gem as the shiny ones, but they're typically far cheaper. If you want a piece of tourmaline for its metaphysical properties, there's no reason except vanity to shell out the big bucks for a beautifully shaped stone. Even if the seller is a rock hound and their stones aren't artificially shaped, the more visually appealing (i.e., symmetrical, pointed, lustrous, et cetera) stones are priced higher. If you have the money and you want to buy the pretty, sparkly stone, go for it. But, if you're on a budget, you can typically find a lovely sample to call your own for a fraction of the price.

Don't forget what is important to you about the crystal-buying process. For example: Are you wanting an amethyst because it's an amethyst? Do you find value in the crystal structure itself? Plenty of people who work with crystals magically believe that the unique respective structures belonging to each type of crystal are part of what make them an indispensable part of witchcraft. But perhaps the story of where the crystal came from is more important for you or you've found a new passion for crystals, and your joy is in building out a large and varied collection. Maybe you just want a few standbys that will serve you no matter what your needs are. Deeply consider *your* reason for purchasing that crystal and don't feel pressured in any one direction by social media.

Do consider lab-grown or synthetic crystals. One way of circumventing the harm of the mining industry is to purchase lab-grown or synthetic crystals. This solves a lot of problems. They're able to be procured in various shapes—like spheres, points, even animals—without destroying the environment to do so. They can be purchased online without needing to physically attend a gem or mineral show, which assists with accessibility. They are the same crystal structure as a crystal dug out of the ground, just made in a laboratory setting using the same methods used by nature (heat, pressure, combination of specific minerals or elements, et cetera). These can also present a more economical alternative to higher-end crystals.

If you'd like to start your own crystal collection, Kathleen had one last tip about that, too. She recommended the following starter set: magnetite, pyrite, and clear quartz. Magnetite is associated with attraction. Pyrite is an iron sulfide mineral also called fool's gold and, because it mimics gold, is associated with prosperity. (Remember to be watchful if you live in an especially humid area.) Clear quartz is, according to just about any book you'll find on crystal magic, good for just about everything else. Typically when performing magic, you're seeking to attract something to you or boost your prosperity in some form or fashion, and the first two stones accomplish that. For everything else, clear quartz is your friend. It also could very well be found in your own backyard (no I'm not kidding) or somewhere within driving distance. It is one of the most abundant minerals on the planet and can be found ethically and cheaply.

Plants

If you're not a crystal goblin, chances are you're a plant parent. Sorry, I don't make the rules. If you salivate over bundles of herbs drying in sun-dappled windows or filling every inch of your room with verdant new leafy friends, you're probably in the latter category. Plants have been part of myth and folklore and magic since time immemorial.

Odysseus protected himself against Circe with a magical herb gifted to him by the messenger god Hermes. Shakespeare's famous Weird Sisters from *Macbeth* kick off the play by crafting a magical brew that included "wool of bat" and "toe of frog," which are alternative names for holly leaves and buttercups, respectively. Rapunzel's magic hair came from a flower in the Disney movie *Tangled* and plenty of other movie plots revolve around obtaining some special herb or plant to complete a mystical concoction. Plant magic is everywhere, and it is one of the big reasons why so many witches can't pass up an opportunity to buy jars in bulk. Seriously, every witch (myself included) dreams of hearing about some malady that has befallen a friend and going to their wall of jars to select the perfect ingredients for a curative potion.

Plant magic, like other forms of magic derived from the natural world, might appear to be complex at first. The endless lists of correspondences and methods of procurement and trying to figure out whether that grimoire you're reading from literally means tongue of dog or it's simply referring to a flower can be confusing. Let's simplify it.

THE MECHANICS OF PLANT MAGIC

The magic of plants can be broken down into two basic types just like crystals: passive and active. Passive plant magic is basically any time you're putting a plant into a setting to infuse that setting with an energy the plant possesses. One example of this from pop culture is found in the book and movie *Practical Magic*, wherein the character Sally Owens advises us to "keep rosemary by your garden gate; plant lavender for luck." Keeping a certain plant associated with love, luck, prosperity, protection, et cetera, can act as (to use my earlier example) a radiator continually putting out that energy. This can work whether the plant is alive or freshly cut or dried. Cut plants can be bound and hung as a charm or worn in small bags—called sachets—around your neck or kept under a pillow, in a drawer, your car, et cetera.

Active plant magic is charging a plant, or combination of plants, with a specific intent and then incorporating them into a spell to accomplish that intent. Similar to crystals, this can take the form of placing the plant in some form around your home, workspace, or keeping it on your person. Maybe an herb is dried and placed in a sachet to keep around your neck or in your purse, and you can even incorporate the plant into a candle or oil that is then used to accomplish a specific purpose.

Plant magic at its core can be quite simple, but, naturally, there are some key things one should know before beginning. Once again, as with crystal magic, this list should serve as the basis for your own research and does not represent the end-all, be-all of plant magic use or knowledge. However, I hope it assists with filling in some of the gaps as you're researching plant magic and aids in providing context as you continue your path.

WHAT TO DO WITH PLANTS

So, you maxed out a credit card at the garden store and brought home all the herbs, vegetables, succulents, and other plants you could fit into your home. They've been drying in bundles in your window or growing in your garden, but what do you actually do with all these plants magically? Do you cook with them? Make them into perfume? Crush them up and blow them in someone's face when you need a fast getaway? Yes, yes, and only if you really want to start a fight. Making magic with plants can be simple and inexpensive (even free!) if you follow these tips.

Harvest What Grows in Your Area

Both the internet and your local library will have loads of free resources about what kind of plants grow not only in your state but right down to your county. Witches, historically, used what they had on hand and made connections with the land around them. An economical way to perform plant magic is to simply learn what grows in your area and then work with it directly. You might find that you can source various magical herbs, roots, and other plants safely and for free simply by taking a walk in the woods behind your house or taking a stroll through a local park.

Grow What Is Native to Your Area

It doesn't take much more than a windowsill and at least a little light to start growing plants for use in magic. If you grow from seed and use up-cycled containers (or, if you have the outdoor space, in the ground), the up-front cost can be pennies per plant. Growing your own plants provides a unique and personal connection that some witches find quite powerful. Many witches revere the natural cycles of the earth, and witnessing the life cycle of local plants is one way of attuning with that energy. It also is a good reminder—from a magical, practical, and economical sense—that all things have a season and that you can make whatever magic you need to make out of whatever is available.

Make Magic with Living Plants

You can perform both passive *and* active magic with a living plant. Plenty of witches I know have brought certain plants into their homes or work-spaces for active magic, either to protect against a certain person or to aid in some other endeavor. You can easily tie a ritual to the care and mainte-nance of a plant, with your watering and fertilizing acting as feeding the spell and the flourishing of the plant powering your intent. You can even get really granular (literally) with it and infuse the soil with your intent either nonverbally, verbally, or by writing down your intent on a piece of paper or an eggshell and putting it in the soil before you add the plant. Plants don't have to be exotic or difficult to care for if you don't have the time or resources to do so. As always, make the magic personal. Choose a plant you like and can care for. I keep succulents for this reason, and they're great! In addition, choosing a plant that can grow in your climate will help ensure you can keep your magic going longer if you need.

Make Magic with Dried Plants

They're everywhere: the little plastic packets or bottles of dried herbs, flowers, roots, leaves, et cetera. They're in witchy shops and grocery stores alike, and you can make plenty of magic with them. Making magic with dried plants allows you the flexibility of choosing plants that either don't grow in your area or possess a specific property you wish to add to your magic. Getting plants from a local witchy shop usually means the plant will be packaged with its name and metaphysical properties on it, which can be helpful when selecting plants for a spell. Of course, there's nothing stopping you from buying what you need at a grocery store if that's more accessible or affordable for you. There is nothing inherently more magical about the rosemary you found at a witchy store than the rosemary you got in the spice aisle.

Consume Plants (with Caution)

I would be remiss if I did not acknowledge that you can, in fact, eat plants. Lots and lots and lots of books of magic include plenty of recipes meant to be eaten, as do goodness knows how many fairy tales and myths. Love spells baked into apple pies. Pea soup made to increase your prosperity. And, of course, we cannot forget the infinite combinations of foods prepared on New Year's Day to ensorcell your New Year with luck, money, love, et cetera. Some witches also turn plants into oils that are used to anoint candles or (depending on the kind of oil) added to foods. And, of course, plenty of self-care products such as bath salts and lotions are made from these oils. All of these are ways you can interact with plant magic. **However** . . .

WHAT NOT TO DO WITH PLANTS

Don't Consume Plants without Researching Them

Not all plants are safe for use in all forms or by all people. Just because it was made by a witch under the light of a full moon in a sacred ritual doesn't mean it cannot harm you. Many plants that are included in recipes, self-care products such as lotions or bath salts, and oil blends might have a deleterious effect on you in some way. If you are unfamiliar with a plant or unfamiliar with how it's being used or prepared, spend some time researching it. Ask your healthcare provider or a local pharmacist to see if it might be something you could be allergic to or has known side effects.

One classic example in witchy circles is mugwort. Mugwort is said to have all sorts of magical properties, and some practitioners do, indeed, use it in teas, bath salts, et cetera. However, mugwort can also be harmful to use if you are a person with a vagina and is not recommended by doctors if you are pregnant. Mugwort can cause the uterus to contract or begin menstruation, which can lead to miscarriage. Some users have reported that use of mugwort has altered their period cycle or caused them to bleed more than normal, and very high dosages consumed orally are associated with causing mania. In addition, mugwort can set off a number of allergic reactions in some people.

When you ask makers of products that include plants like mugwort, or any other plant that is associated with witchcraft but not typically found in your grocery store as a commonly consumed food, you might be told that there is not enough of the plant in the bath salt or lotion or tea blend, et cetera, to cause a problem. Unfortunately, unless that person is your doctor, they aren't the best source for this information. Recommended dosage depends on a number of factors such as height, weight, age, and medical history. The ethical creator will be up front about any possible side effects of their products and will usually list them right there on the website.

It is inadvisable to consume the plants that you get from a metaphysical supplier, especially if they're bagged and labeled with the shop's own packaging. Plants that are packaged and sold to grocery stores and other retailers must meet certain standards for health and safety. These same standards do not apply if something is sold for a metaphysical use. While it might not be true of every shop, it is common that plants arrive in large packages from a supplier that might not provide food-grade plants. They are then divvied up into smaller containers for resale, sometimes with a shared scoop or an employee's hands. Suffice to say, the methods are not uniform, nor do they meet a rigorous safety standard. If you didn't get it from a grocery store or grow it yourself (after verifying it is a consumable plant), don't eat it.

JUST BECAUSE IT'S "NATURAL" . . .

Plenty of witches get hung up on the idea of something being "natural" and therefore safe to consume. If it came from the earth, it's "natural" and somehow immune from causing harm. Obviously, this is false. Plenty of things are natural that are not advisable to consume. Asbestos is natural. Lead is natural. Arsenic is natural. All of these things are created naturally without human intervention, and all of them can cause serious harm or death. Treat the natural world with respect, do your research, trust science, and consume consciously.

Don't Use Every Single Plant

Everyone, myself included, has at one time or another seen a package of some dried, crushed plant with an obscure name and list of properties that perfectly matched a spell they wanted to perform and purchased it. I've bought devil's shoestring, slippery elm, and more because of the unique name and property associated. But . . . then I had a plant I wasn't going to use except for that one time. Sure, you sprinkle a bit of slippery elm into a sachet and tie a knot to stop some gossip, but then what do you do with the rest of the bag? There are plants that serve a dual purpose: bay leaves, basil, garlic, et cetera. But there might also be plants you solely buy for magical use. That's fine, but think critically about purchasing a plant that is only serving one use in your home. How often do you plan on using it? Are you buying this for an ongoing spell lasting days, weeks, months? Or are you buying it for a onetime use and keeping the extra for when you want it down the road?

Don't Keep It Forever

Remember that, unlike crystals, plants have a shelf life. They die and decay and eventually all you have in that jar is dust with an interesting name. We all want to be that witch with a wall of jars, but it's doing no good having dozens of different plant samples if they're not being used. This goes for oils, bath salts (especially if they contain oils or plants), lotions, and anything else with an expiration date. They have an expiration date for a reason. Oils can go rancid, the plants decay, et cetera. The energy the plant once held has been returned to the universe to be recycled and used anew. Consider dual-purpose plants or products when possible, as you're less likely to waste them.

Don't Harvest Wherever You Please or However You Want

Before wandering off to harvest a plant growing naturally in your area, please ensure you are researching the rules around doing so first. Some preserves ask that you not remove any living plants. Some plants have limits on the amount you're allowed to harvest or the time of year you're allowed to do so. If you only need part of a plant, such as flowers, a few leaves, or even a small limb, research the mechanics of harvesting that plant specifically. Some plants might need to have certain parts harvested in specific ways in order to keep the plant alive. Hacking off parts of a plant without knowing how or where to cut, or using the wrong tool, can kill the plant, which affects the environment around it.

I've discussed it before, but one of the many problems with the use of white sage is that many people and companies who harvest it—even when doing so in the wild—destroy the plant in the process, making it more scarce for Native people who need it for religious and personal use. If it's a plant that feeds other life, killing it reduces that animal's food supply, which impacts the surrounding area in all sorts of ways.

Don't Get Bogged Down in Correspondences

I know I have said this quite a lot in this book, but an effective practitioner is nothing if not resourceful and creative. Is the plant the book says you need difficult or pricey to obtain? Get creative. Think about what you're trying to do and let that inform what plant you use. Think about what is accessible to you *right now*.

For example: Are you dealing with a lot of lies or gossip? While there are some plants associated with gossip, they might require a trip to a specialty store to obtain. You know what you might have nearby? Dandelions. Dandelions have long been used as a wishing plant, but who's to stop you from using them to represent a gossiping person? Think about the ways gossip spreads, like dandelions flying off through the air in patterns both predictable and unpredictable, coming to rest in all sorts of places. Just like lies and gossip. Want to stop gossip? Put a dandelion in a jar of water and freeze it.

Plant magic can be an enriching addition to your spiritual practice but, like most areas of witchcraft, requires a bit of consideration before diving in. Don't worry, though; with a bit of research and common sense you'll soon be the greenest of green witches and the natural world will be your apothecary.

Other Nature Magic

There are, of course, more wonders of the natural world than just crystals and plants. Calling on the elements and certain forces of nature is a common and helpful magical tool. As you explore what works for you, here are a few quick tips for working with other types of magic derived from the natural world. I will provide further resources at the back of the book that teach you to employ these types of magic. Here my goal is simply to say the quiet part out loud and provide some safety reminders and context for safely interacting with these types of magic.

WATER MAGIC

The use of water in magic is everywhere. It is used often, because it has three forms that are easily seen and modified by people using equipment we have readily available. Because of this, it can be a powerful tool of witchcraft all on its own. Peering into water can be an act of divination; boiling it can assist with causing rain; infusing it can take your crystal or plant magic to new levels.

You might see a spell somewhere in the world that requires the collection of rainwater, snow, icicles, pond water, et cetera. Moon water, water that sat beneath the light of the moon, is quite trendy and plenty magical, but even that should be treated with caution if the water came from a natural source or if you left it outside in an open container. Be cautious before consuming this water and do a quick internet search about the type of water you're planning to drink. Some water, like spring water, might be naturally filtered and advisable for consumption. Other types of water, like icicles found on the edge of a roof or water from a still pond, are not.

Here in Chicago it's pretty common to make snow cream, ice cream made from snow. However, it's not advisable to consume anything except lily-white snow. If the snow is close to the ground, by a roadway, or any color other than pure white, it's not advised to consume it directly. Consider boiling and/or filtering the water first, or simply use it outwardly to wash your hands. Bathing in certain types of unfiltered/untreated water might also be a problem, as you are exposing sensitive areas to water that could cause infection.

FIRE MAGIC

Fire is a powerful force (and, if it wasn't obvious, a personal favorite of mine) that provides heat, cooks food, and transforms objects from one thing to another—like wood into charcoal. People use fire magic to rid themselves of unwanted things (remember my example in the introduction of burning your ex's stuff?), sparking passion, or even foretelling the future by burning certain woods or plants and looking for symbols in the fire and smoke. Whatever use you're employing, it's important to keep a few key things in mind when dealing with fire.

Whether you're lighting a candle for protection or lighting a bonfire at Samhain, being a witch doesn't stop that fire from causing harm if not treated with care. I realize I sound like a bit of a Boy Scout here, but if you take steps to practice good fire safety beforehand you can enjoy dancing around a fire under the stars chanting and laughing to your heart's content. Blow out your candles if you're leaving your home and nobody else will be there to monitor them. Yes, even that candle that's doing that very important witchy thing. Even that candle. That candle might burn your house down, and it's hard to practice witchcraft when you're running around trying to put a fire out. As you can tell from my chosen craft name, I love a good fire spell, but I'm also the first to dump sand and stomp the fire out at the end of a ritual.

STORM MAGIC

At this point I feel like I'm your concerned dad spouting off last-minute safety tips before you go to your first sleepaway camp, but here we are. Lots and lots of magic can be done during a storm. I have yet to meet a witch who doesn't love the boost of energy felt in the air when the wind is howling and lightning is flashing in the distance. The air is literally crackling with energy, and magical practitioners can use that time to boost the effectiveness of whatever spell they're working by using the extra energy as a kind of jump start on a car.

That said, please do not go wandering off into a storm intentionally to perform your ritual. Getting struck by lightning isn't a badge of honor,

nor are the wet conditions or possible tornado worth it. Instead, consider setting out a bucket to collect the storm water if you wish to use it for magic, and if lightning struck somewhere you can collect a bit of the struck wood or dirt from the struck ground.

Pro Tip: If Reese Witherspoon in *Sweet Home Alabama* taught me anything it's that you can collect some pretty sweet natural glass if you can find a spot where lightning struck sand.

Tuning in to the natural world around us is part and parcel of being a witch. Be conscious. Do your research. Take only what you need. Make sensible substitutions. Before you know it, you'll be the crystal goblin / plant parent you've always dreamt of being.

CHAPTER 14

MODERN MAGICAL TOOLS

The bubbling cauldron. The flying broomstick. The lit candle. The book of spells. These are more than the makings of a really fun Friday night: They're part of the iconography of the witch. No matter how cheesy the TV show or movie is, if it's about witches it typically includes some version of each of these. The classical tools of the witch, however, aren't really practical for most of us, nor are they always necessary. They were practical for people a few hundred years ago, though.

The cauldron was simply what was in the hearths of many homes to prepare food for the family. The broom was for cleaning. Candles warded away the night. Books, if you were lucky enough to afford them and were literate, kept family records, recipes for food and healing, prayers, et cetera. We place mystical qualities on them because they've entered into the zeitgeist of history and myth, but do not fret for one moment about trying to find room for a giant cast-iron cauldron in your studio apartment.

Social media can make you believe that to perform effective spell craft one must own a bejeweled knife and a three-footed cauldron and a wand wrapped in silver wire with crystals and pewter symbols attached. That's simply not the case. The modern witch is a resourceful witch who has all sorts of ways to make effective, ethical, cost-effective magic using items and appliances that are either already in their home or able to be purchased on the cheap.

Note: If you wish to buy something you don't currently have, you do not need to buy it brand-new. Thrift stores, charity shops, antique stores, garage sales, and online marketplaces are phenomenally inexpensive places to get everything you need to cast all sorts of spells. In addition, don't be afraid of purchasing items from those dollar stores where everything is literally $1. Magic will be made whether your candle cost $45 for a single blessed beeswax pillar rolled in sacred herbs, anointed with oil, and filled with crystals or $1 for a pack of ten at Dollar Tree.

It's all about figuring out what you need the item for, how often you'll be using it for witchy purposes, and whether you wish to buy something solely for magical use or to serve a dual purpose in your home. If you plan on using your witchy wares for both mundane and magical use, a very thorough cleaning should be done when switching uses. You don't want to pick belladonna out of your teeth when you thought you were making potato soup.

The Modern Cauldron

At times the cauldron has been used in story to brew up all sorts of magical potions. Other times it is a tool of divination. It has been associated with transformation, summoning, and even raising the dead. While we imagine great iron or copper vessels bubbling over the hearth, the truth is that you can use anything from a cereal bowl to a potpourri pot to do the same thing. (Except, you know, for the raising the dead bit.)

When most people think of cauldrons, they think of potion making. This can be brews, stews, and other magical concoctions meant to infuse a physical substance with magic that can be used by yourself or someone else to achieve a desired effect. Common uses for a modern cauldron range from literally cooking food to peering into a pool of water to look for signs to setting something on fire safely. When choosing a modern cauldron for magical recipes, you have to ask yourself one question: Are you eating it, bottling it, or burning it?

EDIBLE BREWS

Sometimes known as potions, brews are any concoctions you create for a magical purpose that you plan on consuming. If you plan on making something edible, drinkable, or in one way or another going to enter your body, here are some food-safe, modern options you can source in a store near you:

★

Cast-Iron Dutch Oven—this is perhaps the most direct cognate of the classical cauldron. It's cast iron, which means, with care, it might easily become an heirloom passed down to a new generation. It is food safe. It can be used on the stove, in the oven, carried out into the woods for use on a campfire, or used just as a large bowl. And, double-plus bonus, it can be used for other types of cauldron magic such as divination or as a brazier.

- **Pros:** Comes in a variety of sizes. Food safe and capable of lasting a lifetime. Serves a dual purpose in your home. Can be found in most stores that sell homewares.
- **Cons:** This is one of the more expensive options in this chapter. Unless you're getting a very small Dutch oven, the starting price is around $40–$50, and name-brand, enamel-coated versions can cost hundreds of dollars. (Though, in my humble opinion, the cheaper stuff is no less durable or useful and is what I own.)

Work-around: Buy thrifted, secondhand, or rummage around a relative's home to see if they have any that are unwanted. Chances are, you'll come across one. Even if you find one that has completely gone to rust, true cast-iron cookware can come back to being completely food safe and usable with some elbow grease and patience. Search the internet for how-to videos on cast-iron rejuvenation.

Glass Cookware—if you have a large Pyrex glass mixing bowl, you have a cauldron. There are a number of brands of stovetop-safe glass bowls and Dutch ovens. Some people prefer glass because it can be thrown in a dishwasher, doesn't carry tastes over from one dish to the next, and gosh, it looks pretty to see your magical brew bubbling from all angles.

- **Pros:** Functionally similar to a cast-iron Dutch oven (as long as you check that it is both oven and stove safe). Large size and color range. Dishwasher safe. The price range is a bit less than cast iron, too.
- **Cons:** Not as durable as cast iron. One good drop and you're picking slivers of glass out of your food. You're also not as likely to take it with you to cook over a campfire.

Coffeepot—oh boy, howdy, are you going to love making magic with a coffeepot. Granted, you're probably not going to make big food-based magical concoctions with it, but if you're making a witchy tea blend or a potion that you're planning to stick in a spray bottle, the coffeepot is an affordable and easy modern cauldron. Pop in a filter, load with your loose plants (herbs, flowers, et cetera), fill the water vessel, and push a button. If an electric version isn't your speed, buying a French press or stovetop teapot with a basket is another way to brew up some magic on a budget.

- **Pros:** Most parts are dishwasher safe, and if you're using plants that you don't want to mix with your food you can use a disposable filter. You do not have to spend very much money on an electric coffeemaker if you buy new, and you can spend even less if you buy a nonelectric version. They come in all sorts of shapes and sizes to match your magical aesthetic.
- **Cons:** This is where you start getting into items with fewer uses. Yes, it can make a brew, but it's not a one-size-fits-all item. You might still need to pull out a cooking pot for a witchy stew once in a while. From

a food-safety perspective, it should be remembered that this should be used for food-safe plants only. Toxins from harmful plants can seep into the plastic of a coffeemaker. Also, while it's cheaper up front, that can mean you're buying a new one more often.

Crock-Pot—between the electric coffeepot and the Dutch oven lies the favorite of midwestern football wives everywhere: the Crock-Pot. You dump your ingredients into it, turn it on, and come back to it later. There are a lot of sizes and price points, and it can be used for brews, soups, stews, et cetera.

- **Pros:** Another mostly universal tool with the added bonus that many of them can be cleaned in a dishwasher. Flexible price point means that if you are on a budget you can pick one up starting around $15.
- **Cons:** If you need to make magic fast, this is not the tool for you. It's also not as portable as other options.

INEDIBLE BREWS AND BOTTLED POTIONS

If you plan on making something that is not meant to be eaten (room spray, hand wash, anointing oil, et cetera), the options open up a bit. Of course, you could always procure any of the preceding options and keep it solely for baneful or poisonous plants, but how many people have "two Dutch ovens" money or space these days?

☆

Mason Jars—while traditional canning jars are ideal, any glass jar with a tight lid can serve. If you're from the southern United States you've probably heard about or made "sun tea," which is when you stick a bunch of tea bags in a jar or pitcher of water to brew tea by leaving it out in the sun all day. You can do the same thing to make a witchy brew. Stick your herbs, leaves, roots, et cetera, in a jar of water and place in a very sunny window or outside in direct sunlight. I didn't put this in the "edible" section earlier because food scientists are pretty iffy about drinking sun tea, since the water isn't boiled (and is sealed and kept in a warm environment), it can be a great place for bacteria to proliferate. But for non-eating magical purposes? Gosh, it's a great way to make a brew, plus it soaks up all that lovely solar energy. For an added energetic boost, you can leave it out for a whole day to brew and leave it out at night to be blessed by the light of the moon.

- **Pros:** Cheap, accessible, easy to use, and portable.
- **Cons:** Breakable, small, and takes a while to steep. If you're on a time crunch, this might not be the best method.

Oil and Wax Burners—these come in a variety of types, nonelectric and electric. You might see these as simple vessels for the wax or essential oil on top with a place for a tea light on the bottom. Other common varieties include those that use a lightbulb or hot plate for the heating source. If you are only needing a small amount of brew or you're wishing to make an oil blend quickly, you can consider using one of these. They're typically found for under $10, with the tea light type costing far less. These could be used to cleanse or recharge a room or to make a small amount of brew or oil to place in a bottle for later use.

If you want to make an oil, start with a neutral base oil with a high smoke point (such as avocado oil) and add in the other plant materials. Let it slowly diffuse over several hours (at least . . . depending on the plants and oil you could let it steep for longer), strain, and bottle. The oil can be used to anoint candles, magical tools, et cetera. You can, of course, use a combination of unscented wax (like beeswax) with essential oils and plants to create a wax for later magical use.

- **Pros:** Cheap, accessible, easy to use, and portable. You can find nonelectric options.
- **Cons:** Results in very small amounts of brew, oil, or wax, but if it's for personal use that doesn't tend to

be a problem. If you choose the type of burner that uses a tea light or other flame resource, I would not recommend burning an oil over it as it can catch fire.

Work-around: Use flame-based warmers to create brews or waxes. Start with a little water; add a few drops of oil as well as your plant matter (ensuring the plant matter is small enough to be submerged by the water so it doesn't hang over the edge and catch fire).

Potpourri Pots—while these have gone out of style in recent years, you can still find them in a lot of stores. They are small electric pots that resemble a Crock-Pot and are used to keep potpourri warm. Since they're already made to house a blend of scented liquid and plants, they're perfect for making up small batches of brews you don't plan on eating. Plus, they're small enough that they can be tucked away in a cabinet or larger drawer without taking up much space. Some of them even have a lid!

- **Pros:** Fairly inexpensive, easy to use, already made to house nonedible plants and liquids. No open flame!
- **Cons:** Not as portable because they're electric. And, again, small batches.

THE BURNING POT AND DIVINING BOWL

There remain two uses for a cauldron that do not require an electric cord or cooking capability. One is as a brazier, which is a fancy term for a bowl in which you burn things. You can light a fire to throw either written messages or representations of feelings or relationships from which you'd like to free yourself. This could be any firesafe bowl, meaning a bowl that doesn't break when it gets too hot, thereby letting the fire spill out. The other is as a divining bowl. In this, you fill the bowl with water and gaze into it in a meditative state in order to divine the future by letting your vision go soft and seeing what symbols or scenes come to mind. Alternatively, you could melt a candle and let the wax drip into the water and divine any symbols you see. (Really, there are a lot of uses for a bowl of water. I'll put some good books on the subject in the "Resources" section at the back of this book for you to explore the topic and practice in depth.)

★

Decorative Cauldrons—right around Halloween, lots and lots of stores start getting decorative cauldrons. Sometimes they're ceramic, but other times they're made of non–food grade metal. I've purchased both. Because these are typically painted or otherwise coated in something that I might not want flaking off into a brew, I don't recommend using them for edible or bottled potions, but they're perfect to serve as a brazier or divining bowl. I have a few of these, but my favorite is a decently sized metal one that came from HomeGoods a couple of years ago that I bought for less than $10 and have used for both purposes.

- **Pros:** All sorts of styles and sizes and prices.
- **Cons:** If you're short on storage, it's an extra tool you might not need.

Pottery Planters—most pottery can withstand a good bit of heat. Depending on your use, you might choose one with a drainage hole in the bottom, which helps the fire burn faster and better. You can get these in a number of sizes, from a teeny-tiny pot smaller than a tennis ball to a giant, ornate planter. Choose your price and needs.

- **Pros:** These are *everywhere* and you can often find them for free in an online marketplace where someone is giving them away to make extra room around spring or fall. You can decorate them with painted symbols or images that match your spiritual path or intentions.
- **Cons:** Once again, it's one more thing to store. If it has a hole it serves less of a use, but it burns better.

You can get creative when it comes to mixing up witchy potions or foretelling the future. I am someone who doesn't like a lot of clutter, and so anything that can serve dual magical and mundane purposes in my home is wonderful. If you're going to use plants that are not advised to be ingested, I would recommend getting a separate appliance and brewing method so there's little chance of crossover and accidental poisoning. Also, once again, don't make a big fire in your house. Go outside to an area where you will not catch other things on fire accidentally and do your witching there.

The Modern Broom

Brooms and witches go together like peanut butter and chocolate, like frogs and ponds, like philosophy majors and being a barista in a coffee shop. Brooms are not only useful for keeping your floors clean but also relied upon to sweep out negative energy, bring in prosperity, protect against nasty spirits, summon rain, and even foretell a surprise visitor's arrival. Brooms are practical as well as magical, but these days a lot of people have other types of flooring that aren't cleaned easily with a broom. Thus, we have dual-purpose cleaning wands that mop and sweep at the same time and robots that tidy your floors on a daily schedule and all sorts of other contraptions for cleaning. While the good old broom will never truly be replaced, if you don't need a full-size broom in your house or don't want to purchase one purely for magical purposes, you can get by just fine with these!

★

Vacuum Cleaners—not only can these bad boys clean whatever type of floor you have, but they can be used to magically get rid of negative energy as well! Here's how I do it: I choose a dried plant that I associate with cleansing and add it to a bit of baking soda. Then I sprinkle the mixture lightly on my carpet or floor while speaking my intent. I vacuum it up and toss it out! Literally, take it out of my house. You don't want to leave all that piled-up negativity sitting in your trash can. I often use basil for this, because it's said that wherever basil is scattered no evil can remain.

- **Pros:** You probably already have one! You can even clean the air with it. No, seriously, a lot of vacuums have air filtration settings (or you can just take the wand out of the holster and wave it around in the air).
- **Cons:** If you don't have one, this is an expensive and likely unnecessary option.

Spray Mops—these handy things have become not only popular but also affordable in recent years. They're a combination of a washable microfiber pad and a spray bottle that sprays a solution onto your floors for easy mopping. These are primarily used by people who don't have carpet, so if most of your home has a hard surface flooring type this could be a fun and witchy way to use it. Best part? You can fill the solution vessel with your own witchy concoction.

- **Pros:** These can be relatively inexpensive. I purchased mine for around $15, and it can serve a dual purpose as a sweeper and mop. Plus, the microfiber pad is reusable after a wash. Because you're using a sprayer, you control how much goes on the floor. No accidental puddles!
- **Cons:** If you already have a broom and mop, buying another cleaning tool is something extra. Judge what you need based off your budget, space allowance, and home.

Try This: 2 cups water, ½ cup white vinegar, ¼ cup rubbing alcohol. Add 5–10 drops of essential oil of your choice, or infuse the water with plant essence beforehand with cleansing plants of your choice. Fill the vessel and off you go!

The Modern Grimoire

No witch is complete without that hefty book of spells bound in leather and filled with pages stained with leftover remnants of that time your banishing brew had a little too much "toil and trouble" after the double double. I have had a lot of different books of spells in my witchy life. In high school I got this small, glittery journal that I wrote some really interesting spells in. Later on I had multiple different versions of journals and notebooks and finally I got my giant, leather-bound grimoire. It's beautiful. It's an heirloom-quality piece. And, I'll be honest, I have to force myself to use it. I'm a busy person! Writing for me—whether it's spiritual, poetry, or fiction—happens in a spurt of inspiration while I'm on the train, at work, or on the couch at a friend's house, and you know what I don't usually have handy? My one-thousand-page leather-bound grimoire.

I've tried a bunch of different tools over the years, and any of these may work well for you as a place to keep your witchy workings.

★

Notes App/Cloud-Based Document—if you have a smartphone there is a very good chance that you already have a notes app that came as part of the standard operating system. Whether you're on your computer or using your phone, you can likely access a cloud-based document, such as a Google Doc or Airtable, too. If you don't like it, there are a massive number of apps available for free—some that are tailored as spiritual journals.

- **Pros:** They're free, always in your pocket, and often cloud based, which means you can access it from anywhere on earth with an internet connection. You can print off the pages later if you want to kick-start a physical book. Plus, you can organize and reorganize to your heart's content. Also, it's easy to share with a friend.
- **Cons:** It is intangible, so if your battery dies or you're somewhere that using an electronic device is infeasible, you'd better hope you have a good memory. Also, I get it. There's something about a physical book you can't replace.

Three-Ring Binder—now, there are a lot of ways of using this. You can buy a cheap plastic binder and put printouts, handwritten musings, spells, recipes, et cetera, in it. Or you can get really creative! You can turn a cheap plastic binder into a beautiful statement piece using scissors, hot glue, fabric, and cotton batting. Cut the batting so that it covers the outside and inside flaps. Glue it down. Cut the fabric of your choice so that it covers the batting; fold and glue it down over the batting inside and out. My first time doing this I ended up cutting two extra panels and gluing them on the inside flaps to cover my poor folding. I also bought sheet protectors so that my pages had a bit more heft to them and could survive humidity, splashes, et cetera. That actually served me for years, and what I love about a three-ring binder is that you can move it around so easily and insert page dividers to create sections. You can also buy books made to be grimoires with beautiful, ornate covers that are post bound, so they function similar to a three-ring binder with the slight added hassle that you have to unscrew the posts first.

- **Pros:** Very inexpensive if you don't already have some floating around your house. Honestly, check around your place of work. Most workplaces and schools have an overabundance of these and would likely be willing to let you have one for free.
- **Cons:** Flimsy? I guess? I don't have many qualms with the three-ring binder method. If you don't choose to dress it up, it can look a bit dull, but who said your magical tools had to look a certain way? Certainly not this guy.

Get creative! Anything you can use to take notes—a journal, an old recipe box—can be used to organize your witchy information. The most interesting way I've ever seen is a Rolodex. I'm not going to lie, I've often thought a witchy Rolodex would be an incredibly fun and compact way to organize your magical knowledge.

From Mundane to Magic and Back Again

The witches of old used the tools of their home and hearth to make the magic they needed. There is no fundamental difference between them and you, except you have a smartphone and access to many more options than they did thanks to internet shopping. The point of this chapter is to get you out of your own head when it comes to wanting to decorate your space with the tools of witchcraft.

Social media and pop culture have led many new seekers to believe that magic is done with shelves upon shelves of bottled herbs with funny names and sacred blades and mirrors kept beneath dark cloths. This is exacerbated by the fact that so many creators and shop owners sell outrageously overpriced tools that either are from an overseas drop-ship site or are something cheap with a crystal hot-glued onto it whose obscene markup is often attributed to some blessing bestowed upon the item or possibly its association with a certain deity or even the shop owner themselves. There are some incredible smiths and glass artists and jewelers and woodworkers and painters and makers of all types in our community, and they should absolutely be paid what they're worth for making handmade goods. Those pieces have their place, and they might be something you want down the road, but they are not necessary.

You don't need any of those tools to make magic. Besides, so many of the things you see might not end up being applicable to your practice. Your magic might end up mostly being done in the kitchen with your spice rack or you might make sigils with ink and paper or you might make magic with your sewing kit.

You may not need a sacred blade. I've owned three and they pretty much all sat in a drawer, because I ended up using scissors or a kitchen knife to do what I needed to do instead. I get it, though. This is new, and like anything new you want to get all the accessories. That's fine. It's encouraged. Anything to keep you excited and learning more. However, remember, a wand is just a stick. A cauldron is just a cooking pot. A grimoire is just a diary.

The truth is absolutely everything can be a tool for magic. Anything can be a part of ritual. You are the magic, and you don't need anything beyond yourself to work wonders.

PART

5

SPELL
CANVASES

Remember back in chapter 12 when I talked about the different types of magic? Well, I have always found sympathetic magic to be the easiest and most useful introduction into performing effective spell craft, because it gives me something visual and/or tactile to focus on that helps get me into the right headspace. That is the type of magic I'll be using in the following pages.

So, no, you're not going to find spells labeled "Love Spell" or "To Manifest a New Job" in this part of the book. Instead, I'm providing what I call spell canvases. These are rituals that I've adapted for a magical purpose, but what that purpose is will be left up to you. I will present the ritual and then, on the following pages, provide a list of possible ways to use it as a spell. I invite you to take any of them, none of them, or freely adapt them for a new purpose. Use what you've learned in this book about how to employ your senses, leverage correspondences, hone your intention, and incorporate what feels meaningful to *you* in creating this magic. Because, in the end, the action itself is just another tool. Your intention, purpose, belief—everything *you* bring is what makes it magic.

In addition, I've always felt that the most effective witchcraft . . . well . . . *looked* like witchcraft. So, in that spirit, there are spells in which you will make things fly. You will create clouds and summon snow and set fire to objects that will not burn. My hope is that you'll open yourself up to the possibility of what magic can look like in the modern day, using things you either already have in your home or can easily access via the internet or your nearest grocery store.

None of the spells require any specific plants or crystals, and I believe the most expensive item used cost me around $7 to obtain. I want you to believe, if even for a moment, that magic is real and that you can perform it in a way that is noncapitalist, non-appropriative, and filled with a sense of wonder at the world around you.

The FLYING TEA BAG

his is easily one of my favorite spells, and I perform it multiple times a year for different reasons. It's really fun to do with someone who might be new to magic, as it's visually impressive. You're going to make something fly and, in my opinion, there's absolutely nothing cooler than that.

Some of the power and opportunity of this spell comes from what you inscribe on the bag. Before you begin, take time to set your intention, reflect on your purpose, and choose the words, images, or symbols that will be meaningful to you.

WHAT YOU NEED:

- Tea bag (the cheap kind with the staple at the top! No pyramid-looking fancy tea sachets. Go to the store-brand section of the tea aisle and pick a tea flavor you like or that you associate with your end goal.)
- Scissors
- Pen
- Lighter/matches

WHAT YOU DO:

- Holding the staple at the top of the bag, shake slightly so that the leaves fall to the bottom of the bag.

- Cut the tea bag straight across the top underneath the staple. Discard the top portion with the string, and dump the loose tea into a small container or tea strainer.
- Unfold the tea bag.
- Using your pen, write or draw on the tea bag.
- Open it so that it looks like a cylinder.
- Stand one end of the cylinder on a flat surface so that the bottom end is fully flush against the flat surface.
- If you wish, speak your intention aloud clearly.
- Using the lighter or matches, set the top of the cylinder on fire.
- Let it burn completely and watch the bag take flight!

Note: The tea bag will typically not fly more than a couple feet in the air. Still, you should always practice fire safety by clearing a space and having either water or salt on hand.

Afterwards, reward yourself with a cup of tea made from the loose leaves if you choose.

Possible Uses

A Spell of Release—if there is a situation, emotion, or person from which you wish to be released, this is a really fun spell to perform. No matter how often I see that bag fly into the air, if I've given it plenty of intention and focus I get little tingles down my spine every time and feel lighter.

Spells of release work best for me when I spend as much time as needed focusing on the thing I'm releasing. If it is the stress of work, for example, I close my eyes and try to put myself back at work in different moments of stress. I try to feel the situation both specifically (remembering specific instances that created stress) and generally (remembering how the issue affects my life as a whole). Emotionally, mentally, and spiritually connect to the issue at hand. While in that state of connection, write it down on the bag.

Then I imagine what my life will feel like without it. How would my life be better without this in it? This situation, this person, this feeling? Spend as much time as you need on that. Then, in that state of release, light the bag.

★

A Spell of Manifestation—have you ever made a wish and released a balloon into the air? You know what that results in? A nondecomposing Mylar balloon finding a home out in the woods or clogging up a drain or coming to rest who knows where. It results in more trash out in the world, and it's a waste of a good balloon. Or perhaps you've seen the spell performed in movies where you write a wish down on a leaf and release it into the wind. If, like me, you live where the air hurts your face for several months out of the year, you might not want to go outside and throw leaves in the wind.

Instead of writing what you want to get rid of on the bag, write down what you want to bring into your life and release it to the universe to work on your behalf. Some people think of this as asking spirits of the air for assistance, or spirits of fire.

Your thought process will be the reverse of the release spell. First, emotionally, mentally, and spiritually visualize and connect with your life as it exists now, thinking of how it is lacking what you wish to manifest. Write that down on the bag. Then visualize how your life will be changed for the better after your desire manifests. Light the bag.

★

A Spell of Communication—perhaps you see this is a way of sending a message to a loved one on the other side or petitioning a deity. It is common in many cultures to use fire as a way of sending a letter or message to "the other side" (whatever that means to you). A great way to do this in a space with limited fire capabilities is to use a tea bag.

VARIATION

Instead of a tea bag, you can use flash paper, which is a magician's tool you can purchase online or in shops that sell magicians' equipment. It comes in little packs that usually look like note cards. While it won't fly, it will typically give a quick flash of fire and light immediately after being set on fire. Write your words, speak your intention, light the paper on fire, and throw it in the air. Magic.

MAGICAL PAPER
SEED BOMBS

This is a fun spell to do if you want to feel like an ecologically minded ninja. It's fun because you get to tear stuff up, but then later you get flowers. (Or herbs. Or trees. Or, you know, whatever.)

WHAT YOU NEED:

- 3–5 sheets of paper (These can be blank sheets, recycled newspaper, junk mail, diary entries—whatever you want! If you're using recycled paper, try to choose something that represents your goal.)
- Pen/marker
- Bowl/bucket
- Water
- 1 seed packet (I like wildflowers, but choose something that works for you and aligns with your goal. Research your area and do *not* choose an invasive species of plant.)
- Blender
- Strainer
- Drying rack
- Optional: cookie cutters in a shape representative of your goal, paper towel

WHAT YOU DO:

- Write down your intention on the paper.
- Tear the paper into small pieces, and put into the bowl.
- Fill the bowl with water until it just covers the paper.
- Leave paper to soak thoroughly (5–10 minutes, though you can leave it longer without damaging the end product).
- Put the soaked paper in the blender and add an extra splash of water.
- Blend paper and water until it's approximately the consistency of oatmeal.
- Dump the pulp into the strainer and press with your hands to get rid of the excess water, but don't let it get too dry, as the moisture helps the seed bomb retain its shape.
- Return pulp to the bowl and add seeds to mixture. Knead thoroughly.
- Roll the mixture into balls or press into cookie cutters. Using a paper towel, you can put the ball in it and give it a light squeeze to get rid of that last bit of moisture. If you're using shapes, press the paper towel on it, then lightly turn it over and press the other side.
- Leave untouched on a drying rack until thoroughly dry.
- Go out in the world and drop them where they can grow and manifest your desires.

Friendly reminder: Do not put these on someone else's private property. Think a nature walk, public park, et cetera.

Possible Uses

A Spell of Manifestation—it's not exactly a veiled metaphor to associate growing a plant from seed with bringing something into your life that currently exists only as possibility. For this spell type, focus your intention on the words, the seed type, and where you end up placing your seed bombs. I have found that this works best with longer-term goals (such as goals that could be attained in the time it takes the plant to grow fully).

- Choose positive words and simple, declarative statements such as "I will exercise three times a week" or "I will find a job that suits my need for ____." Alternatively, you could write a letter warmly inviting that thing into your life. It's sheets of paper, so you have room to be as detailed as you want.
- Choose seeds that inspire you or remind you of your end goal. For my examples earlier, perhaps you associate sunflowers with energy and exercise or basil with employment. Once again, remember to choose something that 1) will grow in your climate and 2) is not considered an invasive species.
- For manifestation, I would choose a place where you're likely to see the product of your magic. Your favorite walking trail, for example. This will not only mean you're more likely to walk by your enchanted plant and get that little metaphysical boost, but also the sight of the flowers will serve as a psychological reminder of your end goal. We love a spell that does double duty!

A Spell of Letting Go—there are lots of magical ways to take something you don't want and send it away from you. This can be one of those ways. Is it a feeling, a situation, a habit, or even someone's prying eyes? This can be a way of putting some distance between you and something or someone else.

- Choose simple, declarative statements such as "I rid myself of fear" or go bigger and write a detailed letter about the way a particular memory is not allowing you to grow and wish it farewell.

- Choose plants you associate with departure, banishment, et cetera.
- Choose a location you are unlikely to visit. If you're able, look up a park or nature trail in a neighboring town and go on a quick road trip. Speak words of farewell when you place the seed bombs.

COLOR-BLENDING
SPELL

This one is fun, fast, and beautiful! This can be done with disposable materials or with items you want to keep with you as a talisman depending on your purpose.

WHAT YOU NEED:

- 3 small bowls
- Water
- 2 different colors of food coloring / natural dye made from a plant aligning with your goal
- 2 paper towels or white fabric squares
- Optional: plants, stones, or other objects that represent your desire

WHAT YOU DO:

- Set up the three bowls in a line before you.
- Fill the first and third bowls about ¼ full with water; leave the second bowl empty.
- In the first bowl add 2–4 drops of your first food coloring/dye; in the third bowl do the same with your second color. Give the water a quick swirl to mix.
- Roll up paper towels or fabric squares, placing one end in the first cup and the other in the second and so on.

- Watch patiently as the colored water will be pulled up from the bowls through the paper towels or fabric scraps and drip into the empty cup in the middle, blending the two colors.

Possible Uses

Mending a Strained Relationship—if you and someone you care about aren't quite seeing eye to eye, you can use this as a spell to "meet in the middle" or find a compromise in a situation.

- Choose one color that represents you and one that represents the other person.
- As you are filling each cup and taking the action of putting the paper towels or fabric in the cups, you can speak your intention clearly and declaratively.
- If you choose, using white fabric scraps will result in colored fabric that you can keep and sew together as a talisman. If you choose this method, you can fill the interior with plants, stones, or other objects representing your desire to mend the relationship.

Inspiring an Emotion—do you know someone who could use a little compassion? Perhaps *you* could use a dose of peace or calm? Label one cup with the emotion and the other as the person in question. As they meet in the middle, it should instill the desired emotion.

- Once again you can use the scrap fabric to create a talisman filled with plants, stones, or other objects that align with your goal.

VARIATION

Drawing Out Something Unwanted: For this version, you would only use 2 cups, one with the colored liquid and the other empty.

- Name the cup with liquid with what you wish to draw out of you, speaking your intention clearly and declaratively. Visualize how this is impacting your life negatively and how your life would be better without it.
- As the liquid is drawn into the other cup, view that as the negative emotion, trait, attachment leaving you.
- Throw the liquid somewhere you will not visit regularly and dispose of the paper towel outside your home.

SNOW DAY SPELL

W hat is more magical than mixing ingredients and watching snow appear in your kitchen? Nothing. Absolutely nothing. This is a spell adapted from a kid's toy to help inspire a sense of magic and wonder. In all likelihood you might not be able to purchase one of these items from a nearby store—unless it's seasonally available at a hardware store or supermarket—but it can be purchased for between $6–$8 online.

WHAT YOU NEED:
- Sodium polyacrylate (This is sold under lots of names, like Instant Snow, or Snow to Go, or Snow Slime. It's all the same thing and you don't need much, especially as you are unlikely to use this often.)
- Cup
- Water
- Pen
- Slip of paper
- Optional: black pepper

WHAT YOU DO:
- Follow the instructions on the packaging of the sodium polyacrylate and put a small amount of water in the cup.

- Write a name (yours or someone else's) on the paper and put it in the cup.
- Sprinkle the sodium polyacrylate into the water.
- Watch as it becomes snow!

You can mold it into shapes, like a snowball, or simply leave it as fluff just like snow!

Possible Uses

Inspiring Joy—if you or someone else needs to feel the sense of joy, relief, and fun of a snow day from childhood, you can put your name or someone else's on the paper and speak clearly and declaratively your intention. As you sprinkle the "instant snow" into the water, focus your intention on images of laughter and snow and happy times.

Pro Tip: If you do have a cauldron of any kind—even a decorative, ceramic one—making this in the cauldron is incredibly fun and very witchy.

★

Buried under Snow—I'll be honest, I did not originally think of this as a possible use. I suppose I tend to think of what ways spells can improve your life and not how they can . . . well . . . annoy others. This use came from a friend of mine who reminded me that not all people associate a snow day with happy memories. Some people view it as yet more labor one must perform, such as shoveling one's driveway or commuting on slushy roads. This might not wholly be a negative thing. Perhaps someone is in your business and you wish to slow them down or deter them.

- If you are so inclined, name the person who you desire to affect in such a way. Add their name to the cup.
- Speak your intention clearly and declaratively.
- As the snow manifests, add black pepper to represent the dirty, slushy snow that is the bane of midwestern commuters everywhere.

HARD CANDY MAGIC

Sweet. Quick. Cheap. Colorful. This type of magic can be used for a number of effects depending on what your intention is, but all of them result in a sweet bit of magic. To get the most out of this spell, choose a candy that is aligned to your intention in some way (type, color, flavor, smell, a memory, et cetera). Choosing a translucent hard candy will result in a talisman you can see through while something like a caramel will not.

WHAT YOU NEED:

- Cookie sheet or nonstick sheet pan
- Aluminum foil
- Hard candy of your choice
- Optional: cookie cutters, nonstick cooking spray, crystals or dried plants, heat-protective gloves, skewer or toothpick, ribbon or string, container or jar, fresh or dried fruit, oven-safe bowl or Pyrex measuring cup, stones, objects, et cetera

WHAT YOU DO:

- Preheat your oven to 250°F.
- Line your pan with the aluminum foil and arrange the hard candy on top.
- If you'd like to use a cookie cutter to guarantee a specific shape, thoroughly grease it up and put the

candies inside. You might want to crush them up a bit first to ensure that as much of the interior surface of the cookie cutter is filled as possible.

- Put in the oven until melted (approximately 3–6 minutes, depending on the type and amount of candy).
- When you pull the candy out of the oven, it will not reharden immediately. This gives you an opportunity to shape the candy, but be careful if you do this because it will be very hot and liquid sugar burns are no fun. However, working directly with the candy gives you the opportunity to add a special magical touch—literally—in your working.
- If you are adding an optional ingredient—such as crystals, plants, objects, et cetera—now is the time to quickly and firmly press them into the candy. Heat-protective gloves should be used if you are a normal person and not someone like me who dives in headfirst and worries about burning themselves later. If the candy gets too hard, pop it back in the oven to warm up.
- **Note:** If you'd like to be able to hang your resulting candy spell, stick a skewer or toothpick through an area and slowly work it in a circle until you've formed a small opening. Some cookie cutters have the hole built in if they were part of a holiday ornament set. Please remember that if you add nonedible items to your candy, do not eat them or serve them to others. Keep them away from kids.

Possible Uses

Home Talismans—want to make a talisman for protection? Promote wellness? Inspire creativity? If you're not going for a specific effect but more so want to give you or your space a magical boost make a large, ornament-size talisman.

As you're working with the candy, focus your intention on the feeling you wish to inspire (tranquility, creativity, et cetera). Recall times when you've felt that way and visualize that memory being imbued into the candy talisman. You can think of it as light coming from your hands, a cloud of energy, or if you're not a visual person simply know that you have done so. Hang it with a ribbon or string—you can make this color correspond to your intention as well—in an area out of direct light (as it might melt in direct light on a warm enough day). Let it infuse your space with energy.

Note: This is literally sugar, so don't be surprised if it attracts bugs or dust. If it becomes unsightly, simply toss it in the garbage and make another one! Or, if you want to keep it longer, wrap it in clear cling wrap before you hang it.

★

Magical Candy—if you've seen a few movies about witches, you know that eating or drinking something to create a magical effect has long been a part of the lore of the witch. What if you had a little jar of "protection" in your home and you took a little with you before leaving the house? What if you kept a tin of "attraction" in your purse and pulled one out when you saw a cutie from across a crowded room? Here's how to do that!

Perform the same focusing and instilling of energy. This is an edible spell, so do not add anything to the candy that you cannot safely ingest. Choose small, bite-size cookie cutters (I like stars, because that feels so witchy to me) or simply break up your sheet of melted candy after it cools into bite-size pieces. Keep your candies in a container that you keep with you or fill a jar with them in an area where you could use a magical boost. Maybe you need to fill a jar with "Motivation" at your place of work and pop a candy when you need to get busy. You can pair the action of eating a candy with words, speaking your intention clearly to assist in directing the magic.

Fun fact: If you pour melted candy on a bit of fruit . . . you get candy-coated fruit! Yet another way of adding in a bit of magic is by choosing a fruit that aligns with your goal. Maybe you make attraction apple slices or motivating mango. You can use fresh or dried fruit.

✶

Slow Down a Person or Situation—is someone getting a bit too nosy? Are you suddenly the topic of someone's gossip? If someone needs to be put on pause, magically stick them in some candy for a while.

- Instead of melting the candy in a flat pan, melt it in an oven-safe bowl to make it easier to pour. Using a Pyrex measuring cup works best in my experience, as you get a handle and spout.
- Write the nosy person's name on a slip of paper, or choose an object that represents them, and pour the candy over it speaking your intention clearly and directly.
- When sufficient time has passed—use your best judgment—and the clouds of gossip are firmly in the distance, simply break the candy to release the person from the sticky situation.

WRITTEN *in* SALT

This one is so simple you're going to kick yourself for not thinking of it. It's so universally applicable that it can be used to accomplish all sorts of magical tasks from protection to divination. This spell is also easy to vary by using sugar, dried plants (flowers, herbs, et cetera), pepper, glitter, dirt or sand from a particular location, or any spice or crushed plant that aligns with your goals instead of salt.

WHAT YOU NEED:
- Liquid glue (the cheap white kind like you used for crafts as a kid)
- Paper (can be as large or small as you wish. Can use recycled paper)
- Pen
- Salt
- Optional: Sugar or sweet-smelling dried plants/ spices, bitter herbs or other malodorous plant matter, or dirt or sand (either from a place far away or that you associate with protection or justice), crushed plants (associated with either your purpose or divination, et cetera), fire

WHAT YOU DO:
- Using the liquid glue, write a name or draw a shape

on the paper while speaking your intention clearly and declaratively.

- Sprinkle the paper generously with salt.
- Shake off extra salt over a garbage can or sink.
- Keep as an ongoing talisman or ritually dispose of it with fire or water.
- **Note:** If you choose water, you could combine this with the Magical Paper Seed Bomb spell in an act of transformative magic.

Possible Uses

A Spell of Protection—write down names of people you wish to protect in the middle of the paper speaking your intention clearly and declaratively. Using the glue, draw a circle around the names (or, if you associate a different symbol with protection, draw that). Sprinkle salt over the glue, give it a moment to set, and dust off the excess. Keep in a safe place as a talisman of protection, or, if the person is willing, give it to them to keep on their person or in a place of their choosing.

☆

A Spell to Sweeten Disposition—use the glue to write a person's name and sprinkle sugar or sweet-smelling plants/spices onto it. Keep as a talisman or place underneath their bed to work as they sleep.

☆

A Spell to Deter an Unwanted Person—use the glue to write a person's name, but this time sprinkle bitter herbs or other malodorous plant matter, or choose the dirt or sand from a place either far away or that you associate with protection or justice. If you choose, you could then fold the paper into a boat and send it down a nearby creek or river in a direction opposite of your home.

A Spell of Divination—use the glue to write a few words or sentences (depending on how deft you are with the liquid glue) describing a situation. Sprinkle salt, plants associated with either your purpose or with divination, et cetera. Fold the paper loosely and cast into a fire. Let your sight become soft and generally gaze at the fire, the burning paper, and the smoke looking for symbols or images. Write them down as you see them, but don't focus on their meaning at this time. Simply write what you witness from the moment the paper ignites until it is fully consumed. Later, spend time reviewing the symbols and review how they make you feel or what associations you have to them.

WRITTEN *in* FIRE

This is very similar to the last spell with one key difference: you're going to set things on fire and they will not burn. (Please remember your fire safety!)

WHAT YOU NEED:

- Hand sanitizer gel (I prefer the travel size with the squirt top, but whatever cheap alcohol-based brand you have handy is perfect.)
- Heat-resistant surface (I use a plate or silicone cutting board.)
- Matches/lighter
- Optional: pen and paper, a crystal you associate with passion

WHAT YOU DO:

- While speaking your intention clearly and declaratively, write on the plate or silicone mat with the hand sanitizer gel.
- Light with match or lighter.
- Watch the gel burn cleanly until the alcohol in the gel has been consumed.

VARIATION

Coat a nonflammable object that aligns with your purpose (such as a crystal) in the gel and, while speaking your intention, set it ablaze.

Possible Uses

Circle of Protection—nothing says "keep away from my loved one" like a giant wall of fire. Write the person's name you wish to protect on a small piece of paper and place it in the middle of a circle of the gel. Make sure the circle is large enough that the paper won't catch fire. Speak your intention and light the gel on fire. Stay with it until the fire dies. Repeat as needed.

★

Inspire Passion—are things a little lacking in the bedroom? Try igniting your and your partner's fire by drawing a symbol, both of your names, or coating a crystal you associate with passion. If you can safely do so, perform the spell in your bedroom—or wherever you plan on spicing things up. Speak your intention and set it ablaze. Stay with it until the fire dies. Have fun!

MAKE IT RAIN

Have you ever wanted to conjure a rainstorm in your kitchen? Literally? Well, this spell uses a simple bit of sympathetic magic that you can use for prosperity, protection, or weather manipulation.

WHAT YOU NEED:

- 2 cups of water
- Small pot or kettle
- Optional: pen and paper, plants or water-based crystal you associate with prosperity, a bay leaf or basil, plants you associate with protection
- Vase with a large opening
- Bowl that will fit in the vase opening
- Ice

WHAT YOU DO:

- Bring water to a rolling boil in a small pot or kettle.
- Pour boiling water into vase.
- If you are adding paper or plants, do so now.
- Set bowl on top of vase opening, ensuring it is covered completely.
- The hot water will create rolling clouds inside the vase. Let these build for a few minutes until they are thick.
- Add ice to the bowl without moving it from the

opening. The sudden change in temperature will cause the clouds to change from condensation to precipitation and create rain that drips down the sides of the vase and from the bowl on top.

Possible Uses

Weather Magic—loads of weather spells exist, and they often take the form of basically boiling a pot of water and throwing it outside as if to say, *Hey! Sky! Get with it!* If you don't want to yell at the sky because you don't want to give your neighbors more reasons to gossip about you, here's a way to do the same thing. Hold your hands near the vase as the clouds form and visualize the sky becoming cloudy and, after you add the ice, gentle rain falling.

★

Prosperity Magic—the phrase "make it rain" is an idiom used by people to refer to receiving a sudden windfall of cash. While I'm not normally a fan of puns, you can certainly use this miniature rainfall as a bit of sympathetic magic to rain prosperity on yourself or someone else. If the spell is not for you, add the person's name to the vase before pouring the water to ensure the magic is aimed correctly. In addition, you can add plants or non-water-soluble crystals you associate with prosperity to the water and fill the clouds with enhanced magic. Try adding a bay leaf or basil, as both have been associated with wealth, but as always choose what works best for you. Speak your intention clearly and declaratively as the clouds form and as the rain falls.

★

Clouding a Situation—perhaps there's a busybody who is poking their nose in your business. For this version, you won't need the ice. Add the person's name to the vase before adding the water. You may choose to add plants or crystals you associate with protection. As the clouds form, speak your intention clearly and declaratively that their vision become clouded when it comes to you.

FLOWER
TRANSFORMATION

This is adapted from a craft project our teachers had us do as children every year around homecoming. Homecoming is really big in Texas because football is a way of life there, and this trick came in handy for making color-coordinated team decor. But what if you gave it a magical twist? This kind of magic is all about transforming yourself or a situation from one thing to another or adding a missing element into a situation. You can get really creative with different flowers, water blends, and colors.

WHAT YOU NEED:

- Vase
- Water
- 3–20 drops of food coloring or natural plant dye you've made (the more you add, the bolder the color)
- Optional: plants or herbs associated with your goal
- Fresh-cut flowers (while white flowers work best, you can choose any light-colored flower associated with your goal)
- Optional: pen and paper, tissue

WHAT YOU DO:

- Fill a vase ¼–⅓ full with water.
- Add food coloring or natural plant dye you've made.
- If you are planning to steep plants or herbs

associated with your goal in the water, add them now. This can be done well in advance like tea so that you can allow the water to cool, or you can steep the plants for at least 8 hours in your refrigerator or on the counter.

- Add fresh-cut flowers.
- Wait a few hours for the flowers' color to change.
- Place the transformed flowers in an area associated with the needed change, or give them to the person in question. Likewise, you can press and keep the flowers as talismans.

Possible Uses

A Spell of Transformation—the flowers here represent yourself or a situation in need of transformation. Use plants or colors associated with your goal to infuse the flowers with the energy that is needed but is currently missing. Focus on the situation as it exists currently. Fully visualize it in your mind to the best of your ability. If you are not a visual person, consider writing down the situation as it currently exists. Then change the narrative and visualize (or write!) what the situation *will* look like once the transformation takes place. Speak your intention clearly and declaratively as you add the water and flowers to the vase.

★

A Plant Talisman—perhaps you do not necessarily need a situation to change in the immediate future, but you'd rather carry a talisman to generally infuse your daily life with a particular energy. Simply focus on times when you felt the energy you wish to infuse in the flower and let that flow into the water. Once the flower has changed color—or if you're simply using a plant brew once a few hours have passed—press the flower between some tissue in a thick book and keep it either with you or in a special place.

FAST ICE

You remember back in chapter 2 where I talked about writing down what's bothering you and sticking it in a jar in the freezer? So, this is the same principle, but you get to hit things. Plus, the effect is really fun and witchy.

WHAT YOU NEED:

- Pen
- Paper
- Water bottle with lid (do not use a glass water bottle)
- Water
- Timer

WHAT YOU DO:

- Write down what's troubling you.
- Fold it small and put it in the bottle.
- Fill almost to the top with water.
- Seal the lid tightly so there are no spills.
- Put the bottle in the freezer, and set a timer for approximately 2 hours and 45 minutes. (Time in the freezer will depend on the size of the water bottle and the freezer setting, but basically you want the temperature of the water to get as close to freezing as possible.)

- When the time is up, take the bottle out of the freezer.
- Speak your intention clearly and declaratively.
- Whack the bottle with your hand or on a countertop.
- Watch it instantly become a block of ice.

Possible Uses

Freezing a Situation—personally speaking, when I feel stressed about something, it can spiral quickly. My anxiety can trick me into believing that I'm less in control of myself and my environment than I may be (or should be). If you feel that something is getting away from you, it might be time to put it on ice. Write down the situation in a few words, speak your intention, and when the time comes give it a good whack. Putting something in a jar in the freezer feels nice, but whacking something and turning it to ice feels better.

This can, of course, apply to a person as well. Perhaps someone is getting a bit too nosy or gossipy and their actions need to be halted. Write their name and the situation on the paper instead.

★

Weather Magic—I mean, you're turning water into ice with a tap of your finger. That could easily be used as a sympathetic weather manipulation spell. While summoning up icy weather isn't my thing—we get plenty of it naturally here in the Midwest—there's nothing stopping you from giving it a try! Just be careful on the roads!

EGG TRANSFORMATION

Eggs are used in all sorts of magical ways all over the world from fertility to curse removal and all uses in between and beyond. They pop up in most cultures and for most of human history. This bit of magic finds an updated and fun use for eggs that's all about transformation and resilience and is adapted from a viral science experiment video.

WHAT YOU NEED:

- 1 egg
- Pen or marker
- Small glass
- 1 cup white vinegar
- Optional: needle

WHAT YOU DO:

- Place the egg in the glass.
- Pour in the vinegar, ensuring the egg is fully submerged.
- Wait 24 hours. (The water will have a scummy white film floating in it.)
- Take your egg out of the glass; rinse it off.
- Bounce it! The egg has been transformed into a bouncing balloon.
- If you poke it with a needle, it will deflate similar to a water balloon.

Possible Uses

A Spell of Strength—are you feeling a bit fragile? Could you use a boost of courage, strength, or confidence? Use this as sympathetic magic to turn your fragile exterior into something a bit more durable—even if temporarily. Need to get through a big meeting or weather a tough family dinner?

The day before your event, start the spell. Write your name on the egg—or simply include in your statement of intention clearly and declaratively that the egg will represent you—and spend a moment thinking on the ways in which you see yourself as fragile. Don't dwell on this, but acknowledge and accept it. Then see yourself as strong, confident, or otherwise transformed into a version of yourself capable of handling tough situations. You could reflect on a time in your life when you felt more resilient, or, if that's difficult, perhaps think of a character in a movie or book you enjoy who you feel handles tough situations well. Put this energy into the egg knowing that as it transforms from one thing to another so, too, shall you.

★

A Spell to Break Down Barriers—part of what happens during this transformation is the dissolving of the eggshell. In this version of the spell, we're not focusing on the resilience of the end product but on the way in which the shell goes from something hard and protective of its contents to bubbly foam. So, if something is standing in your way, this could be a spell to help you get rid of that barrier.

- Using a pen, marker, or simply including it verbally in your statement of intention, name the egg with the barrier that needs to be removed. Maybe this is a bit of bureaucratic red tape or a restriction preventing you from taking a needed action. Whatever it is, focus on how it is preventing you from doing what you need to do, then visualize what it will be like to not have that barrier impeding you. Speak your intention clearly and declaratively and proceed with the spell—while taking mundane action to resolve the matter—knowing that as the shell dissolves so, too, will your barrier dissolve.

CONCLUSION

As my dear friend Velma Nightshade would say, "back in the long, long ago" she and I had a conversation on our on-again, off-again joint podcast *Inciting A BrewHaHa* about the magical use of fake flowers. And when I say "conversation," I mean we had an actual argument over whether you could only make magic with real flowers or if the synthetic variety could be sufficient. I genuinely don't remember which side of the argument I was on at the time, as it's been well over a decade since then and we've made a promise to ourselves never to go back and listen to that train wreck. Occasionally, longtime listeners of my podcast will bring up the legendary "fake flower" episode of that show and I'll shudder. Thankfully, time and distance have made it an inside joke we can laugh about and a lesson learned.

I've grown a lot since that conversation. I've become less precious about the rules of magic, of spiritual seekership. I've become more open-minded and realized that the work has little to do with the tools and everything to do with the one using them.

Is it what you have access to? Is it something that speaks to you? Do you see results when you use it in a spell? Then yes. Of course. You can make magic with it. Witches are resourceful people and can make magic out of just about anything. There are no rules. There is no witch's council that will come in and poke you with their broomsticks and tell you that you're doing it wrong.

And, yet, there are rules in a way. They might not necessarily be rules of the practice of witchcraft, but they are rules about the social contract we have with one another, what we owe to one another. They're rules we don't often like to think about or bring up in what some call polite conversation or when we would much rather talk about something fun like the history of flying ointments or the elemental associations of wands and athames. Nonetheless, we owe it to ourselves, to our magical community, and to our fellow man to have some of these uncomfortable conversations. To ask, "Why?," when we are told that something has always been done a certain way. To challenge not only convention but also our leaders and ourselves to learn better and do better. To listen in order to hear, instead of listening while waiting to speak. To give something up, even though we like it, when we realize it is harming someone else.

Thank you for going on this journey with me. I know it wasn't easy or comfortable the entire time, but I hope you found it worthy all the same. It's my sincerest wish you understand that this book could never represent the summation of all the various and nuanced ways that our spiritual community was built or how to ethically navigate it. I do hope that it has made you realize that the study and practice of magic is a bit deeper than you may have thought. It has a rich history yet isn't without its pitfalls.

In having an honest discussion of what magic is and can do, I believe we can be empowered to dig deeper and allow it to be a tool of betterment in our lives. By acknowledging that magic doesn't always work or might not work in the way you thought it did, we can dive headfirst into the possibility of what it is and how it can help you.

I hope also that you'll be more prepared to ask tough questions of yourself and others, to speak the quiet part out loud when necessary, and know how to spot good resources you can use to further your spiritual journey. Because the purpose of learning isn't to reach an end point, a place where you can confidently say you know all the things. The purpose is to realize that there is not going to be an end point.

A spiritual journey is a lifelong pursuit. There's no one right way to go about it, and who you are going to be ten years in the future is going to look very, very different from who you are now. That should excite you. You're going to grow in ways you never thought possible. You'll brew potions in your coffeepot on Sunday mornings and keep a cherished crystal on your nightstand (or in your pocket or bra), run around during a storm yelling at the sky, and do a cleansing spell every time your mother comes into town until, one day, you look around and notice that the life you're living looks a little more like the one you intended to be living when you started out on this whole journey. Almost like magic.

ACKNOWLEDGMENTS

I carry the privilege of being white, cisgender, and from a home that never lacked for basic needs. While I also have intersectional areas of oppression, my perspective is inherently skewed. This book represents a fixed point in time and one privileged author's perspective and should by no means be taken as the entirety of knowledge or the true and only way to craft a magical life. If this book has taught you nothing else, let it be that.

It should also be said that one day, perhaps sooner than I would like, this book will become outdated. The research and information used to support the arguments made in this book will be replaced by new research and better information and one day read by those who look back and wonder how I could have ever made such a silly argument in the first place. And to that I say, "Yes. Drag me. I'm sure I deserve it." I hope that the future spiritual seekers reading this book understand that I did the very best I could with the information I could access and the opportunity I was presented but know that if our community has progressed to a point without implicit bias or predators masquerading as leaders, I am celebrating that moment alongside them.

On a lighter note, I would very much like to thank Meg and Kate for putting up with my imposter syndrome and authorial histrionics as I wrote this book in a time of anxiety and trepidation while the world was falling apart. I would also like to thank them for telling me that I *could* write this book, which is a very necessary thing for people to hear and we need to do more of that. "Can" allows for possibility, allows for magic, and is the secret sauce for being a creative person. It is a lesson I needed to learn and a series of continuing education courses I'm sure I will be taking for the rest of my life. For two people far more talented than me, I am humbled you shared a bit of your wisdom and guidance along the way.

To my dear friend, spiritual sister, sometimes co-host, and Pagan Pride Day tent buddy Velma Nightshade, I cannot begin to express how grateful I am that you came into my life. You helped get me out of my shell and graciously taught me that I don't know everything. I love you. I'm proud of you. Now, could you please bring back your podcast?

Cory, Kathleen, Crystal, Katrina, Rommy, Amanda, Beth, Kayti, Nicole, Georgia, Mark, Robyn, Lilith, Marika, Moon, Via, Tiffany, and people whose names are currently escaping me because being faced with the prospect of thanking everyone who's had an influence over me and, by extension, this book is causing my brain to play this fun game where it cannot think of anyone's names . . . thank you. So many of you have graciously had uncomfortable conversations with me, challenged me, and made me a better person when you didn't need to do it.

If you held space for me in your shop or at your event, thank you. If you left a sweet comment for my podcast, thank you. If you wrote a scathing opposition to something I said that helped me to realize I spoke out of turn or needed to dig deeper or unpack my privilege, thank you most of all. I wouldn't have grown without you.

To my editor, Hannah, who dug through all my chaos and helped me to find my words, thank you.

To the diverse, brilliant group of people who beta read this book and provided their unique perspective and critical eye, I am endlessly grateful for your input and for ensuring this book was worthy of the community I wish to serve. Critique is an invaluable part of one's journey, especially when that person finds themselves in the unique position of having a platform like the one this book and my podcast have provided. Good critique makes both me and my work better and, in turn, creates a better tool for others to use. Thank you. Thank you. Thank you.

I began my magical journey when I discovered a book called *Earth, Air, Fire & Water* by Scott Cunningham in high school. It taught me that magic was possible and that other people practiced it. It opened up an entire world to me and invited me along to build a life filled with wonder and reverence for the cycles of seasons, for life and death, and for the intricate web surrounding me at all times in ways I couldn't usually see. Mostly, though, Cunningham's work taught me that magic, that a spiritual life in general, didn't have to be complicated. It could look like picking up a fallen feather and speaking softly into the breeze.

The craft I practice today, all these many years later (*yikes, I'm old!*), is birthed from that spirit of simple practices, of making the mundane magical. Seeing the world around me as filled with possibility, and knowing that magic is simply another tool available to me as a being who exists in this universe. Because of this I believe that there is no line between the scientific and the spiritual. I have a reverence for the natural world as eminently sacred, and I believe that magic is simply a part of that natural world. This is why I examine magic, witchcraft, and connection with Spirit through a lens that is both spiritual and scientific and filled with historical and social context and find immeasurable value in using one as a check and balance against the other. Smart witches are informed witches who value critical analysis and peer review, as my friend Kathleen Borealis might say.

Most of all, this book would not have been possible without the love and support of my husband. He sees me in ways that I oftentimes don't feel I deserve, and I'm grateful that we have continued to choose each other for over fifteen years.

Now go. Find your next book. Find your next podcast, video series, documentary, class, or community event. Learn. Grow. Dig inside yourself and unpack what you find. Don't be afraid of being uncomfortable or wrong, because you will be. A lot. Ask good questions. Analyze the answers you're given. Make ethical choices. Most important, pursue magic wherever you find it.

Love and Lyte,
Fire Lyte

RESOURCES

The following are recommendations for further learning. The articles listed are articles cited throughout this book that I wanted to highlight, while the "Further Reading" section represents books that inspire me or provide valuable historical or sociological context to what has been discussed in this book. In addition, if you're like me, you enjoy the occasional blog, podcast, or YouTube video. I've listed a few to get you started. These recommendations by no means represent a complete and exhaustive list of everything I personally love or learn from. It's simply a list I felt married well with the content of this book.

Articles

Anderson, Elijah. "'The White Space.'" *Sociology of Race & Ethnicity* 1, no. 1 (January 1, 2015): 10–21. https://doi.org/10.1177/2332649214561306.

Atkin, Emily. "Do You Know Where Your Healing Crystals Come From?," *The New Republic*, May 11, 2018. https://newrepublic.com/article/148190/know-healing-crystals-come-from.

Burton, Nylah. "Is Burning Sage Cultural Appropriation? Here's How to Smoke Cleanse in Sensitive Ways." *Bustle*, July 19, 2019. https://www.bustle.com/p/is-burning-sage-cultural-appropriation-heres-how-to-smoke-cleanse-in-sensitive-ways-18208360.

Cargle, Rachel Elizabeth. "When Feminism Is White Supremacy in Heels." *Harper's Bazaar*, August 16, 2018. https://www.harpersbazaar.com/culture/politics/a22717725/what-is-toxic-white-feminism/.

Forer, B. R. "The Fallacy of Personal Validation: A Classroom Demonstration of Gullibility." *Journal of Abnormal and Social Psychology* 44 (1) (February 1949): 118–23.

Harvard Health Publishing. "The Power of the Placebo Effect." Harvard Health, May 2017. https://www.health.harvard.edu/mental-health/the-power-of-the-placebo-effect.

Oster, Emily. "Witchcraft, Weather and Economic Growth in Renaissance Europe." *Journal of Economic Perspectives* 18, no. 1 (Winter 2004): 215–28. Accessed February 9, 2021. http://www.jstor.org/stable/3216882.

Picciotto, Gabriela, Jesse Fox, and Félix Neto. "A Phenomenology of Spiritual Bypass: Causes, Consequences, and Implications." *Journal of Spirituality in Mental Health* 20, no. 4 (2018): 333–54, https://doi.org/10.1080/19349637.2017.1417756.

Further Reading

Adler, Margot. *Drawing Down the Moon*. New York: Penguin, 1979.

Alden, Temperance. *Year of the Witch: Connecting with Nature's Seasons through Intuitive Magic*. Newburyport, MA: Weiser Books, 2020.

Altglas, Véronique. *From Yoga to Kabbalah: Religious Exoticism and the Logics of Bricolage*. Oxford: Oxford University Press, 2014.

Blanton, Crystal, ed. *Shades of Ritual: Minority Voices in Practice*. Stafford, UK: Megalithica Books, 2014.

Blanton, Crystal, Taylor Ellwood, and Brandy Williams, eds. *Bringing Race to the Table: Exploring Racism in the Pagan Community*. Stafford, UK: Megalithica Books, 2015.

Boyer, Paul S., and Stephen Nissenbaum. *Salem Possessed: The Social Origins of Witchcraft*. Brantford, ON: W. Ross MacDonald School, Resource Services Library, 2008.

Cameron, Euan. *Enchanted Europe: Superstition, Reason and Religion, 1250–1750*. Oxford: Oxford University Press, 2013.

Carr-Gomm, Philip, and Richard Heygate. *The Book of English Magic*. London: Hodder & Stoughton, 2014.

Cross, J. Allen. *American Brujeria: Modern Mexican-American Folk Magic*. Newburyport, MA: Weiser Books, 2021.

Cunningham, Scott. *Earth, Air, Fire & Water: More Techniques of Natural Magic*. Woodbury, MN: Llewellyn, 2015.

Davies, Owen. *The Oxford Illustrated History of Witchcraft and Magic*. Oxford: Oxford University Press, 2017.

Davies, Owen. *Popular Magic: Cunning Folk in English History*. London: Hambledon Continuum, 2007.

Dorsey, Lilith. *Orishas, Goddesses, and Voodoo Queens: The Divine Feminine in the African Religious Traditions*. Newburyport, MA: Weiser Books, 2020.

Games, Alison. *Witchcraft in Early North America*. Lanham, MD: Rowman & Littlefield, 2010.

Hedera, Via. *Folkloric American Witchcraft and the Multicultural Experience: A Crucible at the Crossroads*. Winchester, UK: Moon Books, 2021.

Hutcheson, Cory Thomas. *New World Witchery: A Trove of North American Folk Magic*. Woodbury, MN: Llewellyn, 2021.

Hutton, Ronald. *The Witch: A Quest for the Roots of an Ancient Fear*. New Haven: Yale University Press, 2017.

Illes, Judika. *The Weiser Field Guide to Witches: From Hexes to Hermione Granger, from Salem to the Land of Oz*. San Francisco, CA: Red Wheel/Weiser, 2010.

Kunz, George Frederick. *The Curious Lore of Precious Stones*. Philadelphia: J. B. Lippincott, 1913.

Lightfoot, Najah. *Good Juju: Mojos, Rites & Practices for the Magical Soul*. Woodbury, MN: Llewellyn, 2019.

Mooney, Thorn. *Traditional Wicca: A Seeker's Guide*. Woodbury, MN: Llewellyn, 2018.

Owens, Susan. *The Ghost: A Cultural History*. London: Tate Publishing, 2019.

Ryan, W. F. *The Bathhouse at Midnight: An Historical Survey of Magic and Divination in Russia*. University Park: Pennsylvania State University Press, 1999.

Snow, Cassandra. *Queering Your Craft: Witchcraft from the Margins*. Newburyport, MA: Weiser Books, 2020.

Snow, Cassandra, and Beth Maiden. *Queering the Tarot*. Newburyport, MA: Weiser Books, 2019.

Thiselton-Dyer, T. F. *The Folk-Lore of Plants*. New York: D. Appleton and Company, 1889.

Valentine, Robyn. *Magickal Tarot: Spreads, Spellwork, and Ritual for Creating Your Life*. Beverly, MA: Quarto, 2021.

Washuta, Elissa. *White Magic*. Portland, OR: Tin House Books, LLC, 2021.

Wen, Benebell. *The Tao of Craft: Fu Talismans and Casting Sigils in the Eastern Esoteric Tradition*. Berkeley, CA: North Atlantic Books, 2016.

Online Media

At the Crossroads: Intersections in African Spirituality. https://anchor.fm/atthecrossroads/.

Borealis Meditation. https://katborealis.com.

Code Switch. https://www.npr.org/sections/codeswitch/.

Coffee and Cauldrons. https://anchor.fm/coffeeandcauldrons.

Invoking Witchcraft. https://www.invokingwitchcraft.com.

Little Juju Podcast, A. https://www.itsjujubae.com.

MinDat.org. https://www.mindat.org.

New World Witchery. https://newworldwitchery.com.

Occultism With a Side of Salt. https://www.youtube.com/c/OccultismWithaSideofSalt.

Oh No, Ross and Carrie! https://ohnopodcast.com.

Pop Occulture. https://lilithdorsey.com/pop-occulture-show.

Thorn Mooney. https://thornthewitch.wordpress.com.

Voodoo Universe. https://www.patheos.com/blogs/voodoouniverse/.

Witches & Wine. https://www.patheos.com/blogs/witchesandwine/author/ckoo/, https://www.youtube.com/channel/UCDv-aJ7fNmryRC8tD2e4qUA.

NOTES

Chapter 1: Pop Culture and Witchcraft

1. Lilith Dorsey, "The Voodoo Truth about Papa Legba," January 10, 2014, https://www.patheos.com/blogs/voodoouniverse/2014/01/the-voodoo-truth-about-papa-legba/.

2. Mediamatters4america, "Pat Robertson Blames Haiti's 'Pact to the Devil' for Catastrophe," YouTube video, 1:23, January 13, 2010, https://www.youtube.com/watch?v=mPyyXQN8cG0.

3. N. J. Schweitzer and Michael J. Saks, "The *CSI* Effect: Popular Fiction about Forensic Science Affects the Public's Expectations about Real Forensic Science, *Jurimetrics* 47 (Spring 2007): 357–64.

Chapter 3: When Magic Fails

1. David J. Ley, "6 Reasons People Lie When They Don't Need To," *Psychology Today*, January 23, 2017, https://www.psychologytoday.com/us/blog/women-who-stray/201701/6-reasons-people-lie-when-they-don-t-need.

Chapter 4: The Rise of the Political Witch

1. Emily Oster, "Witchcraft, Weather and Economic Growth in Renaissance Europe," *Journal of Economic Perspectives* 18, no. 1 (Winter 2004): 215–28, accessed February 9, 2021, http://www.jstor.org/stable/3216882.

Chapter 5: Why Are You Here?

1. "'Nones' on the Rise," Pew Research Center, Pew Forum on Religion & Public Life, October 9, 2012, https://www.pewforum.org/2012/10/09/nones-on-the-rise/.

2. Michael Lipka and Claire Gecewicz, "More Americans Now Say They're Spiritual but Not Religious," Pew Research Center, September 6, 2017, https://www.pewresearch.org/fact-tank/2017/09/06/more-americans-now-say-theyre-spiritual-but-not-religious/.

3. "Why America's 'Nones' Don't Identify with a Religion," Pew Research Center, August 8, 2018, https://www.pewresearch.org/fact-tank/2018/08/08/why-americas-nones-dont-identify-with-a-religion/.

Chapter 7: The Ethics of Dabbling

1. Rachel Elizabeth Cargle, "When Feminism Is White Supremacy in Heels," *Harper's Bazaar*, August 16, 2018, https://www.harpersbazaar.com/culture/politics/a22717725/what-is-toxic-white-feminism/.

2. Gabriela Picciotto, Jesse Fox, and Félix Neto, "A Phenomenology of Spiritual Bypass: Causes, Consequences, and Implications," *Journal of Spirituality in Mental Health* 20, no. 4 (2018): 333–54, https://doi.org/10.1080/19349637.2017.1417756.

3. Elijah Anderson, "The White Space," *Sociology of Race and Ethnicity* 1, no. 1 (January 1, 2015): 10–21, https://doi.org/10.1177/2332649214561306.

4. Andrew Bentley, "Off the Reservation," Partnership With Native Americans, September 13, 2012, http://blog.nrcprograms.org/off-the-reservation/.

5. Nylah Burton, "Is Burning Sage Cultural Appropriation? Here's How to Smoke Cleanse in Sensitive Ways," *Bustle*, July 19, 2019, https://www.bustle.com/p/is-burning-sage-cultural-appropriation-heres-how-to-smoke-cleanse-in-sensitive-ways-18208360.

6. Véronique Altglas, "Religious Exoticism," Discover Society, October 6, 2015, https://discoversociety.org/2015/10/06/religious-exoticism/.

7. Lindsay Dodgson, "People of Color Explain the Difference between Cultural Appropriation and Appreciation," *Insider*, September 5, 2020, https://www.insider.com/difference-between-cultural-appropriation-and-appreciation-2020-9.

8. "#OwnVoices" is a term coined by the writer Corinne Duyvis and refers to an author from a marginalized or underrepresented group writing about their own experiences/from their own perspective, rather than someone from an outside perspective writing as a character from an underrepresented group.

Chapter 8: Can I Make Sh*t Up?

1. Melody, "Lepidolite," essay in *Love Is in the Earth: A Kaleidoscope of Crystals Updated*, 3rd ed. (Wheat Ridge, CO: Earth-Love Publishing House, 1995), 379–81.

2. Scott Cunningham, "Lepidolite," essay in *Cunningham's Encyclopedia of Crystal, Gem & Metal Magic*, 2nd ed. (Woodbury, MN: Llewellyn, 1998), 131–32.

3. Judy Hall, "Lepidolite," essay in *The Crystal Bible* (Cincinnati, OH: Walking Stick Press, 2003), 176–77.

Chapter 9: Spotting a Fraud

1. B. R. Forer, "The Fallacy of Personal Validation: A Classroom Demonstration of Gullibility," *Journal of Abnormal and Social Psychology* 44(1) (February 1949): 118–23, https://doi.org/10.1037/h0059240.

2. D. H. Dickson and I. W. Kelly, "The 'Barnum Effect' in Personality Assessment: A Review of the Literature," *Psychological Reports* 57, no. 2 (October 1985): 367–82, https://doi.org/10.2466/pr0.1985.57.2.367.

3. Bernie I. Silverman, "Studies of Astrology," *The Journal of Psychology* 77, no. 2 (1971): 141–49, https://doi.org/10.1080/00223980.1971.9916861.

4. C. R. Snyder, R. J. Shenkel, and C. R. Lowery, "Acceptance of Personality Interpretations: The 'Barnum Effect' and Beyond," *Journal of Consulting and Clinical Psychology* 45(1) (February 1977): 104–14, https://doi.org/10.1037/0022-006X.45.1.104.

5. Dany J. MacDonald and Lionel G. Standing, "Does Self-Serving Bias Cancel the Barnum Effect?," *Social Behavior and Personality: An International Journal* 30, no. 6 (September 2002): 625–30, https://doi.org/10.2224/sbp.2002.30.6.625.

Chapter 11: UPG ... What Now?

1. Rob Stein, "Brains of Dying Rats Yield Clues about Near-Death Experiences," NPR, August 12, 2013, https://www.npr.org/sections/health-shots/2013/08/12/211324316/brains-of-dying-rats-yield-clues-about-near-death-experiences.

2. Stein, "Brains of Dying Rats Yield Clues about Near-Death Experiences."

3. Owen Davies, "Hag-Riding in Nineteenth-Century West Country England and Modern Newfoundland: An Examination of an Experience-Centred Witchcraft Tradition," *Folk Life* 35, no. 1 (1996): 36–53, https://doi.org/10.1179/043087796798254443.

Chapter 12: Making Magic
1. Harvard Health Publishing, "The Power of the Placebo Effect," Harvard Health, May 2017, https://www.health.harvard.edu/mental-health/the-power-of-the-placebo-effect.

2. James Frazer, "Sympathetic Magic," chap. 3 in *The Golden Bough* (New York: Macmillan, 1922; New York: Bartleby, 2000), part 1: "The Principles of Magic."

3. Joseph R. Ferrari, Catherine A. Roster, Kendall P. Crum, and Matthew A. Pardo, "Procrastinators and Clutter: An Ecological View of Living with Excessive 'Stuff,'" *Current Psychology* 37 (September 2017): 441–44, https://doi.org/10.1007/s12144-017-9682-9.

Chapter 13: Nature's Magic
1. Emily Atkin, "Do You Know Where Your Healing Crystals Come From?," *The New Republic*, May 11, 2018, https://newrepublic.com/article/148190/know-healing-crystals-come-from.

ABOUT THE AUTHOR

For more than ten years, **Fire Lyte** has interviewed self-identified witches, fairy experts, goblin hunters, paranormal investigators, and even a werewolf on his podcast *Inciting A Riot*. His thousands of listeners worldwide tune in as he examines magic, witchcraft, Paganism, and spiritual seekership through a diverse, inclusive lens with a balance of modern science, critical thought, and pop culture. He lives in the Chicago suburbs with his husband and vast array of fur children.